Afro-American
Literature and Culture
Since World War II

AMERICAN STUDIES INFORMATION GUIDE SERIES

Series Editor: Donald Koster, Professor of English Emeritus, Adelphi University, Garden City, New York

Also in this series:

AMERICAN ARCHITECTURE AND ART—*Edited by David M. Sokol*

AMERICAN FOLKLORE—*Edited by Richard M. Dorson**

AMERICAN HUMOR AND HUMORISTS—*Edited by M. Thomas Inge**

AMERICAN LANGUAGE AND LITERATURE—*Edited by Henry Wasser**

AMERICAN POPULAR CULTURE—*Edited by Marshall W. Fishwick and Larry Landrum**

THE AMERICAN PRESIDENCY—*Edited by Kenneth E. Davison**

AMERICAN RELIGION AND PHILOSOPHY—*Edited by Ernest R. Sandeen and Frederick Hale*

AMERICAN STUDIES—*Edited by David W. Marcell**

ANTHROPOLOGY OF THE AMERICAS—*Edited by Thomas C. Greaves**

EDUCATION IN AMERICA—*Edited by Richard G. Durnin**

HISTORY OF THE UNITED STATES OF AMERICA—*Edited by Ernest Cassara*

NORTH AMERICAN JEWISH LITERATURE—*Edited by Ira Bruce Nadel**

SOCIOLOGY OF AMERICA—*Edited by Charles Mark*

THE RELATIONSHIP OF PAINTING AND LITERATURE—*Edited by Eugene L. Huddleston and Douglas A. Noverr*

TECHNOLOGY AND HUMAN VALUES IN AMERICAN CIVILIZATION—*Edited by Stephen Cutliff, Judith A. Mistichelli, and Christine M. Roysdon**

WOMAN IN AMERICA—*Edited by Virginia R. Terris**

*in preparation

The above series is part of the
GALE INFORMATION GUIDE LIBRARY

The Library consists of a number of separate series of guides covering major areas in the social sciences, humanities, and current affairs.

General Editor: Paul Wasserman, Professor and former Dean, School of Library and Information Services, University of Maryland

Managing Editor: Denise Allard Adzigian, Gale Research Company

Afro-American Literature and Culture Since World War II

A GUIDE TO INFORMATION SOURCES

Volume 6 in the American Studies Information Guide Series

Charles D. Peavy

Professor of English
University of Houston
Houston, Texas

Gale Research Company
Book Tower, Detroit, Michigan 48226

Z
1229
.N39
P4

Library of Congress Cataloging in Publication Data

Peavy, Charles D
    Afro-American literature and culture since World
War II.

    (American studies information guide series ; v. 6)
    (Gale information guide library)
    Includes indexes.
    1. American literature—Afro-American authors—
Bibliography. 2. American literature—20th century—
Bibliography. 3. Afro-Americans—Bibliography.
4. United States—Civilization—1945- —Bibliography.
5. Reference books—Afro-Americans—Bibliography.
I. Title.
Z1229.N39P4   [PS153.N5]   016.810'8'0896073   73-17561
ISBN 0-8103-1254-9

VITA

Charles D. Peavy is a professor of English at the University of Houston where he teaches courses in American and Afro-American literature. He received his Ph.D. from Tulane University, New Orleans. He is the past president of the Texas College Conference of Teachers of English and the American Studies Association of Texas. He has served seven years on the National Council of the American Studies Association.

Peavy is the recipient of grants from the National Endowment for the Humanities, American Council of Learned Societies, Danforth Association, and the University of Houston. His published research includes several bibliographies, monographs, books, and articles.

CONTENTS

Contents

Contents

FOREWORD

Although Charles D. Peavy is a professor of English at the University of Houston, he has been very active in the field of American Studies, with a special interest in twentieth-century Afro-American literature and culture. He is the author of numerous scholarly articles related to that interest, and his knowledge of black American writers and the unique culture that has produced them is most unusual.

Professor Peavy has chosen to concentrate his book on the period since World War II. I believe his choice to be wise, not because there was an inconsiderable body of black American literature before that time but because the giant strides made in virtually all the arts, and perhaps particularly in literature, by black Americans since then have dwarfed what preceded them. Furthermore, much of the work that preceded the war was done within the context of the predominantly white social structure. In large measure the civil rights movement, the increased urbanization of black Americans, the developing knowledge of black American history, and a sense of pride in their roots has materially changed the basic approach of our black artists.

Professor Peavy's book will, I feel, be of genuine value to all students of Afro-American literature and culture, covering, as it does, not only the work of all major figures of the period but also that of a great many who, although relatively minor, deserve to be known by all who wish to be solidly grounded in the field.

Donald N. Koster
Series Editor

INTRODUCTION

This bibliography embraces the general subject of Afro-American literature and culture during the three decades immediately following World War II. I have chosen this period in black American history because of the revolutionary cultural changes that occurred during this time and because of the role that Afro-American literature played in these changes. Black Cultural Nationalism, for instance, was a natural concomitant to the Black Power Movement; the mood that sparked the riots in Watts, Detroit, and New York was reflected in the revolutionary black drama produced by rapidly emerging theater groups in the urban ghettoes. Black poetry and prose emphasized Black Pride and Black Identity. Militant black leaders stressed the essentially revolutionary nature of the new literature. During this period, Maulana Ron Karenga, founder of the Black Nationalist Cultural Organization, consistently stressed the importance of a cultural revolution preceding any attempt at revolutionary social change. "The battle we are waging now," he said, "is the battle for the minds of black people; if we lose this battle, we cannot win the violent one." Similarly, LeRoi Jones, founder of the Black Arts Repertory Theatre and School in Harlem and of Spirit House in Newark, and Ed Bullins, cofounder of the Black Arts/ West in San Francisco and Minister of Culture of the Black Panther Party, insisted that the new black literature should be directed exclusively toward the black audience, addressing itself to the fears, frustrations, and aspirations of Black America. It is natural, then, that much of the literature covered by this bibliography reflects the cultural revolution of the age and differs radically from the protest, integrationist, or assimilationist literature of earlier decades before the war.

I have been selective in choosing those cultural aspects which I felt best reflected the Zeitgeist of this period, and thus have included sections on such subjects as the Black Muslims and the Black Panthers, the Civil Rights Movement and the Black Power Movement, riots, prison writing, and the psychology of blacks. In selecting writers and their works, I have again been selective in including that literature which best expresses the spirit of the time.

In establishing the format for this volume, I have avoided what seemed the impossible task of annotating entries for poems in the bibliography. The fact that a work is a poem is indicated by the word "poetry" after the title. In all other instances, the entries are annotated as an aid for the student and re-searcher.

Charles D. Peavy

Part 1

SUBJECTS

ANTHOLOGIES

Adoff, Arnold, ed. BLACK OUT LOUD: AN ANTHOLOGY OF MODERN
POEMS BY BLACK AMERICANS. New York: Macmillan, 1970. 86 p.

An anthology of sixty-seven poems "compiled to introduce Black
Poetry to the young brothers and sisters. . . ."

_____. I AM THE DARKER BROTHER: AN ANTHOLOGY OF MODERN POEMS
BY BLACK AMERICANS. New York: Macmillan, 1968. 128 p.

An anthology of twenty-eight black poets such as Gwendolyn Brooks,
Arna Bontemps, and LeRoi Jones.

AFRO-ARTS ANTHOLOGY (ANTHOLOGY OF OUR BLACK SELVES). Newark,
N.J.: Jihad Productions, 1969. Unpaged.

First edition (1966) originally published as AFRO-AMERICAN FESTI-
VAL OF THE ARTS MAGAZINE 1966. Articles, essays, poetry,
and plays by Sonia Sanchez, L.P. Neal, E. Spriggs, LeRoi Jones,
Ben Caldwell.

Barksdale, Richard [K.], and Kinnamon, Keneth, eds. BLACK WRITERS OF
AMERICA: A COMPREHENSIVE ANTHOLOGY. New York: Macmillan, 1972.
917 p.

Part 6 of the anthology is entitled "The Present Generation: Since
1945" and contains selections of postwar fiction, poetry, drama,
and essays as well as excerpts by racial spokesmen such as Martin
Luther King, Jr., Malcolm X, and Eldridge Cleaver.

Bullins, Ed, ed. THE NEW LAFAYETTE THEATRE PRESENTS; PLAYS WITH AES-
THETIC COMMENTS BY 6 BLACK PLAYWRIGHTS. Garden City, N.Y.: Doubleday, 1974. 301 p.

Contains Ed Bullins, THE FABULOUS MISS MARIE; J.E. Gaines,
WHAT IF IT HAD TURNED UP HEADS; Clay Goss, ON BEING HIT;
Oyamo, HIS FIRST STEP; Sonia Sanchez, UH, UH; BUT HOW DO
IT FREE US?; Richard Wesley, BLACK TERROR.

_____. NEW PLAYS FROM THE BLACK THEATRE. New York: Bantam Books, 1969. 304 p.

Contains WE RIGHTEOUS BOMBERS by Kingsley B. Bass; IN NEW ENGLAND WINTER by Ed Bullins; THE KING OF SOUL OR THE DEVIL AND OTIS REDDING and FAMILY PORTRAIT OR MY SON THE BLACK NATIONALIST by Ben Caldwell; EL HAJ MALIK by N.R. Davidson; THE RISE by Charles H. Fuller, Jr.; THE MAN WHO TRUSTED THE DEVIL TWICE by Herbert Stokes; and GROWIN' INTO BLACKNESS by Salimu.

Chapman, Dorothy H. INDEX TO BLACK POETRY. Boston: G.K. Hall & Co., 1974. 541 p.

Index to over five thousand poets in ninety-four books and pamphlets and thirty-three anthologies.

Childress, Alice, ed. BLACK SCENES. Garden City, N.Y.: Doubleday, 1971. 154 p.

A drama anthology which contains THE BIRD CAGE by Floyd Barbour; TO FOLLOW THE PHOENIX by William Branch; NATURAL MAN by Theodore Brown; A SON COME HOME by Ed Bullins; ONE LAST LOOK by Steve Carter; THE AFRICAN GARDEN by Alice Childress; PURLIE VICTORIOUS by Ossie Davis; TO KILL A DEVIL by Roger Furman; A STREAK OF LEAN by Abbey Lincoln; 417 by Julian Mayfield; LAND REYOND THE RIVER by Loften Mitchell; SHOES by Ted Shine; and DAY OF ABSENCE by Douglas Turner Ward.

Coombs, Orde, ed. WE SPEAK AS LIBERATORS: YOUNG BLACK POETS. New York: Dodd, Mead, 1970. 252 p.

An anthology of fifty-seven black poets of the 1960s. Most of the poets included were previously either unpublished or infrequently published.

Couch, William, Jr., ed. NEW BLACK PLAYWRIGHTS. Baton Rouge: Louisiana State University Press, 1968. 258 p.

Contains GOIN' A BUFFALO by Ed Bullins; CEREMONIES IN DARK OLD MEN by Lonne Elder; A RAT'S MASS by Adrienne Kennedy; FAMILY MEETING by William Wellington Macky; and DAY OF ABSENCE and HAPPY ENDING by Douglas Turner Ward.

Emanuel, James A., and Gross, Theodore, eds. DARK SYMPHONY. New York: Free Press, 1968. 604 p.

Last two sections contain selections from the works of major Afro-American writers since 1945.

Gayle, Addison, Jr., ed. THE BLACK AESTHETIC. Garden City, N.Y.: Doubleday, 1971. 432 p.

An important anthology of essays dealing with various aspects of the black aesthetic. The essays are divided into five categories: theory, music, poetry, drama, and fiction.

Hill, Herbert, ed. SOON, ONE MORNING: NEW WRITING BY AMERICAN NEGROES, 1940-1962. New York: Alfred A. Knopf, 1963. 617 p.

Anthology divided into three sections: essays, fiction, and poetry. Contains much previously unpublished material. Also contains a selection from original version of Ellison's INVISIBLE MAN.

Hughes, Douglas A. FROM A BLACK PERSPECTIVE: CONTEMPORARY BLACK ESSAYS. New York: Holt, Rinehart and Winston, 1970. 247 p.

Includes essays by Claude Brown, James Baldwin, Nathan Hare, Nathan Wright, Jr., John Oliver Killens, Stokely Carmichael, LeRoi Jones, Eldridge Cleaver, Julian Bond, Malcolm X, Julius Lester, Dick Gregory, and others.

James, Charles L., ed. FROM THE ROOTS. New York: Dodd, Mead, 1970. 370 p.

An anthology of short stories by black Americans. Last two sections, "Toward Literary Assimilation, 1940-1950," and "Toward A Black Art, 1950-1969," contain short fiction by post-World War II Afro-Americans.

Kearns, Francis E., ed. THE BLACK EXPERIENCE: AN ANTHOLOGY OF AMERICAN LITERATURE FOR THE 1970'S. New York: Viking Press, 1970. 650 p.

Includes works by forty-two writers (not all black) about the black experience in America.

King, Woodie, [Jr.], and Milner, Ron[ald], eds. BLACK DRAMA ANTHOLOGY. New York: Columbia University Press, 1972. 671 p.

Contains ALL WHITE CASTE by Ben Caldwell; BLACK CYCLE by Martie Charles; A MEDAL FOR WILLIE by William Branch; LADIES IN WAITING by Peter DeAnda; THE CORNER by Ed Bullins; JUNKIES ARE FULL OF (SHHH. . .) and BLOODRITES by LeRoi Jones; CHARADES ON EAST FOURTH STREET by Lonne Elder; GABRIEL by Clifford Mason; BROTHERHOOD by Douglas Turner Ward; THE MARRIAGE by Donald Greave; THE ONE by Oliver Pitcher; THE OWL KILLER by Philip Hayes Dean; REQUIEM FOR BROTHER X by William W. Macky; THREE X LOVE by Ron Zuber; MOTHER AND CHILD by Langston Hughes; WHO'S GOT HIS OWN by Ron Milner; TOE JAM by Elaine Jackson; and STRICTLY MATRI-

MONY by Errol Hill. The introduction, "Evolution of a People's Theater," is by LeRoi Jones.

Major, Clarence, ed. THE NEW BLACK POETRY. New York: International Publishing Co., 1969. 156 p.

An anthology of post-World War II poetry which indicates the contemporary awakening of black consciousness.

Margolies, Edward, ed. A NATIVE SON'S READER. Philadelphia: J.B. Lippincott, 1970. 361 p.

An anthology of primarily post-World War II novels. Selections arranged in categories to best express various aspects of the Afro-American experience, such as migration, city, children, church, music, anger, and men and women.

Randall, Dudley, ed. BLACK POETRY: A SUPPLEMENT TO ANTHOLOGIES WHICH EXCLUDE BLACK POETS. Detroit: Broadside Press, 1969. 48 p.

An anthology of contemporary black poetry.

Reed, Ishmael, ed. 19 NECROMANCERS FROM NOW: AN ANTHOLOGY OF ORIGINAL AMERICAN WRITING FOR THE 70'S. Garden City, N.Y.: Doubleday, 1970. 369 p.

An anthology of plays and fiction of Afro-American, Indian-American, and Chinese-American writers. Reed sees these writers as representative of the movement he calls "Neo-hoodooism."

Schulberg, Budd, ed. FROM THE ASHES: VOICES OF WATTS. New York: World Publishing Co., 1969. 277 p.

An anthology of short stories, plays, essays, poetry, and novels-in-progress produced in Schulberg's Watts Writers Workshop, founded after the 1965 riots in Watts.

Singh, Raman K., and Fellowes, Peter. BLACK LITERATURE IN AMERICA. New York: Thomas Y. Crowell, 1970. 354 p.

An anthology of poetry, fiction, essays, and drama, designed for use in college freshman courses in composition as well as courses in Afro-American literature.

Turner, Darwin T. BLACK AMERICAN LITERATURE. Columbus, Ohio: Charles E. Merrill, 1969. 142 p.

Contains short fiction by Richard Wright, Frank Yerby, Ralph Ellison, James Baldwin, William M. Kelley, and Kristin Hunter.

_____. BLACK DRAMA IN AMERICA. New York: Fawcett, 1971. 630 p.

This anthology does not confine itself to contemporary Afro-American drama but it does have such plays as EMPEROR OF HAITI by Langston Hughes, OUR LAN' by Theodore Ward, THE TOILET by LeRoi Jones, and PURLIE VICTORIOUS by Ossie Davis.

Wilentz, Ted, and Weatherly, Tom, eds. NATURAL PROCESS: AN ANTHOLOGY OF NEW BLACK POETRY. New York: Hill and Wang, 1970. 181 p.

Contains poetry by David Henderson, Nikki Giovanni, Clarence Major, Sonia Sanchez, Carolyn M. Rodgers, and others.

Williams, John [A.]. BEYOND THE ANGRY BLACK. New York: Cooper Square Publishers, 1966. 198 p.

A collection of works by post-World War II black writers which reflects the angry mood that characterized the period leading to the black power movement; also contains the works of a few white writers.

BIBLIOGRAPHIES

Benoit, Bernard, and Fabre, Michel. "A Bibliography of Ralph Ellison's Published Writings." STUDIES IN BLACK LITERATURE 2 (Autumn 1971): 25-28.

A useful index to Ellison's work published prior to 1971.

"Books and Articles Related to Black Theatre Published from 1/1960 to 2/1968." DRAMA REVIEW 12 (Summer 1968): 176-80.

A somewhat confusing bibliography because of the format followed: plays are listed by author in chronological order; articles are listed in chronological order.

Corrigan, Robert A. "Afro-American Fiction: A Checklist 1853-1970." MID-CONTINENT AMERICAN STUDIES JOURNAL 11 (Fall 1970): 114-35.

An extended version of the checklist which originally appeared in STUDIES IN BLACK LITERATURE, vol. 1, no. 2.

Covo, Jaqueline. "Ralph Ellison in France: Bibliographic Essays and Checklist of French Criticism, 1954-1971." CLA JOURNAL 16 (June 1973): 519-26.

The definitive bibliography on the subject.

Deodene, Frank, and French, William P. BLACK AMERICAN FICTION SINCE 1952, A PRELIMINARY CHECKLIST. Chatham, N.J.: Chatham Bookseller, 1971. 25 p.

A most useful checklist for postwar Afro-American fiction.

Dickinson, Donald C. A BIO-BIBLIOGRAPHY OF LANGSTON HUGHES, 1902-1967. Hamden, Conn.: Archon Books, 1967. 273 p.

An expansion of Dickinson's University of Michigan dissertation.

Fuller, Hoyt W. "Books by Arna Bontemps, Compiled 1969, Revised and Amended,

1971." BLACK WORLD 20 (September 1971): 78-79.

> Lists Bontemps' publications as well as his collaborations with
> Langston Hughes, Jack Conroy, W.C. Handy, and others.

Graham, James D. "Negro Protest in America, 1900-1955. A Bibliographical
Guide." SOUTH ATLANTIC QUARTERLY 67 (1968): 94-107.

> A review-essay and bibliographic guide to the literature and
> scholarship concerned with Negro protest in America. The last
> section, entitled "The Literature of Negro Protest, 1940-1955"
> (pp. 104-7), is relevant to the subject examined in this bibliog-
> raphy.

Houston, Helen R. "Contributions of the American Negro to American Culture:
A Selected Checklist." BULLETIN OF BIBLIOGRAPHY 26 (July-September
1969): 71-83.

> "The purpose of this bibliography is to furnish titles which will be
> of value in a study of the American Negro's effect on American
> culture and its effect on him." Categories of listings include
> general, autobiography and biography, art, folklore, music, liter-
> ature, and theater.

Hudson, Theodore R. A LEROI JONES (AMIRI BARAKA) BIBLIOGRAPHY: A
KEYED RESEARCH GUIDE TO WORKS BY LEROI JONES AND TO WRITING
ABOUT HIM AND HIS WORKS. Washington, D.C.: The author, 1971. 18 p.

> A reprint of material apparently taken from Hudson's unpublished
> dissertation, "From LeRoi Jones to Amiri Baraka" (Howard Univer-
> sity, 1971). Though certainly incomplete, Hudson's bibliography
> is useful in that it notes the various names Jones used in his pub-
> lications, for instance, LeRoi Jones, Amiri Baraka or Imamu Amiri
> Baraka, Ameer Baraka or Imamu Ameer Baraka.

Jahn, Janheinz. A BIBLIOGRAPHY OF NEO-AFRICAN LITERATURE FROM
AFRICA, AMERICA, AND THE CARIBBEAN. New York: Praeger, 1965.
359 p.

> This book contains writings in three languages (with translations)
> by writers described by Jahn as "neo-African." Among the U.S.
> "neo-Africans" are Langston Hughes, Richard Wright, and LeRoi
> Jones.

Kaiser, Ernest. "Recent Literature on Black Liberation Struggles and the Ghetto
Crisis (A Bibliographical Survey)." SCIENCE AND SOCIETY 33 (1969): 168-
96.

> A comprehensive bibliographical survey and review essay.

Bibliographies

Krash, Ronald, et al. BLACK AMERICA: A RESEARCH BIBLIOGRAPHY. St. Louis, Mo.: St. Louis University, 1972. 113 p.

Most of the material listed in this collection was published after World War II.

Leffall, Dolores C. BIBLIOGRAPHIC SURVEY. THE NEGRO IN PRINT. FIVE YEAR SUBJECT INDEX 1965-1970. Washington, D.C.: Negro Bibliographic and Research Center, 1971. 166 p.

Somewhat difficult to use, this bibliography contains listings of important post-World War II publications.

Levi, Doris J., and Milton, Nerissa L. DIRECTORY OF BLACK LITERARY MAGAZINES. Washington, D.C.: Negro Bibliographic and Research Center, 1970. 19 p.

Lists the editors, publishers, frequencies of publication, and subscription and single rates. Also contains brief comments regarding the contents of the journals.

McPherson, James M. BLACKS IN AMERICA. Garden City, N.Y.: Doubleday, 1971. 430 p.

Bibliographical essays on blacks in American culture. Sections 7, 8, and 9 contain bibliographical essays on Afro-American subjects from 1945 to 1970.

Meyers, Carol. "A Selected Bibliography of Recent Afro-American Writers." CLA JOURNAL 16 (March 1973): 377-82.

A useful checklist for the period through 1972.

Porter, Dorothy B. A WORKING BIBLIOGRAPHY ON THE NEGRO IN THE UNITED STATES. Ann Arbor, Mich.: University Microfilms, 1968. 128 p.

A useful bibliography. Contains listing of recent black journals and newspapers.

Querry, Ronald, and Fleming, Robert E. "A Working Bibliography of Black Periodicals." STUDIES IN BLACK LITERATURE 3 (Summer 1972): 31-36.

Schatt, Stanley. "Contemporary Afro-American Drama: An Annotated Checklist of Primary and Secondary Sources." WEST COAST REVIEW 8 (October 1973): 41-44.

A good checklist for contemporary black drama. Also lists anthologies of black drama.

_____. "Le Roi Jones: A Checklist to Primary and Secondary Sources."

BULLETIN OF BIBLIOGRAPHY AND MAGAZINE NOTES 28 (April-June 1971): 55-57.

A very brief bibliography of works by and about Jones, useful in its annotations of the secondary sources but unfortunately containing errors in the listings of the primary sources.

Schutz, Walter. DIRECTORY OF AFRO-AMERICAN RESOURCES. New York: R.R. Bowker, 1970. 485 p.

Directory lists 2,108 institutions and 5,365 collections of resource materials. Institutions include college, university, public, government, and business libraries; and federal, state, local, and private agencies.

Shockley, Ann, and Chandler, Sue. LIVING BLACK AMERICAN AUTHORS: A BIOGRAPHICAL DIRECTORY. New York: R.R. Bowker, 1973. 220 p.

Besides biographical entries the book contains selected bibliographies.

Standley, Fred J. "James Baldwin: A Checklist, 1963-1967." BULLETIN OF BIBLIOGRAPHY 25 (May-August 1968): 135-37.

A useful reference tool for research on Baldwin.

Turner, Darwin T. AFRO-AMERICAN WRITERS. New York: Appleton-Century-Crofts, 1970. 117 p.

A useful compendium of bibliographic references to black writers, not all of them contemporary.

Walton, Hanes, Jr. THE STUDY AND ANALYSIS OF BLACK POLITICS. Metuchen, N.J.: Scarecrow Press, 1973. 161 p.

A comprehensive listing of articles, books, and dissertations on every aspect of blacks in politics.

Welsch, Erwin K. THE NEGRO IN THE UNITED STATES. Bloomington: University of Indiana Press, 1965. 142 p.

A critical Introduction to the principal sources for research in Afro-American culture. Included are sources on history, literature, music, art, biography, sociology, and religion.

Williams, Daniel T. EIGHT NEGRO BIBLIOGRAPHIES. New York: Kraus Reprint, 1970. Various pagings.

First five sections concentrate on Afro-American history of the 1960s: (1) The Freedom Rides, (2) The Southern Students' Protest Movement, (3) The University of Mississippi and James Meredith, (4) The Black Muslims, and (5) Martin Luther King, Jr.

Bibliographies

Williams, Ora. AMERICAN BLACK WOMEN IN THE ARTS AND SOCIAL SCIENCES. Metuchen, N.J.: Scarecrow Press, 1973. 141 p.

A bibliography of more than one thousand entries and close to two thousand works.

____. "A Bibliography of Works Written by American Black Women." COLLEGE LANGUAGE ASSOCIATION JOURNAL 15 (March 1972): 354-77.

An excellent checklist on black female writers.

BLACK AESTHETIC

Barksdale, Richard K. "Urban Crisis and the Black Poetic Avant-Garde."
NEGRO AMERICAN LITERATURE FORUM 3 (Summer 1969): 40-44.

For the poet of the black avant-garde there will never be any
"searing apocalyptic vision" but only "the cobweb of creative
insecurity."

"The Black Aesthetic: A Debate." BLACK WORLD 24 (December 1974):
30-48.

The opponent in the debate, Martin Kilson, sees the new black
art as nothing but an ideology; the defender, Addison Gayle, Jr.,
defends the new black art on aesthetic grounds.

Clarke, John Henrik, ed. WILLIAM STYRON'S NAT TURNER: TEN BLACK
WRITERS RESPOND. Boston: Beacon Press, 1968. 120 p.

Because there were no major black reviews of Styron's sensational
fictionalization of the confessions of the black slave revolutionary,
Nat Turner, a book which many black intellectuals found not only
inaccurate but racist, ten black writers responded with their views
on Styron's work. In addition to Clarke, the writers included are
Lerone Bennett, Jr., Alvin F. Poussaint, Vincent Harding, John
Oliver Killens, John A. Williams, Ernest Kaiser, Loyle Hairston,
Charles V. Hamilton, and Mike Thelwell.

Crouch, Stanley. "Toward a Purer Black Poetry Aesthetic." JOURNAL OF
BLACK POETRY 1 (Fall 1968): 28-29.

Street speech and street song are two very different things; many
young black poets do not understand this.

Dickstein, Morris. "The Black Aesthetic in White America." PARTISAN RE-
VIEW 38 (Winter 1971-72): 376-95.

An examination of James Baldwin, Cecil Brown, James Alan Mc-

Pherson, Ishmael Reed, and others in the context of the developing black aesthetic of the late sixties.

Dixon, Melvin. "Black Theater: The Aesthetics." NEGRO DIGEST 18 (July 1969): 41–44.

"A functional, viable black aesthetic grows from an alliance of the artist with the community. The artist and his audience become one in search of the spiritual truth of blackness in a righteous effort to create an indigenous black art, a living theater, a living aesthetics."

Emanuel, James A. "Blackness Can: A Quest for Aesthetics." In THE BLACK AESTHETIC, edited by Addison Gayle, Jr., pp. 192–223. Garden City, N.Y.: Doubleday, 1971.

Emanuel feels that "those who accept the responsibility of charting a course for black authors and critics, bearing in mind that such activity is anathema to many of its assumed beneficiaries, must look backward as well as forward."

Evans, Mari. "Contemporary Black Literature." BLACK WORLD 19 (June 1970): 4, 93–94.

A statement concerning black literature from the perspective of "black consciousness."

Fabio, Sarah Webster. "A Black Paper." NEGRO DIGEST 18 (July 1969): 27–31, 76–89.

A response to David Littlejohn's BLACK ON WHITE and also an attack on his opposition to the institution of a course in Afro-American literature at the University of California.

Ford, Nick Aaron. "A Blueprint for Negro Authors." PHYLON 11 (1950): 374–77.

Outlines three requirements for black writers: (1) mastery of craftsmanship, (2) the continued use of racial themes, (3) the use of social propaganda subordinated so skillfully to the purposes of art that it will not insult the average reader.

Fowler, Carolyn. "A Contemporary Black-American Genre, Pamphlet/Manifesto Poetry." BLACK WORLD 23 (June 1974): 4–19.

A discussion of the "survival ethos" as it is implanted in the black aesthetic.

Fuller, Hoyt W. "The Black American Writer." NEGRO DIGEST 19 (April 1970): 96.

Ostensibly a review of C.W.E. Bigsby's two-volume work concerning black literature, this "review essay" is actually an attack on all white critics of black literature. The essay is one of many of Fuller's editorial statements that symptomize his increasing alienation with white experts in the late 1960s and early 1970s (see also statements on page 95 of the same issue of NEGRO DIGEST, and BLACK WORLD 19 [July 1970]: 87).

_____. "The Black-White War for Control of Image." BLACK WORLD 21 (November 1971): 77-78.

Fuller attacks the NEW YORK TIMES BOOK REVIEW for not utilizing black critics to review black literature and for what appears to be an effort to keep its readers from being exposed to black consciousness and the black aesthetic.

_____. "The Black-White War for Control of Image--Continued." BLACK WORLD 21 (May 1972): 90-91.

Another of Fuller's many editorials concerning the "hold" white publishers and critics have on the publication and success of literature written by black authors. In this statement, Fuller attacks poet Louis Simpson's casual dismissal of the work of Gwendolyn Brooks, Richard Gilman's contempt for contemporary black drama, as well as the authoritative stance assumed by Robert Bone.

_____. "Introduction toward the Black Aesthetic." NOMMO 1, no. 1: 3. Slightly variant text appears in THE BLACK AESTHETIC, edited by Addison Gayle, Jr., pp. 3-12. Garden City, N.Y.: Doubleday, 1971.

A statement of the goal of the Organization of Black American Culture (OBAC) in Chicago: to establish a black aesthetic.

_____. "The New Black Literature: Protest or Affirmation." In THE BLACK AESTHETIC, edited by Addison Gayle, Jr., pp. 346-69. Garden City, N.Y.: Doubleday, 1971.

A discussion of the new black writer's concern with image and myth: "They are about the business of destroying those images and myths that have crippled and degraded black people, and the institution of new images and myths that will liberate them."

_____. "The Task of the Negro Writer as Artist--A Symposium." NEGRO DIGEST 15 (April 1965): 54-83.

The symposium consists of the statements made by thirty-six black writers in response to the question asked by Hoyt Fuller, editor of NEGRO DIGEST: "What is the task of the Negro writer concerned with creating a work of art in a segregated society and how does his task differ from that of the white writer--if it differs at all?"

_____. "Toward a Black Aesthetic." CRITIC 26 (April–May 1968): 70-73.

Seminal essay in the movement to establish a black aesthetic.

Gayle, Addison, Jr. "Cultural Strangulation: Black Literature and the White Aesthetic." NEGRO DIGEST 18 (July 1969): 32-39. Reprinted in his THE BLACK AESTHETIC, pp. 39-46. Garden City, N.Y.: Doubleday, 1971.

A rebuttal to white critics' opposition to the anthology BLACK FIRE, and to their contention that there is no black aesthetic.

_____. "The Function of Black Literature at the Present Time." In his THE BLACK AESTHETIC, pp. 407-19. Garden City, N.Y.: Doubleday, 1971.

Gayle writes in this concluding essay in his anthology that "the black writer at the present time must forego the assimilationist tradition and redirect his art to the strivings within the race."

_____. Preface to his BLACK EXPRESSION, pp. vii-xv. New York: Weybright and Talley, 1969.

Black writers should dedicate themselves to the proposition that "literature is a moral force for change as well as an aesthetic creation."

_____, ed. THE BLACK AESTHETIC. Garden City, N.Y.: Doubleday, 1971. 432 p.

An anthology of essays concerning the black artists' attempts to define a black aesthetic in the various genres: drama, music, fiction, and poetry. An important collection on the subject.

Gerald, Carolyn F. "The Black Writer and His Role." NEGRO DIGEST 18 (January 1969): 42-48.

"What is new [in black literature] is the deliberate desecration and smashing of idols, the turning inside-out of symbols. . . . Bitterness is being replaced by wrath; a sense of frustration is giving way before a sense of power."

Hagopian, John V. "Mau-Mauing the Literary Establishment." STUDIES IN THE NOVEL 3 (Summer 1971): 135-47.

Insisting that blacks have a unique experience, language, and literature which whites cannot understand, militant black writers have intimidated publishers, critics, and other black writers who repudiate the ethics and aesthetics of violence. The result has been a corruption of the artistry of black literature.

Hannerz, Ulj. "The Significance of Soul." In BLACK EXPERIENCE: SOUL, edited by Lee Rainwater, pp. 15-30. New Brunswick, N.J.: Transaction Books, 1973.

An essay on the meaning of soul, which Hannerz sees as "the essence of Negroness."

Karenga, [Maulana] Ron. "Black Cultural Nationalism." In THE BLACK AESTHETIC, edited by Addison Gayle, Jr., pp. 32-38. Garden City, N.Y.: Doubleday, 1971.

"All art must reflect and support the Black Revolution, and any art that does not discuss and contribute to the revolution is invalid. . . ."

Keller, Joseph. "Black Writing and the White Critic." NEGRO AMERICAN LITERATURE FORUM 3 (Winter 1970): 103-10.

Suggests a methodology for white criticism of black literature.

Kgositsile, William Keorapetse. "Paths to the Future." In THE BLACK AESTHETIC, edited by Addison Gayle, Jr., pp. 248-60. Garden City, N.Y.: Doubleday, 1971.

The sixties produced a generation of black poets who were influenced by Negritude, and protest poets and writers like Cesaire, Senghor, Diop, and DuBois.

Kilgore, James C. "A Question of Aesthetics?--The Case for Black Literature." NEGRO DIGEST 18 (July 1969): 11-17.

"Not to teach, in the context of American Literature, that literature which treats honestly the humanity of black Americans is to continue to be, to black and white Americans, academically dishonest, humanistically cruel, and psychologically destructive."

_____. "Toward the Dark Tower." BLACK WORLD 19 (June 1970): 14-17.

An argument for the expression of black consciousness in the new Afro-American poetry.

King, Woodie, Jr., and Milner, Ron[ald], eds. "Evolution of a People's Theater." In their BLACK DRAMA ANTHOLOGY, pp. vii-x. New York: New American Library, 1971.

King and Milner argue that contemporary black drama must be freed from the tastes of the white culture of Broadway and must express the needs and attitudes of the black community.

Lee, Don L. "Toward a Black Aesthetic: Black Poetry--Which Direction?" NEGRO DIGEST 17 (September-October 1968): 27-32.

"Black poets will deal with themselves as 'individuals' first and
then will move toward a concept of 'peoplehood'. . . . They will
move from the _I_ to the _we_ to the _us_ and to the _our_."

_____. "Toward a Definition: Black Poetry of the Sixties (After LeRoi Jones)."
In THE BLACK AESTHETIC, edited by Addison Gayle, Jr., pp. 235-47. Garden City, N.Y.: Doubleday, 1971.

Lee writes that "black poets have discovered their uniqueness, their
beauty, their tales, their history, and have diligently moved to
enlighten their people and the world's people in an art form that's
called poetry, but to them is another extension of black music."

_____. "Voices of the Seventies: Black Critics." BLACK WORLD 19
(September 1970): 24-30.

"What the Black critic must bring to us is an extensive knowledge
of world literature, along with a specialized awareness of our own
literature."

Mayfield, Julian. "You Touch My Black Aesthetic and I'll Touch Yours." In
THE BLACK AESTHETIC, edited by Addison Gayle, Jr., pp. 24-31. Garden
City, N.Y.: Doubleday, 1971.

"The Black Aesthetic, for those trying to create today, is neces-
sarily the business of making revolution."

Miller, Adam David. "Some Observations on a Black Aesthetic." In THE
BLACK AESTHETIC, edited by Addison Gayle, Jr., pp. 397-404. Garden
City, N.Y.: Doubleday, 1971.

Suggests that "it may be that a black aesthetic is inherent in the
black experience and is rendered when we honestly recreate that
experience."

Milner, Ronald. "Black Theater--Go Home." In THE BLACK AESTHETIC,
edited by Addison Gayle, Jr., pp. 307-12. Garden City, N.Y.: Doubleday,
1971.

Black dramatists must return to the black communities because they
"can sustain, assist, and inspire us to essential and brilliant levels
in our new black theater."

Neal, Larry. "Any Day Now: Black Art and Black Liberation." EBONY,
August 1969, pp. 54-62.

Neal discusses the role the black arts movement will play in the
"cultural and spiritual liberation of Black America." In addition,
the black arts movement "seeks to link, in a highly conscious
manner, art and politics in order to assist in the liberation of Black
people."

_____. "The Black Arts Movement." DRAMA REVIEW 12 (Summer 1968): 29-39.

An essay which outlines the total commitment to the black community of the black arts movement. The movement proposes "a radical reordering of the western cultural aesthetic."

_____. "Some Reflections on the Black Aesthetic." In THE BLACK AESTHETIC, edited by Addison Gayle, Jr., pp. 13-16. Garden City, N.Y.: Doubleday, 1971.

An outline indicating what Neal feels to be the categories and elements constituting a black aesthetic.

O'Neal, John. "Black Arts: Notebook." In THE BLACK AESTHETIC, edited by Addison Gayle, Jr., pp. 47-58. Garden City, N.Y.: Doubleday, 1971.

"Our work as Black Artists is to help our People to recognize themselves and the inevitable demands of the struggle that lies ahead."

Perkins, Eugene. "The Changing Status of Black Writers." BLACK WORLD 19 (June 1970): 18-23, 95-98.

"The new Black writers are defining themselves, and in doing so, defining that criteria which they feel is relevant to judging their literature. . . ."

Randall, Dudley. "The Black Aesthetic in the Thirties, Forties, and Fifties." In THE BLACK AESTHETIC, edited by Addison Gayle, Jr., pp. 224-34. Garden City, N.Y.: Doubleday, 1971.

A historical survey of the gradual emergence of a black aesthetic.

Rodgers, Carolyn. "Breakforth. In Deed." BLACK WORLD 19 (September 1970): 13-22.

An expression of the black aesthetic by one of the founding members of the Organization of Black American Culture Writers' Workshop (OBAC) in Chicago.

Stewart, James T. "The Black Revolutionary Artist." In BLACK FIRE, AN ANTHOLOGY OF AFRO-AMERICAN WRITING, edited by LeRoi Jones and Larry Neal, pp. 3-10. New York: William Morrow, 1968. Reprinted in THE BLACK NOVELIST, edited by LeRoi Jones and Roy Neal, pp. 136-41. Columbus, Ohio: Charles E. Merrill, 1970.

The task of the black writer is revolutionary. "He must view his role vis-a-vis White Western civilization, and from this starting point in his estrangement begin to make new definitions founded on his own culture--on definite black values."

. "The Development of the Black Revolutionary Artist." In BLACK FIRE, AN ANTHOLOGY OF AFRO-AMERICAN WRITING, edited by LeRoi Jones and Larry Neal, pp. 3-10. New York: William Morrow, 1968.

Stewart calls for an "estrangement" from the dominant white culture in order to "generate and energize" black artists.

Stewart, Jimmy. "Introduction to Black Aesthetics in Music." In THE BLACK AESTHETIC, edited by Addison Gayle, Jr., pp. 81-96. Garden City, N.Y.: Doubleday, 1971.

A discussion of how the black music of the sixties represents an absolute break with the past and with the aesthetic ideology of the white national culture.

Tatham, Campbell. "Double Order: The Spectrum of Black Aesthetics." MID-CONTINENT AMERICAN STUDIES JOURNAL 11 (1970): 88-100.

The conflict between those who insist upon viewing racial concern as a metaphor for universal questions and those who insist upon revolutionary commitment to black consciousness within a specific and concrete black community.

Toure, Askia Muhammad. "The Crises in Black Culture." BLACK THEATRE 1 (n.d.): 11-15.

One of two "symposium essays" on Harold Cruse's CRISIS OF THE NEGRO INTELLECTUAL published under the title "Two on Cruse" in the first issue of BLACK THEATRE.

Turner, Darwin. "Afro-American Literary Critics." BLACK WORLD 19 (July 1970): 54-67. Reprinted in THE BLACK AESTHETIC, edited by Addison Gayle, Jr., pp. 59-77. Garden City, N.Y.: Doubleday, 1971.

"A new group of Black critics have developed who reject the standards previously applied to works by Afro-Americans and are demanding that literature be judged according to an aesthetic grounded in Afro-American culture."

Wellburn, Ron. "The Black Aesthetic Imperative." In THE BLACK AESTHETIC, edited by Addison Gayle, Jr., pp. 132-49. Garden City, N.Y.: Doubleday, 1971.

"Black musicians should re-evaluate the technological intrusions now threatening our music; times may come when that technology will be useless."

Williams, John A. "The Literary Ghetto." SATURDAY REVIEW, 20 April 1963, pp. 21, 40.

Williams objects to the stereotyping of black authors by white critics and the inability of white authors to create genuine black characters.

BLACK MUSLIMS

Alonzo 4X. "Why I Follow the Honorable Elijah Muhammad." BLACK WORLD 23 (August 1974): 77-80.

A black journalist discusses his reasons for following the head of the Black Muslim organization.

Berger, Monroe. "Black Muslims." HORIZON 6 (Winter 1964): 48-65.

A review of the history of Black Muslims in America and an explanation for their passionate rejection of white America.

Brashler, William. "Black on Black: The Deadly Struggle for Power." NEW YORK 8 (9 June 1975): 44-50, 55-57.

A report on the factional struggles within the Black Muslims since the death of Elijah in February 1975.

Essien-Udom, Essien Udosen. BLACK NATIONALISM: A SEARCH FOR AN IDENTITY IN AMERICA. Chicago: University of Chicago Press, 1962. 367 p.

An examination of "the ideology of black nationalism, its organizations, leaders, and programs, focusing on the Nation of Islam-- a Muslim movement led by Elijah Muhammad."

Hentoff, Nat. "Elijah in the Wilderness." REPORTER 23 (4 August 1960): 37-40.

A comparison of Malcolm X and Elijah Muhammad: "Malcolm X may yet be an executive in the Urban League, but Elijah Muhammad is more likely to end as Marcus Garvey did--with little left but pictures of himself addressing huge crowds years before."

Lightfoot, Claude. "Negro Nationalism and the Black Muslims." POLITICAL AFFAIRS 41 (July 1962): 3-20.

Traces the growth and impact of the Black Muslim movement and places it in the context of black nationalism.

Lincoln, C. Eric. THE BLACK MUSLIMS IN AMERICA. Boston: Beacon Press, 1961. 276 p.

Definitive study of the Black Muslim movement in America.

Lomax, Louis E. WHEN THE WORD IS GIVEN: A REPORT ON ELIJAH MUHAMMAD, MALCOLM X, AND THE BLACK MUSLIM WORLD. Cleveland: World Publishing Co., 1963. 290 p.

An account of the Black Muslim movement based on newspaper articles and interviews over a period of time. Second part of the book contains the texts and addresses of Elijah Muhammad and Malcolm X and an interview by Lomax of Malcolm X.

Mason, Philip. "The Revolt against Western Values." DAEDALUS 96 (Spring 1967): 328-52.

Contains a section on the Black Muslims in the United States as well as millenarian cults such as the Ras Tofaris of Jamaica and the Mau Mau in Africa.

Mufassir, Sulayman Shahid. "Solutions to the Problem of Slavery (Then and Now)." BLACK WORLD 19 (July 1970): 12-18.

A discussion of the solutions Islam offers to "the Black man's present condition of enslavement to institutionalized racism and capitalistic oppressions."

Samuels, Gertrude. "Feud within the Black Muslims." NEW YORK TIMES MAGAZINE, 22 March 1964, pp. 17, 104-7.

A discussion of the "revolt" in Elijah Muhammad's Black Muslim sect caused by Malcolm X's "Black Nationalist" political movement.

Worthy, William. "The Angriest Negroes." ESQUIRE, February 1961, pp. 102-5.

A report on the Black Muslims and their attitudes towards whites.

BLACK PANTHERS

Anthony, Earl. PICKING UP THE GUN: A REPORT ON THE BLACK PAN-
THERS. New York: Dial Press, 1970. 160 p.

> Written by a former Panther "official" who left the group. Anthony
> details the goals and methods of the organization and tells why he
> left it; his early infatuation with the Panthers ends in disillusion-
> ment. Anthony is opposed to the party's affiliation with white
> radicals.

Arlen, Michael J. AN AMERICAN VERDICT. Garden City, N.Y.: Doubleday, 1973. 196 p.

> An examination of the 1969 raid in which fourteen armed plain-
> clothesmen broke into the Chicago Panther headquarters and killed
> Fred Hampton and Mark Clark. Concerns also the trial of State's
> Attorney Edward Hanrahan, who was accused of conspiring to ob-
> struct justice in investigating the facts of the raid.

Balagoon, Kuwasi, et al. LOOK FOR ME IN THE WHIRLWIND: THE COL-
LECTIVE AUTOBIOGRAPHY OF THE NEW YORK 21. Introduction by Haywood
Burns. New York: Random House, 1971. 364 p.

> The members of the Black Panthers who were on trial for conspiracy
> tell their stories. Each tells how he or she was motivated to join
> the Panthers.

Baruch, Ruth-Marion. THE VANGUARD. Introduction by William Worthy.
Boston: Beacon Press, 1970. 127 p.

> A photographic essay on the Black Panther party.

Blackburn, Sara, ed. WHITE JUSTICE: BLACK EXPERIENCE TODAY IN
AMERICA'S COURTROOMS. Foreword by Haywood Burns. New York: Harper
& Row, 1971. 289 p.

> Trial transcripts: The People of the State of Illinois v. Brenda

Harris, Blair Anderson, Ronald Satchel, Harold Bell, Deborah Johnson, Louis Truelock. The People of the State of California v. Huey P. Newton. The People of the State of California v. Charles Bursey. The People of the State of California v. Warren Wells. The People of the State of New York v. Alfred E. Cain, Ricardo DeLeon, Jerome West. The State of Connecticut v. Bobby G. Seale.

Chevigny, Paul. COPS AND REBELS: A STUDY OF PROVOCATION. New York: Pantheon Books, 1972. 332 p. Bibliography, pp. 329-32.

Chevigny, a New York ACLU lawyer, defends three Black Panthers accused of criminal conspiracy in 1970.

Erikson, Erik Homburger. IN SEARCH OF COMMON GROUND: CONVERSATIONS WITH ERIK ERIKSON AND HUEY P. NEWTON. New York: W.W. Norton, 1973. 143 p.

Transcripts of two meetings between Erikson and Newton. Newton discusses his theory of "revolutionary intercommunalism."

Foner, Philip S., ed. THE BLACK PANTHER SPEAKS. Preface by Julian Bond. Philadelphia: J.B. Lippincott, 1970. 274 p.

Contains the manifesto of the Black Panther party; excerpts from the Black Panther newspaper, articles, interviews, and "messages" from Panther leaders Huey P. Newton, Bobby Seale, Eldridge Cleaver, David Hilliard, Fred Hampton; contains the Young Lords Party's 13-Point Program and Platform.

Freed, Donald. AGONY IN NEW HAVEN: THE TRIAL OF BOBBY SEALE, ERICKA HUGGINS, AND THE BLACK PANTHER. New York: Simon & Schuster, 1973. 347 p.

A carefully documented analysis of the trial of Seale and Huggins for the kidnapping and murder of Black Panther Alex Rackley.

Hersey, John Richard. LETTER TO THE ALUMNI. New York: Alfred A. Knopf, 1970. 145 p.

Contains a defense of President Brewster of Yale University and the full text of Brewster's remarks about the New Haven trials of Black Panthers.

Kempton, Murray. THE BRIAR PATCH: THE PEOPLE OF THE STATE OF NEW YORK VS. LUMUMBA SHAKUR ET AL. New York: E.P. Dutton, 1973. 282 p.

An examination of the trial of the "Panther 21" who had been indicted for arson, conspiracy, and attempted murder.

Kennebeck, Edwin. JUROR NUMBER FOUR: THE TRIAL OF THIRTEEN BLACK PANTHERS AS SEEN FROM THE JURY BOX. New York: W.W. Norton, 1973. 238 p.

An account of the trial which lasted from October 1970 to May 1971. Black Panthers were accused of conspiracy to blow up police stations, railroad tracks, and department stores in order to incite revolution.

Major, Reginald. A PANTHER IS A BLACK CAT. New York: William Morrow, 1971. 308 p.

An examination of the founding of the Black Panther party in Oakland, California, in 1966 and an analysis of the conditions, such as poor housing, police harrassment, and unemployment which led to its formation.

Marine, Gene. "The Persecution and Assassination of the Black Panthers as Performed by the Oakland Police under the Direction of Chief Charles R. Gain, Major John Reading, et al." RAMPARTS 6 (May 1968): 37-46.

An attack on police action against the Black Panther party, in the form of a drama.

Moore, Chuck. I WAS A BLACK PANTHER. Garden City, N.Y.: Doubleday, 1970. 144 p.

"How and why a high school boy gets involved with the Black Panthers and where it leads him," as told to Moore by a Panther. Written in the form of a novel, the book purports to be a true story.

Moore, Gilbert Stuart. A SPECIAL RAGE. New York: Harper & Row, 1971. 276 p.

An examination of the Black Panther party and its leaders and an analysis of the Huey P. Newton murder trial.

Newton, Huey P. "The Black Panthers." EBONY, August 1969, pp. 106-12.

An article written by Newton while a prisoner at Los Padres Men's Colony at San Luis Obispo, California. Newton discusses the purpose, methods, and political ideology of the Black Panther organization.

_____. TO DIE FOR THE PEOPLE: THE WRITINGS OF HUEY P. NEWTON. New York: Random House, 1972. 232 p.

An outline of the history and goals of the Black Panther party in a compilation of articles, speeches, and interviews by Huey Newton, the founder of the organization.

Riley, Clayton. "Assault on the Panthers." LIBERATOR 10 (January 1970): 4-7.

An examination of the inevitable and systematic plan to destroy the Panthers when they shifted their tactics from self-defense and breakfast for black community children.

Schanche, Don A. THE PANTHER PARADOX. New York: D. McKay Co., 1970. 231 p.

A personal account of a white liberal's activities with the Black Panthers. A history and introduction to the Black Panther party. Contains an interview with Eldridge Cleaver during his exile in Algiers.

Seale, Bobby. SEIZE THE TIME: THE STORY OF THE BLACK PANTHER PARTY. New York: Random House, 1970. 429 p.

"The Nixon-Agnew-Mitchell Administration--hand in hand with the Reagans, the Daleys, the Hoffmans, the Carswells, Rockefellers, DuPonts, the Bank of America and other exploiters--moves closer and closer to open fascism."

_____. SEIZE THE TIME: THE STORY OF THE BLACK PANTHER PARTY AND HUEY P. NEWTON. New York: Random House, 1969. 429 p.

An autobiographical and historical work which attempts to deal with the "misconceptions" that Panthers are antiwhite and committed to the murder of white policemen. Most of the book is a transcription of tapes made in the fall of 1968 and the winter of 1969-70.

_____. "Selections from the Biography of Huey P. Newton [part 1]." RAMPARTS 7 (26 October 1968): 21-34.

A narration and commentary by people who knew Huey P. Newton. In this first part, Seale comments on his early associations with Newton and the organization of the Black Panther party. (See also the sequel, cited below.)

_____. "Selections from the Biography of Huey P. Newton, Part II." RAMPARTS 7 (17 November 1968): 8-16, 49-64.

A continuation of the excerpts from the biography of Newton by Bobby Seale and Eldridge Cleaver. (See Part 1, cited above.)

Sheehy, Gail. PANTHERMANIA: THE CLASH OF BLACK AGAINST BLACK. New York: Harper & Row, 1971. 125 p.

Concerned with the trial of Bobby Seale and Ericka Huggins on conspiracy to murder Alex Rackley in New Haven, Connecticut.

Wolfe, Tom. RADICAL CHIC AND MAU-MAUING THE FLAK CATCHERS.
New York: Farrar, Straus & Giroux, 1970. 153 p.

RADICAL CHIC appeared in a slightly variant form in NEW YORK
magazine, June 1970.

BLACK POWER MOVEMENT

Anderson, S.E. "The Fragmented Movement." NEGRO DIGEST 17 (September-October 1968): 4-10.

A "black critical analysis" of the five major factions within the black power movement: (1) the integrationist, (2) the city-statesman, (3) back to Africa-ism, (4) black nation concept, (5) revolutionary nationalism.

Antarah, Obi [L.C. Richmond, Jr.]. "A Blueprint for Black Liberation." BLACK WORLD 22 (October 1973): 61-66.

An attempt to coordinate the various schools of thought represented by Pan-Africanism, Imamu Baraka's Black Cultural Nationalism, Elijah Muhammad's Black Muslimism, and Black Integrationists.

Ascoli, Max. "This Negro Revolution." REPORTER 29 (10 October 1963): 22.

An editorial, written from a "Northern point of view," on racial unrest in the South.

Bailey, Peter. "What African-American Nationalism Means to Me." NEGRO DIGEST 17 (December 1967): 31-33.

Bailey feels that African-American nationalism is an ideology which can serve as an umbrella to insure the human resources and group stability of black people.

Barbour, Floyd, ed. THE BLACK POWER REVOLT. Boston: Porter Sargent, 1968. 287 p.

A collection of essays and poetry concerned with the black power movement (first section deals with the background from 1791 to 1923). Following are views of Carmichael, LeRoi Jones, Malcolm X, Ron Karenga, and others.

Bennett, Lerone, Jr. THE CHALLENGE OF BLACKNESS. Chicago: Johnson Publishing Co., 1972. 250 p.

A collection of essays and speeches concerned with the political and social implications of the black struggle for freedom.

_____. "Of Time, Space and Revolution." EBONY, August 1969, pp. 31-39.

A black historian examines the black power struggle and concludes that "America is going to become a democracy, or America is going to become a North American South Africa."

"Black Power: A Discussion." PARTISAN REVIEW 35 (Spring 1968): 195-232.

Norman Mailer, Charles Hamilton, Robert Coles, William M. Kelley, and others respond to an article on black power by Martin Duberman (see page 32).

THE BLACK REVOLUTION. Chicago: Johnson Publishing Co., 1970. vii, 234 p.

First published as a special issue of EBONY magazine, August 1969. Contains essays by Lerone Bennett, Larry Neal, Huey P. Newton, A.B. Spellman, James Turner, and others concerning events in the black power struggle from 1963 to 1970.

Boggs, James. "Black Power--A Scientific Concept Whose Time Has Come." In BLACK FIRE, AN ANTHOLOGY OF AFRO-AMERICAN WRITING, edited by LeRoi Jones and Larry Neal, pp. 105-18. New York: William Morrow, 1968.

An attempt to analyze the theoretical work that has been done concerning the concept of black power.

Boggs, James, and Boggs, Grace Lee. "Uprooting Racism and Racists in the United States." NEGRO DIGEST 19 (January 1970): 20-22, 70-79.

A blueprint for the alleviation of racism in America by a husband and wife team who were activists in the labor movement and who are social theoreticians.

Bond, Julian. BLACK CANDIDATES: SOUTHERN CAMPAIGN EXPERIENCES. Atlanta: Southern Regional Council, 1969. 57 p. Illus.

An analysis by an astute black politician and statesman.

Broderick, Francis L., and Meir, August, eds. NEGRO PROTEST THOUGHT IN THE TWENTIETH CENTURY. Indianapolis: Bobbs-Merrill, 1965. 444 p.

Parts 3 and 4 contain addresses and essays by leading black freedom advocates since World War II. Manifestoes and pronouncements by NAACP, CORE, and SNCC are included.

Black Power Movement

Brown, H. Rap. DIE NIGGER DIE. New York: Dial Press, 1969. 145 p.

A political and autobiographical statement by one of the most revolutionary of the black militants in the 1960s. Brown, the former chairman of the Student Non-Violent Coordinating Committee, writes of his rise to militant involvement in the black power struggle.

Carmichael, Stokely. "Toward Black Liberation." In BLACK FIRE, AN ANTHOLOGY OF AFRO-AMERICAN WRITING, edited by LeRoi Jones and Larry Neal, pp. 119-32. New York: William Morrow, 1968.

Carmichael argues that "without the power to control their lives and their communities, without effective political institutions through which to relate to the total society," black communities will continue to exist in "a constant state of insurrection."

_____. "We Are All Africans." BLACK SCHOLAR 1 (April 1970): 15-19.

A speech by Carmichael for the dedication ceremony of the Malcolm X Liberation University in Durham, North Carolina, in October 1969.

Carmichael, Stokely, and Hamilton, Charles V. BLACK POWER: THE POLITICS OF LIBERATION IN AMERICA. New York: Random House, 1967. 198 p.

A call for the black community to unite in order that blacks may participate on all levels of decision making in the United States.

Chrisman, Robert. "The Formation of a Revolutionary Black Culture." BLACK SCHOLAR 1 (June 1970): 2-9.

The development of a revolutionary black culture is essential for black survival in a country bent upon the systematic elimination of black cultural development.

Clay, William L. "Emerging New Black Politics." BLACK WORLD 21 (October 1972): 32-39.

Clay, a black congressman from the state of Missouri, says, "Our politics at one time was based on the theory of appeasing the white majority. . . . We now couch our thinking in the fundamental concept that 'what's good for minorities is good for the nation.'"

Cleaver, Eldridge. POST-PRISON WRITINGS AND SPEECHES. New York: Random House, 1969. 211 p.

Edited with an appraisal by Robert Scheer.

Collins, Larry. "Students Leave Racist College." LIBERATOR 11 (May 1971): 18.

The actions of BASA (Black Action Students Association) at Defiance College, Ohio.

Conot, Robert E. RIVERS OF BLOOD, YEARS OF DARKNESS. New York: Bantam Books, 1967. 497 p.

> An account of the Watts riot.

Conyers, John, Jr. "Politics and the Black Revolution." EBONY, August 1969, pp. 162-66.

> Conyers, a black congressman (1st District, Michigan) feels that "it may be the supreme irony of history that the ethnic group that has been most abused by the country may turn out to be the country's salvation."

Cook, Mercer, and Henderson, Stephen E. THE MILITANT BLACK WRITER IN AFRICA AND THE UNITED STATES. Madison: University of Wisconsin Press, 1969. 136 p.

> Henderson's section of the book, entitled "'Survival Motion': A Study of the Black Writer and the Black Revolution in America," is concerned with jazz artists and black writers (particularly poets) who are involved in the creation of "black consciousness" in the United States. Cook's section deals solely with African writers.

Cunningham, James. "Ron Karenga and Black Cultural Nationalism." NEGRO DIGEST 17 (January 1968): 4, 76-80.

> A critique of Karenga's concept of black cultural nationalism by a member of the Chicago-based Organization of Black American Culture (OBAC).

Darden, Clifford E. "Organizational Development in the Black Community." NEGRO DIGEST 18 (June 1969): 35-44.

> "The Black community is caught between the moribund ethos of fatalism and the nascent ideology of 'Black Power'--or progressivism."

Davis, Milburn. "Fad Prone Negroes." BLACK DIALOGUE 3 (Winter 1967-68): 5, 8.

> Attacks black support of white fads which tend to make the black race seem inferior, such as processing hair or wearing blonde or red wigs.

Diop, Alioune. "Three Objectives of a Cultural Policy." BLACK WORLD 22 (October 1973): 38-41.

> "Black civilization is a common project and, like the nation, a threshold of awareness: the shared conviction that our cohesion

exists and is justified by common historical experiences, common languages, and a common spiritual heritage."

Draper, Theodore. THE REDISCOVERY OF BLACK NATIONALISM. New York: Viking Press, 1970. 211 p.

A review of the various movements for black nationalism or black autonomy in America. The examination includes biographical sketches of leaders of black nationalism such as Finley, Delany, Turner, Carmichael, Garvey, Malcolm X, DuBois, Cleaver, and Newton.

Duberman, Martin. "Black Power in America." PARTISAN REVIEW 35 (Winter 1968): 34-48.

"Black Power is both a product of our society and a repudiation of it. Confronted with the continuing indifference of the majority of whites to the Negro's plight, SNCC and CORE have lost faith in conscience and time. . . ."

Dyson, Jim. "Reflections '68." HABARI BARUA 1, no. 5 [1968]: 8-11.

A review of the significant events of 1968 that were relevant to the struggle for black power in America.

Forman, James. THE MAKING OF BLACK REVOLUTIONARIES. New York: Macmillan, 1972. 568 p.

A personal account of the organization and growth of SNCC (Student Nonviolent Coordinating Committee) in the 1960s, Forman's early life in Mississippi and Chicago, and his experience in the army.

_____. THE MAKING OF BLACK REVOLUTIONARIES: A PERSONAL AC-COUNT. New York: Macmillan, 1972. 683 p.

Forman's account of the activities of SNCC and its relation to the Black Panther party.

_____. SAMMY YOUNGE, JR.: THE FIRST BLACK COLLEGE STUDENT TO DIE IN THE BLACK LIBERATION MOVEMENT. New York: Grove Press, 1968. 282 p.

Sammy Younge was a black activist student who was shot in Tuskegee, Alabama, on 3 January 1966, by a white man who was identified, brought to trial, and acquitted.

Gayle, Addison, Jr. "Black Power: Existential Politics." LIBERATOR 9 (January 1969): 4-7.

"Men who believe in the benevolence of government cannot believe in their own power."

Gethers, Solomon P. "Black Power: Three Years Later." NEGRO DIGEST 19 (December 1969): 4-10, 69-81.

Gethers reviews the various movements toward black power under the headings "The Assimilationist View of Black Power," "The Pluralist View of Black Power," and "The Nationalist View of Black Power," then offers his own theory of black liberation.

Green, Johnny L. "Wake Up Niggers." LIBERATOR 10 (November 1970): 4-7.

Argues for the necessity for blacks to unite for political and economic power.

Halisi, Clyde, and Mtume, James, eds. THE QUOTABLE KARENGA. Los Angeles: US Organization, 1967. 30 p.

Quotations from the speeches and essays of Maulana Ron Karenga, the leader of the California-based US organization. Quotations are arranged under headings black cultural nationalism, revolution, politics, art, religion, liberals.

Hamilton, Charles V. "How Black Is Black." EBONY, August 1969, pp. 45-52.

Hamilton discusses how many blacks emphasize their black conscious-ness in various external ways ("Afro" or "natural" hair styles, wear-ing dashikis), but says that being black is more than skin color or costume, it is an attitude, a state of mind.

Hare, Nathan. "Black Ecology." BLACK SCHOLAR 1 (April 1970): 2-8.

"The real solution to the environmental crisis is the decolonization of the black race."

_____. "It's Time to Turn the Guns the Other Way." BLACK SCHOLAR 1 (May 1970): 28-30.

Attack on Nixon administration's policy on Vietnam and a call to bring black soldiers home from the war to establish a "black do-mestic militia" to defend the black communities.

_____. "New Role for Uncle Toms." NEGRO DIGEST 17 (August 1968): 14-19.

Discusses Uncle Toms and tomism. Hare divides Uncle Toms into two categories--the utilitarian and the pathological. The utilitarian

<u>toms</u> "identify with militancy to varying degrees," the pathological <u>toms</u> have "identified with the aggressor."

_____. "The Plasma of Thinking Black." NEGRO DIGEST 18 (January 1969):
12-18.

"Thinking black" is "questioning whiteness and its values and the contradictions and irrationalities of white society." Hare divides the process of thinking black into a six-part formula, PLASMA: P-physiognomy, L-language, A-artifacts, S-sickness, M-mathematics, and A-audaciousness.

Hedgepeth, William. "The Radicals: Are They Poles Apart?" LOOK, 7 January 1969, pp. 34-35.

An examination of two antipodal leaders of the controversy over the race question: Roy Harris, Georgia segregationist, and Black Panther Minister of Information, Eldridge Cleaver.

Hill, Herbert. ANGER AND BEYOND: THE NEGRO WRITER IN THE UNITED STATES. New York: Harper & Row, 1966. 227 p.

An anthology of essays on black writers in America by Saunders Redding, LeRoi Jones, Arna Bontemps, Ossie Davis, and others.

Hough, Joseph C., Jr. BLACK POWER AND WHITE PROTESTANTS. New York: Oxford, 1968. 228 p.

Well-documented with extensive footnotes, Hough's argument is that white Protestants should realize their responsibilities as Christians and support by political action the efforts of Negro pluralism.

Jackson, Larry R. "Welfare Mothers and Black Liberation." BLACK SCHOLAR 1 (April 1970): 31-37.

The power the black female population wields in the struggle for black power--welfare rights movement is preponderantly led by females.

"Jesse Jackson: One Leader among Many." TIME, 6 April 1970, pp. 14-23.

Jackson's ascendancy in leadership after the murder of Dr. Martin Luther King, Jr., is traced, particularly his activity with Operation Breadbasket, the economic arm of the Southern Christian Leadership Conference.

Job. "Blacker Than Thou." HABARI BARUA 1 (n.d.): 5.

An attempt to stop the controversy concerning the relative "blackness" of various organizations by establishing seven principles or postulates of blackness.

Johnson, Roberta Ann. "The Prison Birth of Black Power." JOURNAL OF BLACK STUDIES 5 (June 1975): 395-414.

Demonstrates the similarity between ghetto and prison and argues that black political awareness emerges in the prisons for the same reason it emerges in the ghetto.

Kaiser, Ernest. "The Literature of Negro Revolt." FREEDOMWAYS 3 (1963): 36-47.

A review of Louis E. Lomax's THE NEGRO REVOLT.

Karenga, [Maulana] Ron. "Ron Karenga and Black Cultural Nationalism--A Response." NEGRO DIGEST 17 (January 1968): 5-9.

An answer to James Cunningham's critique of his concept of black cultural nationalism which appeared in the same issue of NEGRO DIGEST (see page 31).

Killens, John Oliver. BLACK MAN'S BURDEN. New York: Trident, 1965. 176 p.

A black novelist's examination of the racial problem in America.

_____. "The Black Writer and Revolution." ARTS IN SOCIETY 5 (Winter 1968): 395-99.

It is incumbent upon black revolutionary writers to reconstruct the history of the last four hundred years.

Killian, Lewis M. THE IMPOSSIBLE REVOLUTION? BLACK POWER AND THE AMERICAN DREAM. New York: Random House, 1968. 198 p.

An examination of the black protest of the 1950s and black militancy of the 1960s.

King, Larry L. CONFESSIONS OF A WHITE RACIST. New York: Viking Press, 1971. 191 p.

An examination of white racist attitudes.

Lee, Don L. "Notes from a Black Journal." NEGRO DIGEST 19 (January 1970): 11, 85-89.

"Images of goodness do not control the world, but images of power do."

Lincoln, C. Eric. THE SOUNDS OF THE STRUGGLE: PERSONS AND PER-SPECTIVES IN CIVIL RIGHTS. New York: William Morrow, 1968. 252 p.

Eighteen essays analyzing the civil rights movement, the Black

Muslims, the Negro's "Middle-Class Dream," and Malcolm X.

Locke, Hubert G. THE DETROIT RIOT OF 1967. Detroit: Wayne State University Press, 1969. 160 p.

An examination of the riots and violence that wracked Detroit in 1967, with maps and illustrations.

Lomax, Louis E. THE NEGRO REVOLT. New York: Harper & Row, 1962. 285 p.

Chapters on the origin of the "Negro Revolt" in colonial America, the civil rights movement and NAACP, sit-ins, freedom rides, Black Muslims, the Urban League.

McEvoy, James, and Miller, Abraham. BLACK POWER AND STUDENT REBELLION. Belmont, Calif.: Wadsworth Publishing Co., 1969. 440 p.

An anthology of the struggles for making the higher educational system more relevant to black people.

McKissick, Floyd B. "The Way to a Black Ideology." BLACK SCHOLAR 1 (December 1969): 14-17.

"It is the task of black intellectuals to provide the cohesive philosophy which will propel the black-led revolution which must happen if justice is to be achieved in America."

Mahome, Othello. "Incident at Cornell." LIBERATOR 9 (June 1969): 4-7.

Concerned with the seizure of the student union building by one hundred members of the Afro-American Society at Cornell University.

_____. "Review of H. Rap Brown's DIE NIGGER DIE." LIBERATOR 9 (November 1969): 20.

"The same media that cast H. Rap Brown in the role of a fiery revolutionary evangelist has made his rhetoric a cliche."

Mailer, Norman. "Looking for Meat and Potatoes--Thoughts on Black Power." LOOK, 7 January 1969, pp. 57-60.

Mailer's views on a technological culture's confrontation with the demand for black power. Mailer's stance is both liberal and separatist.

Masotti, Louis H., and Corsi, Jerome R. SHOOT-OUT IN CLEVELAND: BLACK MILITANTS AND THE POLICE, JULY 23, 1968. New York: Praeger, 1969. 126 p.

Illustrated account of the Cleveland riot.

Mboya, Tom. "Mboya's Rebuttal." EBONY, August 1969, pp. 90-94.

Kenya's minister for economic planning and development defends his position, which opposed a back-to-Africa movement. This is the last message of the slain Kenya leader to black Americans.

Mkalimoto, Ernie. "Revolutionary Black Culture: The Cultural Arm of Revolutionary Nationalism." NEGRO DIGEST 19 (December 1969): 11-17.

Argues the importance of a cultural underpinning for the black power movement, for "if a given revolution finds itself bathed in the light of brilliant military successes, it is nonetheless true that this very same revolution can discover its political gains reversed if proper attention is not paid to work in the ideological/cultural areas."

Moss, James A., ed. THE BLACK MAN IN AMERICA: INTEGRATION AND SEPARATION. New York: Dell, 1971. 165 p.

Contains statements by leading spokesmen in the black power movement of the 1960s, including Whitney M. Young, Martin Luther King, Jr., James Farmer, Julian Bond, Eldridge Cleaver, Carl B. Stokes, and Dick Gregory.

Muse, Benjamin. THE AMERICAN NEGRO REVOLUTION: FROM NONVIOLENCE TO BLACK POWER, 1963-1967. Bloomington: Indiana University Press, 1968. xii, 345 p.

Important examination of the black struggle for equality and power in the 1960s.

Nadelson, Regina. WHO IS ANGELA DAVIS? THE BIOGRAPHY OF A REVOLUTIONARY. New York: Peter H. Wyden, 1972. 208 p.

Brief biography contains no notes, bibliography, or other research tools.

"National Black Political Agenda." BLACK WORLD 21 (October 1972): 27-31.

Excerpted from the Gary Conference Report. Report notes that there must be an independent black political movement, an independent black political agenda, and an independent black spirit.

Nelson, Truman. THE RIGHT OF REVOLUTION. Boston: Beacon Press, 1968. 148 p.

Argues that black Americans have the right to revolt against the existing American government since they have been deprived of their rights under the Constitution. The argument is based on John Locke's philosophy and the American revolutionary tradition.

Nower, Joyce. "Cleaver's Vision of America and the New White Radical: A Legacy of Malcolm X." NEGRO AMERICAN LITERATURE FORUM 4 (March 1970): 12-21.

Influence of Cleaver and Malcolm X on the young white radicals.

"Other Voices, Other Strategies." TIME, 6 April 1970, pp. 23-27.

Spokesmen for three disparate approaches to the solution of the struggle for black rights are interviewed separately: (1) Julian Bond, one of eight blacks elected to the Georgia House of Representatives in 1965, (2) Bobby Seale, a founder and chairman of the Black Panther party, and (3) Whitney Young, Jr., the executive director of the National Urban League.

Pantell, Dora, and Greenidge, Edwin. IF NOT NOW, WHEN? THE MANY MEANINGS OF BLACK POWER. New York: Delacorte, 1970. 216 p.

A study of the black man in contemporary society, various moderate and militant movements and organizations, problems in housing, schools, and economic development in the ghetto.

Parker, J.A. ANGELA DAVIS: THE MAKING OF A REVOLUTIONARY. New York: Arlington House, 1973. 272 p.

No documentation, notes, or bibliography are contained in this study.

Peavy, Charles D. "The Black Art of Propaganda: The Cultural Arm of the Black Power Movement." ROCKY MOUNTAIN SOCIAL SCIENCE JOURNAL 7 (April 1970): 9-16.

Examines the black arts movement as a concomitant to the black power movement. Discusses the use of film, community theater, and various black journals to spread an essentially revolutionary message.

Poussaint, Alvin F. "A Psychiatrist Looks at Black Power." EBONY, March 1967, pp. 142-52.

Poussaint discusses the psychological implications of the shift from an integration-oriented mentality to self-determination and black consciousness.

Powell, Adam Clayton. KEEP THE FAITH BABY! New York: Trident, 1967. 293 p.

Collection of sermons and speeches delivered at the Abyssinian Baptist Church.

Prothro, James, and Matthews, Donald. NEGROES AND THE NEW SOUTHERN

POLITICS. New York: Harcourt, Brace & World, 1966. 551 p.

A review of the literature of the subject combined with over two thousand interviews. A massive compilation of data.

Riley, Clayton. "Angela Davis, Elegant Sister." LIBERATOR 10 (November 1970): 10-11.

An appreciation of the black female revolutionary.

Ritchie, Barbara. THE RIOT REPORT. New York: Viking Press, 1949. 254 p. Illus.

Illustrated, shortened version of the REPORT OF THE NATIONAL ADVISORY COMMISSION ON CIVIL DISORDER.

Rogers, Ray. "Black Guns on Campus." NATION 208 (May 5, 1969): 558-60.

The battle between Ron Karenga's US organization and the Black Panthers on the campus at UCLA.

Rowan, Carl T. JUST BETWEEN US BLACKS. New York: Random House, 1974. 203 p.

Commentaries drawn from Rowan's "Black Perspectives" broadcasts and covering the black experience, "from collecting welfare to contracting VD, from denigrating blacks on TV and in the press, to insisting on hiring a maid for a dollar an hour."

Rustin, Bayard. "Black Power and Coalition Politics." COMMENTARY 42 (September 1966): 35-40.

"The day-to-day lot of the ghetto Negro has not been improved by the various judicial and legislative measures of the past decade." Rustin feels that it is the growing conviction that Negroes cannot win "which accounts for the new popularity of 'black power.'"

_____. "The Myths of the Black Revolt." EBONY, August 1969, pp. 96-104.

Once considered a radical himself, Rustin warns that black revolutionaries are pursuing the wrong paths to freedom. The essay is divided into seven parts: "The Myth of Black," "The Myth of Black Capitalism," "The Myth of Reparations," "The Myth of Black Studies," "The Myth of Violence," "The Myth of Separatism," and "The Myth of the Black Revolution."

Seale, Bobby. "Revolutionary Action on Campus and Community." BLACK SCHOLAR 1 (December 1969): 4-7.

A revolutionary statement written while Seale was confined in prison after the Chicago conspiracy trial.

Stanford, Max. "Black Nationalism and the Afro-American Student." BLACK SCHOLAR 2 (June 1971): 27-31.

A plea for black unity by the national field chairman of RAM (Revolutionary Action Movement) during the 1960s.

Staples, Robert. "Black Ideology and the Search for Community." LIBERATOR 9 (June 1969): 8-11.

Under the doctrine of black power the tactic of nonviolence will change to one of self-defense.

Storing, Herbert J. WHAT COUNTRY HAVE I? POLITICAL WRITINGS BY BLACK AMERICANS. New York: St. Martin's Press, 1970. 235 p.

An anthology of the political writings of W.E.B. DuBois, Martin Luther King, Jr., Joseph Jackson, Malcolm X, Stokely Carmichael, Eldridge Cleaver, Albert Cleage, Julius Lester.

Strickland, Bill. "The Gary Convention and the Crisis of American Politics." BLACK WORLD 21 (October 1972): 18-26.

A speech given at the third annual meeting of the National Conference of Black Political Scientists, May 5, 1972. Strickland gives his analysis of the National Black Political Convention, held in Gary, Indiana, on March 10-12, 1972.

Toure, Askia Muhammad [Roland Snellings]. "Jihad!; Toward A Black National Credo." NEGRO DIGEST 18 (July 1969): 11-17.

A concept of "revolution" which will "re-link Afro-America with the Afro-Asian East"; a "revolution" which will "restore the mind and Soul of the Black man to his ancestral rhythms and Ancient Spirituality."

Wagstaff, Thomas. BLACK POWER: THE RADICAL RESPONSE TO WHITE AMERICA. Beverly Hills, Calif.: Glencoe Press, 1969. 150 p.

Traces the contemporary black power movement back to its roots in the nineteenth century.

Walters, Ronald. "African-American Nationalism." BLACK WORLD 22 (October 1973): 9-27, 84-85.

After the Panthers, SNCC, SCLC, and other black nationalist organizations have passed from the front of the nationalistic period of the 1960s, a new unifying ideology is necessary. This essay attempts to suggest ways in which "existing variants can be clarified, broadened and made more useful to the goals of the Black community."

_____. "The New Black Political Culture." BLACK WORLD 21 (October 1972): 4-17.

"The Power to legitimize Black leadership and Black demands has largely been exercised by the white power structure, and it will be the heavy mandate of the Black Official, because he is a broker, to assist in the process of legitimacy transference to the hands of the people."

Watts, Daniel H. "The Carmichael/Cleaver Debate." LIBERATOR 9 (September 1969): 3-5.

"There is no one who stands a better chance to destroy a Black revolutionary group than a white romanticist revolutionary."

Weinberg, Kenneth G. BLACK VICTORY: CARL STOKES AND THE WINNING OF CLEVELAND. Chicago: Quadrangle Books, 1968. 250 p.

An account of the successful political campaign of Carl Stokes.

Williams, Robert F. "Interview." BLACK SCHOLAR 1 (May 1970): 2-14.

An interview conducted by the BLACK SCHOLAR on 23 April 1970, shortly after Williams had returned from exile.

_____. NEGROES WITH GUNS. New York: Marzani & Munsell, 1962. 128 p.

Black power writing by a militant black leader who fled to China after being accused of murder during racial unrest in North Carolina.

Wolff, Anthony. "Godfrey Cambridge's Open Door Policy." LOOK, 7 January 1969, p. 76.

An interview with Godfrey Cambridge. Cambridge discusses his views on black revolutionary heroes like Malcolm X and the effect they can have on young black minds.

Wren, Christopher S. "Black Power Shakes the White Church." LOOK, 7 January 1969, pp. 84-85.

An examination of the "black caucus" in the white church and the stance taken by black ministers such as Albert Cleage, Jr., and George Clements.

Wright, Nathan. "Black Power vs. Black Genocide." BLACK SCHOLAR 1 (December 1969): 47-52.

Planned parenthood and birth control measures seen as genocidal in nature.

Wright, Richard. BLACK POWER: A RECORD OF REACTIONS IN A LAND OF PATHOS. New York: Harper, 1954. 358 p.

Wright's reactions after his trip to Africa's Gold Coast in the spring of 1953.

Zinn, Howard. SNCC: THE NEW ABOLITIONISTS. Boston: Beacon Press, 1964. 286 p.

The activities of SNCC in Mississippi, Georgia, and Alabama, including sit-ins and freedom rides.

BLACK SPEECH

Abrahams, Roger D. DEEP DOWN IN THE JUNGLE. Hatboro, Pa.: Folklore Associates, 1964. 287 p.

A study of "Negro narrative folklore from the streets of Philadelphia," but attention is also given to terms and expressions common to urban black life in general.

Claerbaut, David. BLACK JARGON IN WHITE AMERICA. Grand Rapids, Mich.: William Eerdmans, 1972. 89 p.

Treatment of black speech as an identifiable language of a subculture. Contains dictionary of black jargon.

Dundes, Alan, ed. MOTHER WIT FROM THE LAUGHING BARREL: READINGS IN THE INTERPRETATION OF AFRO-AMERICAN FOLKLORE. Englewood Cliffs, N.J.: Prentice-Hall, 1973. 673 p.

Sixty-five articles on every significant aspect of black American folklore, including jokes, tales, music, customs, toasts, and superstitions. Excellent discussion of signifying, playing the dozens, jive talk, and "street smarts."

Fabio, Sarah Webster. "Who Speaks Negro? What Is Black?" NEGRO DIGEST 17 (September-October 1968): 33-37. Also in BLACK EXPRESSION, edited by Addison Gayle, Jr., pp. 115-19. New York: Weybright and Talley, 1969.

"Black language is direct, creative, intelligent communication between black people based on a shared reality, awareness, understanding which generates interaction. . . ."

Jones, Kirland C. "The Language of the Black 'In-Crowd': Some Observations on Intra-Group Communication." CLA JOURNAL 15 (September 1971): 80-89.

The language of the black "in-crowd" is a tool of group cohesion, binding insiders together and excluding all those who do not belong.

Black Speech

Kochman, Thomas. "Rapping in the Ghetto." In BLACK EXPERIENCE: SOUL, edited by Lee Rainwater, pp. 51-76. New Brunswick, N.J.: Transaction Books, 1973.

A discussion of black idiom: "rapping," "shucking," "jiving," "running it down," "gripping," "copping a plea," "signifying," and "sounding."

Lewis, John. "The Slang of Black Folk." BLACK ARTS 1, no. 3 (n.d.): 16-17.

The use of black slang by black writers and spokesmen may be seen as an important extension of the black pride movement.

Loman, Bengt. CONVERSATIONS IN A NEGRO AMERICAN DIALECT. Washington, D.C.: Center for Applied Linguistics, 1967. 164 p.

A transcription and analysis of nonstandard dialect spoken by school-age black children of lower socioeconomic stratum in Washington, D.C., in 1965.

Turbee, Florence. "Black Revolutionary Language: 'Up against the Wall, Mother. . . .'" LIBERATOR 9 (November 1969): 8-10.

"The Black Liberation Movement is developing a new vocabulary to express its new mood."

Wolfram, Walter A. A SOCIOLINGUISTIC DESCRIPTION OF DETROIT NEGRO SPEECH. Washington, D.C.: Center for Applied Linguistics, 1969. 237 p.

Studies the significance of speech as an indicator of status in the black community and the role speech plays in social mobility. Correlates speech differences with social differences.

BLACK STUDIES

Bogle, Donald. "Black and Proud behind Bars." EBONY, August 1969, pp. 65-72.

An examination of the Black Cultural Development Society, an all-black inmate organization formed at the Colorado State Penitentiary in Canon City, Colorado. The group set up its own classes in Swahili and Afro-American history.

Clements, Clyde C. "Black Studies for White Students." NEGRO AMERICAN LITERATURE FORUM 14 (March 1970): 9-11.

Black studies for white students will help insure responsible citizenship in a democratic and pluralistic society by helping whites recognize a black cultural heritage and reducing white stereotyped thinking.

Cudjoe, Selwyn R. "Needed: A Black Studies Consortium." LIBERATOR 9 (September 1969): 14-15.

A plan to pool the financial, faculty, and archival resources at various universities engaged in black studies.

Dixon, Vernon J. "The Black Student and the Brother in the Streets." NEGRO DIGEST 18 (November 1968): 28-35.

"If the black student approaches the black community unhandicapped, he may discover such strengths as nonindividualistic concern for communal interests, the institution of the extended family and rich cultural forms of which the figurative tradition is only one instance."

Ford, Nick Aaron. BLACK STUDIES: THREAT-OR-CHALLENGE. New York: Kennikat Press, 1973. 217 p.

A definitive study of black studies programs--the history, scope, and organizational patterns.

Harding, Vincent. "Black Students and the 'Impossible' Revolution." EBONY, August 1969, pp. 141-48.

The director of the Institute of the Black World reviews black student demands and rebellion at Cornell University, Howard University, and Atlanta University. Black students sense the possibility for revolutionary change; they demand that the "impossible" be redefined in their own generation.

Joyner, Irving. "The Black University." HABARI BARUA 1, no. 5 (n.d.): 12-13.

Many white universities have recruited black militants for their faculties in an attempt to mold black activists into a force that will benefit white America.

Long, Richard A. "Black Studies: International Dimensions." CLA JOURNAL 14 (September 1970): 1-6.

Black studies should be international in its orientation and scope because it is required of the nature of the inquiry itself and also because it is in the general tradition of internationalism.

———. "The Future of Black Studies." CLA JOURNAL 15 (September 1971): 1-6.

The future of black studies lies in its contribution to the wholeness and sanity of the new black person.

McGinnis, James. "Towards a New Beginning: Crisis and Contradiction in Black Studies." BLACK WORLD 22 (March 1973): 27-35.

Predicts that the new mood of the 1970s will result in opportunistic black professionals (who abandoned poverty programs for black studies) abandoning black studies and moving onto the "new bandwagon" of prison reform.

Obatala, J.K. "Where Did Their Revolution Go?" NATION 215 (2 October 1972): 272-74.

A commentary on the decline or disappearance of black student unions on campuses in southern California by a founding member of the black student union at California State University, Los Angeles.

Pentony, Devere E. "The Case for Black Studies." In FROM A BLACK PERSPECTIVE: CONTEMPORARY BLACK ESSAYS, edited by Douglas A. Hughes, pp. 209-20. New York: Holt, Rinehart and Winston, 1970.

Discusses such questions as standards and scholarship and whether "black studies are legal and proper."

Robinson, Armstead L.; Foster, Craig L.; and Ogilvie, Daniel H., eds. BLACK STUDIES IN THE UNIVERSITY. New Haven, Conn.: Yale University Press, 1969. 231 p.

>A transcription of the symposium on black studies held at Yale University in May 1968.

Shepherd, Jack. "Black America's African Heritage." LOOK, 7 January 1969, pp. 18-29.

>Text and photographs concerning the African heritage of Afro-Americans as reflected in the art and artifacts of Nok, Ife, Benin, and Ashanti artisans.

_____. "Who Am I? Ghetto Students Search for Answers in a Black Africa." LOOK, 7 January 1969, p. 30.

>The effect that a trip to Africa has on a group of black ghetto youth from America.

Simpkins, Edward. "Black Studies: Here to Stay?" BLACK WORLD 24 (December 1974): 26-29.

>Simpkins, the black dean of the College of Education at Wayne State University, sees that there will always be a challenge for maintaining black studies programs on American campuses.

Staples, Robert. "Black Studies: A Review of the Literature." BLACK SCHOLAR 2 (October 1970): 53-56.

>A review of the literature concerned with the establishment of black studies programs in higher education.

Sundiata, I.K. "Black Studies: A Cop-out?" LIBERATOR 9 (April 1969): 10.

>The growth of Afro-American studies programs is unhealthy because it is a sop, a palliative--a "cop-out."

Turner, James. "Black Students and Their Changing Perspective." EBONY, August 1969, pp. 135-40.

>The author of this article was a student who organized the black students at Northwestern University in Evanston and who was an activist with various student movements across the United States.

Van Deburg, William L. "Afro-American Studies: A Question of Preservation." NEGRO HISTORY BULLETIN 37 (June-July 1974): 262-64.

>One of the more optimistic views on the future of black studies programs.

Walton, Sidney F., Jr. THE BLACK CURRICULUM: DEVELOPING A PROGRAM IN AFRO-AMERICAN STUDIES. East Palo Alto, Calif.: Black Liberation Publishing Co., 1970. 522 p.

> The work of a revolutionary black intellectual concerned with survival as an "authentic black educator" in a white-dominated institution.

Wilcox, Preston. "Black Studies as An Academic Discipline." NEGRO DIGEST 19 (March 1970): 75-87.

> Before black studies can earn the status of an academic discipline, white-controlled institutions must accept the relevance of such studies.

Williams, Ronald. "Black Studies: The Work to Come." NEGRO DIGEST 19 (January 1970): 30-35.

> A review-essay of the symposium conducted at Yale University and published as BLACK STUDIES IN THE UNIVERSITY (see page 47 under Robinson et al.).

CIVIL RIGHTS MOVEMENT

Batchelder, Alan B. "Economic Forces Serving the Ends of the Negro Protest." ANNALS OF THE AMERICAN ACADEMY OF POLITICAL AND SOCIAL SCIENCE 357 (January 1965): 80-88.

> Factors aiding Negro efforts at economic advancement are technological change, changes in southern urban employment, government backed nondiscriminatory employment opportunities, declining birthrates, military and government training of Negroes.

Clark, Kenneth B. THE NEGRO PROTEST: JAMES BALDWIN, MALCOLM X, MARTIN LUTHER KING TALK WITH KENNETH B. CLARK. Boston: Beacon Press, 1963. 56 p.

> Transcriptions of television interviews with prefatory notes by Clark.

Cothran, Tilman C. "The Negro Protest against Segregation in the South." ANNALS OF THE AMERICAN ACADEMY OF POLITICAL AND SOCIAL SCIENCE 357 (January 1965): 65-72.

> Negro protest is analyzed in terms of ideology, tactics and strategy, leadership, and membership.

Danzig, David. "In Defense of 'Black Power.'" COMMENTARY 42 (September 1966): 41-46.

> Group solidarity is the only road to Negro salvation. "Disillusion with the liberal ideal of color-blindedness and the adoption of a strategy of color-consciousness is characteristic of the Negro militants and is, indeed, at the heart of what 'black power' is all about."

Drinan, Robert F. "Why Direct Action Must Not Cease." NEGRO DIGEST 15 (April 1965): 4-13.

> The dean of the Boston College Law School (now a congressman from Massachusetts) opposes the moratorium on demonstrations and direct

action during the presidential campaign agreed to by major civil rights organizations. "Without direct action, the white majority will try to forget the plight of the Negro."

Dunbar, Leslie W. "The Southern Regional Council." ANNALS OF THE AMERICAN ACADEMY OF POLITICAL AND SOCIAL SCIENCE 357 (January 1965): 108-12.

A brief history of the Southern Regional Council evolvement from the Commission on Interracial Co-operation formed in 1919 through the present shape of the organization formed in 1944.

Fager, Charles. SELMA 1965: THE TOWN WHERE THE SOUTH WAS CHANGED. New York: Charles Scribner's Sons, 1974. 241 p.

An account of the 1965 civil rights march from Selma to Montgomery by one of the participants.

Friedman, Leon, ed. THE CIVIL RIGHTS READER: BASIC DOCUMENTS OF THE CIVIL RIGHTS MOVEMENT. New York: Walker, 1967. 348 p.

The earliest document in this collection is "The Report of the President's Committee on Civil Rights (1947)." Contains articles by Daniel Moynihan, James Tobin, and Bayard Rustin, presidential addresses, U.S. Supreme Court cases, and civil rights laws.

Hansberry, Lorraine. THE MOVEMENT: DOCUMENTARY OF A STRUGGLE FOR EQUALITY. New York: Simon & Schuster, 1964. 127 p.

A collection of photographs assembled with the assistance of the Student Non-Violent Coordinating Committee, with a text and commentary by Lorraine Hansberry.

Hickey, Neil, and Edwin, Ed. A.C. POWELL AND THE POLITICS OF A RACE. New York: Fleet Publishing Corp., 1965. 308 p.

A study of black congressman Adam Clayton Powell.

King, Martin Luther, Jr. STRENGTH TO LOVE. New York: Harper & Row, 1963. 146 p.

The Christian ideals and philosophy that motivated King.

_____. STRIDE TOWARD FREEDOM: THE MONTGOMERY STORY. New York: Harper & Row, 1958. 230 p.

King's examination of the nonviolent Alabama bus boycott, the violent opposition to it, and the ultimate victory of the blacks.

_____. THE TRUMPET OF CONSCIENCE. New York: Harper & Row, 1968. 78 p.

King's creed as he formulated it a few months before his assassination.

_____. WHERE DO WE GO FROM HERE: CHAOS OR COMMUNITY? New York: Harper & Row, 1967. 209 p.

A discussion of nonviolence and its effectiveness in achieving full civil rights for black Americans.

_____. WHY WE CAN'T WAIT. New York: Harper & Row, 1964. 178 p.

Explanation of why black Americans demand their rights immediately. Contains King's "Letter from Birmingham Jail."

Lane, James H. "The Changing Character of Negro Protest." ANNALS OF THE AMERICAN ACADEMY OF POLITICAL AND SOCIAL SCIENCE 357 (January 1965): 119-26.

An examination of the three forms of protest taken in the desegregation movement since World War II: legal (NAACP), educational (Urban League, Southern Regional Council), and activist (CORE, SCLC, SNCC).

Lee, Don L. "The Death Walk against Afrika." BLACK WORLD 22 (October 1973): 29-36.

Lee argues that black people ("Afrikans") must develop a life-style consistent with the struggle to undermine and challenge existing institutions and governments working against Afrikans all over the world.

Lewis, Anthony, and the NEW YORK TIMES. PORTRAIT OF A DECADE: THE SECOND AMERICAN REVOLUTION. New York: Random House, 1964. 322 p.

A compilation of the works of many journalists on the civil rights movement from 1954 to 1964, with particular emphasis on the school desegregation issue.

Lincoln, C. Eric. SOUNDS OF THE STRUGGLE, PERSONS AND PERSPECTIVES IN CIVIL RIGHTS. New York: William Morrow, 1967. 252 p.

Eighteen previously published essays on Black Muslims, the role of the black minister in the civil rights movement, the absence of the father in the black family, and other related topics.

Matthews, Donald R., and Prothro, James W. NEGROES AND THE NEW SOUTHERN POLITICS. New York: Harcourt, Brace & World, 1966. 567 p.

Data gathered from a sample survey of blacks and whites in the South conducted by the Survey Research Center (Michigan), from

Negro college students, and from intensive study of four typical communities.

Miller, William Robert. MARTIN LUTHER KING, JR.: HIS LIFE, MARTYRDOM, AND MEANING FOR THE WORLD. New York: Weybright and Talley, 1968. 319 p.

An illustrated appraisal of King's work in the civil rights movement.

Morsell, John A. "The National Association for the Advancement of Colored People and Its Strategy." ANNALS OF THE AMERICAN ACADEMY OF POLITICAL AND SOCIAL SCIENCE 357 (January 1965): 97-101.

A brief review of the first half-century of the history of the NAACP.

Moss, James A., ed. THE BLACK MAN IN AMERICA: INTEGRATION AND SEPARATION. New York: Dell, 1971. 165 p.

Contains statements by civil rights leaders (who favor integration) and black power leaders (who favor separation).

Peck, James. FREEDOM RIDE. New York: Simon & Schuster, 1962. 160 p.

An examination of the historic freedom rides of 1961.

Proudfoot, Merill. DIARY OF A SIT-IN. Chapel Hill: University of North Carolina Press, 1962. 218 p.

Proudfoot's entries begin on 9 June 1960, and end 24 July. In an "afterword" Proudfoot writes that the sit-ins were largely unsuccessful; ultimately, it was the economic boycott or the threat of it that brought results.

Rose, Arnold M. "The American Negro Problem in the Context of Social Change." ANNALS OF THE AMERICAN ACADEMY OF POLITICAL AND SOCIAL SCIENCE 357 (January 1965): 1-17.

The major changes in race relations from 1940 through 1964 are traced.

Rustin, Bayard. "From Protest to Politics: The Future of the Civil Rights Movement." COMMENTARY 39 (February 1965): 25-31.

"The civil rights movement is evolving from a protest movement into a full-fledged social movement--an evolution calling its very name into question. It is now concerned not merely with removing barriers to full opportunity but with achieving the fact of equality.

_____. "The Lessons of the Long Hot Summer." COMMENTARY 44 (October

1967): 39-45.

> Rustin discusses the importance of voter registration groups in the South, and says that "Southern Negroes, once they have registered and organized themselves politically, will have to seek out allies with whom they can form a majority."

Thompson, Daniel C. "The Rise of Negro Protest." ANNALS OF THE AMERICAN ACADEMY OF POLITICAL AND SOCIAL SCIENCE 357 (January 1965): 18-29.

> "Social controls supporting the biracial system in the United States are primarily corporal and legal and are often in conflict with prevailing moral and religious precepts. . . . The Negro protest is, itself, a clear endorsement of the 'American Creed' and a reaffirmation of the faith Negroes have in the democratic process."

Young, Whitney M., Jr. "The Urban League and Its Strategy." ANNALS OF THE AMERICAN ACADEMY OF POLITICAL AND SOCIAL SCIENCE 357 (January 1965): 102-7.

> A review of the first fifty-four years of the Urban League.

DRAMA

Abramson, Doris E. NEGRO PLAYWRIGHTS IN THE AMERICAN THEATRE, 1925-1959. New York: Columbia University Press, 1969. 335 p.

Excellent study of black theater in America. Extensive bibliography.

Adams, George R. "Black Militant Drama." AMERICAN IMAGO 28 (Summer 1971): 107-28.

A study of RAISIN IN THE SUN, BLUES FOR MR. CHARLIE, and DUTCHMAN as therapeutic warnings to American society.

Bailey, Peter. "The Black Theater." EBONY, August 1969, pp. 127-34.

An article on how the black community theaters take revolutionary drama to the people. Includes discussion of the Performing Arts Society of Los Angeles, the Black Arts Theater in Harlem, and the Black Arts Theater in Milwaukee.

Bullins, Ed, ed. THE NEW LAFAYETTE THEATRE PRESENTS; PLAYS WITH AESTHETIC COMMENTS BY 6 BLACK PLAYWRIGHTS. Garden City, N.Y.: Doubleday, 1974. 301 p.

Includes THE FABULOUS MISS MARIE by Ed Bullins; WHAT IF IT HAD TURNED UP HEADS by J.E. Gaines; ON BEING HIT by Clay Goss; HIS FIRST STEP by Oyamo; UH, UH; BUT HOW DO IT FREE US? by Sonia Sanchez; BLACK TERROR by Richard Wesley.

Cade, Toni. "Black Theater." In BLACK EXPRESSION, edited by Addison Gayle, Jr., pp. 134-43. New York: Weybright and Talley, 1969.

Predicts that the black theater of the 1960s will provide "the lessons for the more genuine, more separate, more black, more liberated revolutionary theater of the seventies."

Couch, William, Jr. NEW BLACK PLAYWRIGHTS. Baton Rouge: Louisiana State University Press, 1968. 258 p.

An anthology of six plays by Douglas Turner Ward, Adrienne
Kennedy, Lonne Elder, Ed Bullins, and William Wellington Mackey.

Dent, Thomas C.; Schechner, Richard; and Moses, Gilbert. THE FREE SOUTH-
ERN THEATRE BY THE FREE SOUTHERN THEATRE. New York: Bobbs-Merrill,
1969. 233 p.

Documentary history of the radical black theater in New Orleans
with journals, letters, poetry, and essays by those involved in its
founding and operation.

Elder, Lonne III. CEREMONIES IN DARK OLD MEN. New York: Farrar,
Straus & Giroux, 1969. 179 p.

Elder's first play. Concerned with a father and his two sons and
their attempt to establish a business and to avoid eviction.

Evans, Don. "The Theater of Confrontation: Ed Bullins, Up against the Wall."
BLACK WORLD 23 (April 1974): 14-18.

Argues that Bullins is not "negative" in his art but is concerned
with "those suicidal practices which render the black man impotent."

Fabre, Geneviéve E. "A Checklist of Original Plays, Pageants, Rituals and
Musicals by Afro-American Authors Performed in the United States from 1960
to 1973." BLACK WORLD 23 (April 1974): 81-97.

Checklist also includes a listing of "collective Creations, Anonymous Plays and Plays by Unknown Authors" (pp. 95-97). Authors
are listed alphabetically and plays in chronological order of first
production.

Gaffney, Floyd. "Black Theatre: Commitment and Communication." BLACK
SCHOLAR 1 (June 1970): 10-15.

A survey of the developments in black theater since World War II.

Gordone, Charles. NO PLACE TO BE SOMEBODY: A BLACK-BLACK COMEDY
IN THREE ACTS. Indianapolis: Bobbs-Merrill, 1969. 115 p.

Harsh, sardonic, militant melodrama that combines comedy and
tragedy in its message of black consciousness.

Hansberry, Lorraine. A RAISIN IN THE SUN. New York: Random House,
1959. 146 p.

A black mother's struggle to instill dignity and black manhood into
her son.

Harris, Henrietta. "Building a Black Theatre." DRAMA REVIEW 12 (Summer

1968): 157-58.

A note on the founding of the Aldridge Players/West in San Francisco in 1964, with comments on its early productions.

Jefferson, Miles M. "The Negro on Broadway, 1947-1948." PHYLON 9
(1948): 99-107.

Review of the year's theatrical season.

————. "The Negro on Broadway, 1952-1953--Still Cloudy, Fair Weather
Ahead." PHYLON 14 (1953): 268-79.

Review of the year's theatrical season.

————. "The Negro on Broadway, 1953-1954: A Baffling Season." PHYLON
15 (1954): 253-60.

Review of the year's theatrical season.

————. "The Negro On Broadway: 1954-1955--More Spice Than Substance."
PHYLON 16 (1955): 303-12.

Review of the year's theatrical season.

————. "The Negro on Broadway: 1955-1956." PHYLON 17 (1956): 227-
37.

Review of the year's theatrical season.

————. "The Negro on Broadway: 1956-1957." PHYLON 18 (1957): 286-
95.

Review of the year's theatrical season.

Johnson, Helen Armstead. "Playwrights, Audiences and Critics." NEGRO
DIGEST 19 (April 1970): 17-24.

A review of the drama of the new black militant playwrights.
"One thing which stands apart from the rhetoric and confusion is
the revolutionary playwright's clearly specified audience. He
chooses to write for Black people in Black neighborhoods."

Jurges, Oda. "Selected Bibliography [of] Black Plays, Books and Articles Related to Black Theatre Published from 1/1960 to 2/1968." DRAMA REVIEW
12 (Summer 1968): 176-80.

A selected bibliography of plays (listed by author in alphabetical
order) and articles (listed in chronological order).

Kaufman, Michael W. "The Delicate World of Reprobation: A Note on the Black Revolutionary Theatre." EDUCATIONAL THEATRE JOURNAL 23 (December 1971): 446–51.

Essentially a comparison of two plays, LeRoi Jones's THE SLAVE and Jimmy Farrett's AND WE OWN THE NIGHT, both about black revolution.

Kgositsile, K. William. "Towards Our Theater: A Definitive Act." In BLACK EXPRESSION, edited by Addison Gayle, Jr., pp. 146–48. New York: Weybright and Talley, 1969.

Kgositsile calls for a theater of "instruction, construction, and destruction" modeled along the lines established in LeRoi Jones's mythic and ritualistic drama, BLACK MASS.

King, Woodie, Jr. "Black Theatre: Present Condition." DRAMA REVIEW 12 (Summer 1968): 117–24.

An examination of various black community theaters operating in 1968, such as the Negro Ensemble Company (New York), Douglas House (Watts), Concept East (Detroit), Spirit House (Newark).

_____. "The Dilemma of Black Theater." NEGRO DIGEST 19 (April 1970): 10–15, 86–87.

A review of black theater since the end of World War II.

King, Woodie, Jr., and Milner, Ron[ald], eds. "Evolution of a People's Theater." In their BLACK DRAMA ANTHOLOGY, pp. 7–10. New York: American Library, 1971.

In this introduction to a coauthored anthology of contemporary black drama, King and Milner argue the necessity to free black drama from the dictates of the "Great White Way," i.e., Broadway.

Miller, Adam David. "It's a Long Way to St. Louis." DRAMA REVIEW 12 (Summer 1968): 147–50.

Discusses the "proper audience" for black drama. Black playwrights should write works about blacks for blacks, addressing themselves solely to the needs and aspirations of the black audience.

Mitchell, Loften. BLACK DRAMA. New York: Hawthorn Books, 1967. 247 p.

A critical study of black drama in America from the seventeenth century to the 1960s. The last two sections are concerned with post-World War II theater, off-Broadway developments, and the drama of LeRoi Jones, James Baldwin, and Lorraine Hansberry.

_____. "The Negro Theatre and the Harlem Community." In BLACK EXPRES-
SION, edited by Addison Gayle, Jr., pp. 148-59. New York: Weybright
and Talley, 1969.

> Mitchell reviews the history of black theaters in Harlem in this
> century and predicts that theater outside the black community will
> remain "a middle class luxury wherein the playwright speaks,
> cajoles, seduces, and lies to an expense-account audience."

Molette, Carlton W. "Afro-American Ritual Drama." BLACK WORLD 12
(April 1973): 4-12.
> Observations based on the "dramatic rituals" of the Afro-American
> church service.

Neal, Larry. "Cultural Nationalism and Black Theatre." BLACK THEATRE
1 (n.d.): 8-10.

> One of two symposium pieces on Harold Cruse's CRISIS OF THE
> NEGRO INTELLECTUAL published under the title "Two on Cruse"
> in the first issue of BLACK THEATRE.

_____. "Toward a Relevant Black Theatre." BLACK THEATRE 4 (April 1970):
14-15.

> An introduction to a recorded symposium on the play, WE RIGH-
> TEOUS BOMBERS.

O'Neal, John. "Motion in the Ocean: Some Political Dimensions of the Free
Southern Theatre." DRAMA REVIEW 12 (Summer 1968): 70-77.

> Traces the role of the Free Southern Theatre in New Orleans in
> the struggle for civil rights and black power.

Paterson, Lindsay, ed. ANTHOLOGY OF THE AMERICAN NEGRO IN THE
THEATRE: A CRITICAL APPROACH. International Library of Negro Life and
History series. New York: Publishers Co., 1967. 306 p.

> Sections 5-8 contain essays on black actors and playwrights since
> World War II. Included are essays by Langston Hughes, Loften
> Mitchell, Ossie Davis, Woodie King, Jr., Ruby Dee, Darwin
> Turner, and Tom Dent.

Peavy, Charles D. "Myth, Magic, and Manhood in LeRoi Jones' MADHEART."
STUDIES IN BLACK LITERATURE 1 (Summer 1970): 12-20.

> An approach to Jones's MADHEART as a psychomythic play contain-
> ing subliminal messages of black consciousness--a black morality
> play with a Blackman-Everyman.

_____. "The Revolutionary Theater and the Black Power Movement." In SOME

REFLECTIONS UPON MODERN AMERICA, pp. 61-74. College Station: Texas A & M, 1969.

A study of RIOT SALE, THE JOB, and TOP SECRET by Ben Caldwell, and DUTCHMAN, THE SLAVE, HOME ON THE RANGE, and POLICE by LeRoi Jones and the psychosocial motivations behind the production of these plays.

_____. Satire and Contemporary Black Drama." SATIRE NEWS LETTER 7 (Fall 1969): 40-49.

The primary motivation for the satire in most contemporary black drama is to correct the misconceptions the black man has about himself and the society in which he lives.

Shelton, Robert. "Theatre." NATION 196 (January 1963): 20.

A review of Langston Hughes's play BLACK NATIVITY, a Christmas "song-play" in two acts.

Silvera, Frank. "Toward a Theater of Understanding." NEGRO DIGEST 18 (April 1969): 33-35.

An assessment of James Baldwin's AMEN CORNER.

Steele, Shelby. "White Port and Lemon Juice--Notes on Ritual in the New Black Drama." BLACK WORLD 22 (June 1973): 4-13, 78-84.

Steele sees a ritualistic pattern in the repetition of symbols, characterizations, themes, and language styles in the new black theater begun by LeRoi Jones and continued by Ron Milner, Ed Bullins, Herbert Stokes, Ben Caldwell.

Teer, Barbara Ann. "To Black Artist, With Love." NEGRO DIGEST 18 (April 1969): 4-8.

A young black actress, producer, and director argues that "if black theaters are to be at all valid, they must meet the psychological needs of all black people" and "bring them closer to an awareness of who they really are."

X, Marvin. "Manifesto: The Black Educational Theatre of San Francisco." BLACK THEATRE 6 (1972): 30-35.

Concerned with the revolutionary function of black theater, based on principles established by Maulana Ron Karenga.

ECONOMICS

Anderson, Talmadge. "Black Economic Liberation under Capitalism." BLACK SCHOLAR 2 (October 1970): 11-14.

"Further attempts at being absorbed in the white system will not result in black and white integration, but black disintegration."

Bailey, Ronald W., ed. BLACK BUSINESS ENTERPRISE: HISTORICAL AND CONTEMPORARY PERSPECTIVES. New York: Basic Books, 1971. 361 p.

An examination of black economic development, "from capitalism to socialism, from integration to separation."

Blaustein, Arthur I., and Faux, Geoffrey. THE STAR-SPANGLED HUSTLE: WHITE POWER AND BLACK CAPITALISM. New York: Doubleday, 1972. 289 p.

An attack on the Nixon administration's program for minority enterprises.

Bloice, Carl. "Black Labor is Black Power." BLACK SCHOLAR 2 (October 1970): 29-32.

The role black labor can play in the revolution.

Boggs, James. RACISM AND THE CLASS STRUGGLE: FURTHER PAGES FROM A BLACK WORKER'S NOTEBOOK. New York: Monthly Review Press, 1970. 190 p.

Boggs contends that "American society faces only three alternatives: to continue rotting away as it is today, naked counter-revolution, or Black Revolutionary Power."

Dreyfuss, Joe. "Where Is Jesse Jackson Going?" BLACK ENTERPRISE 5 (October 1974): 23-27.

A review of the many activities of Jackson, the president and

moving force of PUSH (People United to Save Humanity), an organization devoted to what he calls "civil economics."

Foley, Eugene P. "Small Business Loans and the Negro Community." NEGRO
DIGEST 14 (October 1965): 25-28.

>Concerns the "success story" of Albert E. Watson and the "6 by
6" program begun in Philadelphia (loans up to $6,000 for six years).

Hamilton, Charles V. "Urban Economics, Conduit-Colonialism and Public Policy."
BLACK WORLD 21 (October 1972): 40-45.

>"Government spending in poor communities is as transient as water
in a dishrag. No sooner is money poured into them than private
entrepreneurs wring it out again."

Holsendolph, Ernest. "Blacks in High Finance." BLACK ENTERPRISE 5 (October 1974): 35-39, 61.

>Concerned with the noticeable "influx of blacks into the ranks of
stockbrokers, security analysts, account executives, investment
brokers."

Johnson, Herschel. "Tomorrow's Black Money Managers." BLACK ENTERPRISE
5 (October 1974): 28-31.

>Herschel is optimistic about the future job market for blacks with
M.B.A. degrees who desire roles In financial decision making.

Killens, John Oliver. "Black Labor and the Black Liberation Movement."
BLACK SCHOLAR 2 (October 1970): 33-39.

>"While millions of white workers will see a conflict of interests
between Black Liberation and the white-oriented Labor Movement,
there can be no fundamental contradiction between black labor
and the black community."

Meade, Matthew. "Black Capitalism?" LIBERATOR 10 (March 1970): 16-19.

>"Pulling oneself up by one's own bootstraps not only defies the law
of gravity, but the economic laws as well."

Ofari, Earl. "Black Labor: Powerful Force for Liberation." BLACK WORLD
22 (October 1973): 43-47.

>The author of THE MYTH OF BLACK CAPITALISM (see page 62)
argues that "rising nationalist and class awareness has increased
the militancy of both Black male and female workers alike" and
has "alarmed the corporate capitalist exploiters."

_____. THE MYTH OF BLACK CAPITALISM. New York: Monthly Review Press, 1970. 126 p.

A Marxist analysis of the growth of black capitalism from the ranks of the small but vocal group of free blacks in America.

Poinsett, Alex. "The Economics of Liberation." EBONY, August 1969, pp. 150-55.

A critique of President Nixon's concept of black capitalism as being inadequate for the development of a black economy; also an examination of "economic racism." Article stresses need for broad-based control of black economy by blacks instead of whites.

Turner, James. "Blacks in the Cities: Land and Self-Determination." BLACK SCHOLAR 1 (April 1970): 9-13.

Without control over land, resources, and production, there can be no self-determination for black people.

Vatter, Harold G., and Palm, Thomas, eds. THE ECONOMICS OF BLACK AMERICA. New York: Harcourt Brace Jovanovich, 1972. 296 p.

An anthology of essays concerning the socioeconomic problems of black Americans.

Venable, Abraham S. BUILDING BLACK BUSINESS: AN ANALYSIS AND A PLAN. New York: Graves/Crowell, 1972. 132 p.

Venable, the first black director of the Office of Minority Business Enterprise, examines the fact that less than 1 percent of the business generated in the American economy is an outgrowth of black-owned enterprises.

Wright, Robert E. "Black Capitalism: Toward Controlled Development of Black America." NEGRO DIGEST 19 (December 1969): 27-33.

Analyzes the confusion caused by the term "black capitalism" and points out that the economic programs of Marcus Garvey, W.E.B. DuBois, Elijah Muhammad, and Malcolm X are not essentially different from that of Booker T. Washington.

EDUCATION

BLACK CONSCIOUSNESS AND HIGHER EDUCATION: AN OCCASIONAL PAPER PUBLISHED BY THE CHURCH SOCIETY FOR COLLEGE WORK. Cambridge, Mass.: Church Society for College Work, 1968.

Transcript of a discussion concerning the relation of Afro-Americans to the American system of higher education.

"The Black University Concept: Educators Respond." NEGRO DIGEST 18 (March 1969): 66-77, 96-98.

Hoyt Fuller, editor of NEGRO DIGEST, polled leading black educators to determine their response to the concept of the black university. The article includes the responses of James R. Lawson, president of Fisk University; Benjamin E. Mays, president emeritus of Morehouse College; Samuel D. Proctor, dean, special projects, University of Wisconsin; and Benjamin F. Payton, president of Benedict College.

Brown, Roscoe C. "The White University Must Respond to Black Student Needs.' NEGRO DIGEST 18 (March 1969): 29-32, 87-88.

"The concern of the educator must not be to integrate (by any means necessary) the African-American student into a basically dysfunctional educational system, but rather, if he chooses to work within that system, to work towards its destruction as a source of black oppression."

Davis, Ronald. "The Black University: In Peril before Birth." NEGRO DIGEST 19 (March 1970): 12-18, 59-67.

A response to Vincent Harding's essay, "New Creation or Familiar Death" (see below). Davis fears "for the ebbing but yet unborn and contained Black University."

Harding, Vincent. "New Creation or Familiar Death." NEGRO DIGEST 18 (March 1969): 5-14.

Harding's "letter" was "written in the spirit of black ecumenical concern as we move towards a new humanity." The essay prompted several rejoinders in subsequent issues of NEGRO DIGEST.

Hare, Nathan. "Black Invisibility on White Campuses." NEGRO DIGEST 18 (March 1969): 39-43, 91-94.

"In the effort to make education 'relevant' to the black community-- and by indirection, to the white community--the communities themselves may be transformed, each in its own way, and made relevant to a bona fide education."

Hopkins, Chuck. "Malcolm X Liberation University." NEGRO DIGEST 19 (March 1970): 39-43.

"The over-riding purpose of the University is to provide a framework within which education can become relevant to the needs of Black people."

Hurst, Charles G. "Malcolm X: A Community College with a New Perspective." NEGRO DIGEST 19 (March 1970): 30-36.

A statement of the philosophy for founding Malcolm X College.

"Institute of the Black World: Statement of Purpose." NEGRO DIGEST 19 (March 1970): 20-23.

An outline of the goals of the community of black scholars gathered in Atlanta under the aegis of the Martin Luther King, Jr., Memorial Center.

Jaffe, A.J., et al. NEGRO HIGHER EDUCATION IN THE 1960'S. New York: Praeger, 1968. 290 p.

Primarily concerned with black colleges and black students in the South. Study based on statistical analysis obtained from a series of questionnaires.

Johnson, Roosevelt. "Black Administrators and Higher Education." BLACK SCHOLAR 1 (November 1969): 66-74.

Discusses the importance of an Institute for Black College Administrators to be established at universities centrally located throughout the United States.

Killens, John O[liver]. "The Artist and the Black University." BLACK SCHOLAR 1 (November 1969): 61-65.

The argument for the establishment of an ideal university for black people, the "Black Communiversity."

McNeill, Ann. "The Scandal of 'Black Social Knots.'" NEGRO DIGEST 17 (December 1967): 16-19.

> "Negroes who are responsible for the training of young minds must bear a part of the blame for the insecurities among their people."

McWorter, Gerald A. "Struggle, Ideology and the Black University." NEGRO DIGEST 18 (March 1969): 15-21, 89-90.

> McWorter sees the black university as "an institutional concept of life and liberation," and outlines the dangers facing the black university concept.

Malson, Robert A. "The Black Power Rebellion at Howard University." NEGRO DIGEST 17 (December 1967): 21-30.

> An analysis of the attack on the black bourgeoisie bastion at Howard University.

Martin, Michael. "The Functions of Colonial Education." BLACK WORLD 24 (August 1975): 4-16.

> A study of the negative effect a repressive school hierarchy has on the mental health of black students.

Smith, Calvert H. "In White Universities: Why Black Administrators 'Fail.'" BLACK WORLD 24 (August 1975): 26-29, 53.

> Smith sees no real hope for meaningful employment of black administrators until they are put in traditional line position with legitimate power to implement decisions made. This will not occur, however, until institutions hire black administrators because of their competence and "not to pad affirmative action reports or to pacify the black community."

Wilcox, Preston. "On the Black University." NEGRO DIGEST 19 (December 1969): 19-25.

> Wilcox sees the black university more as a movement than an institution--a physical building; "it has no admissions requirements for Blacks," and it exists "wherever Black people are."

Wilson, William J. "A Rejoinder to Vincent Harding." NEGRO DIGEST 19 (March 1970): 6-11, 57-59.

> A response to Harding's "New Creation or Familiar Death" (see page 63). Wilson questions whether more than a handful of black institutions could create an institution "that would even remotely approximate the Atlanta University Center model."

ENTERTAINERS

Angelou, Maya. I KNOW WHY THE CAGED BIRD SINGS. New York: Random House, 1969. 281 p.

A powerful autobiography of a black girl's initiation into life.

Bailey, Pearl. THE RAW PEARL. New York: Harcourt, Brace & World, 1968. 206 p.

An autobiography of the black singer and actress.

————. TALKING TO MYSELF. New York: Harcourt Brace Jovanovich, 1971. 233 p.

Bailey's thoughts on a variety of subjects, such as religion, politics, and show business.

Bechet, Sidney. TREAT IT GENTLE. New York: Hill & Wang, 1960. 245 p.

A taped and transcribed "spoken autobiography" of the famous clarinet and soprano saxophone player.

Dunham, Katherine. TOUCH OF INNOCENCE. New York: Cassell, 1960. 312 p.

An autobiography that covers the first twenty years of Dunham's life (from the First World War to the Depression).

Holliday, Billie. LADY SINGS THE BLUES. New York: Doubleday, 1956. 250 p.

An autobiography written with the assistance of William Duffy. Contains chronological discography.

Hughes, Langston. FAMOUS NEGRO MUSIC MAKERS. New York: Dodd, Mead, 1955. 179 p.

Biographical sketches of Afro-American musicians written primarily
for juvenile readers.

Hughes, Langston, and Meltzer, Milton. BLACK MAGIC: A PICTORIAL HIS-
TORY OF THE NEGRO IN AMERICAN ENTERTAINMENT. New York: Prentice-
Hall, 1968. 375 p.

A pictorial history of the black artist (dancer, actor, singer, and
composer) from the time of slavery to the 1960s.

Kitt, Eartha. THURSDAY'S CHILD. New York: Duell, Sloan and Pierce, 1956.
250 p.

The autobiography of Eartha Kitt.

Waters, Ethel. HIS EYE IS ON THE SPARROW. Garden City, N.Y.: Doubleday, 1951. 278 p.

An autobiography written with the assistance of Charles Samuels.

_____. TO ME IT'S WONDERFUL. New York: Harper & Row, 1972. 162 p.

A personal account of Waters' "spiritual rebirth" in 1957 through
the inspiration of the Reverend Billy Graham and his religious
crusades. Also contains an abridged discography of Waters' re-
cordings.

FOLKLORE

Abrahams, Roger D. DEEP DOWN IN THE JUNGLE. Hatboro, Pa.: Folklore Associates, 1964. 287 p.

The folklore and street games of black urban streets.

Brown, Sterling A. "Negro Folk Expression." In BLACK EXPRESSION, edited by Addison Gayle, Jr., pp. 3-14. New York: Weybright and Talley, 1969.

An examination of black folktales and aphorisms, "why" stories, and animal stories.

Hughes, Langston, and Bontemps, Arna, eds. BOOK OF NEGRO FOLKLORE. New York: Dodd, Mead, 1958. 624 p.

Collection of folktales, spirituals, gospel songs, blues, work songs, Harlem jive, play songs, and games.

Lester, Julius. BLACK FOLKTALES. Illustrated by Tom Feelings. New York: Richard W. Baron, 1969. 159 p.

Columnist, folk singer, and author Julius Lester retells African and Afro-American folktales in a contemporary vernacular.

Oster, Harry. "The Afro-American Folktale in Memphis: Theme and Function." NEGRO AMERICAN LITERATURE FORUM 3 (Fall 1969): 83-87.

Research conducted in Memphis in 1968 indicates how the folktale still actively performs many important functions for black people.

JEWS

Baldwin, James. "The Harlem Ghetto: Winter 1948." COMMENTARY 5 (February 1948): 165-70. Reprinted in his NOTES OF A NATIVE SON, pp. 57-72. Boston: Beacon Press, 1955.

> Baldwin says that "when the Negro hates the Jew as a Jew he does so partly because the nation does and in much the same pain-ful fashion that he hates himself."

_____. "Negroes Are Anti-Semitic Because They're Anti-White." In BLACK ANTI-SEMITISM AND JEWISH RACISM, edited by Nat Hentoff, pp. 3-12. New York: Richard W. Baron, 1969. Also in NEW YORK TIMES, 9 April 1967, pp. 26-27.

> "The crisis taking place In the world, and in the minds and hearts of black men everywhere, is not produced by the Star of David, but by the old, rugged Roman cross on which Christendom's most celebrated Jew was murdered."

Behran, Sia. "To Albert Shanker: Anti-Semitism???" HABURI BARUA 1 (n.d.): 16-17.

> Controversial poem concerning the black man's indifference to the suffering of the Jews in World War II.

Berson, Lenora E. THE NEGROES AND THE JEWS. New York: Random House, 1971. 436 p.

> An examination of the Jewish-black racial conflict. The Philadel-phia riot of August 1964, during which 632 Jewish stores were broken into and looted is examined. Also examined are the politics of race, Zionism and black nationalism, "White Hipsters and Black Jews."

Berube, Maurice, and Hill, Marilyn G., eds. CONFRONTATION AT OCEAN HILL-BROWNSVILLE. New York: Praeger, 1969. 340 p.

A collection of essays dealing with the nine-week long teachers' strike in 1968. Contains many documents necessary for an objective examination of the strike. See particularly the sections "Anti-Semitism and Racism" and "Decentralization and Community Control."

"The Black and the Jew: A Falling Out of Allies." TIME, 31 January 1969, pp. 55-59.

A TIME cover story prompted by the school crisis in the Ocean Hill-Brownsville School District. New York, says the article, is the center for black anti-Semitism.

Booth, William H. "Racism and Human Rights." In BLACK ANTI-SEMITISM AND JEWISH RACISM, edited by Nat Hentoff, pp. 117-27. New York: Richard W. Baron, 1969.

An examination of the forms of racism in New York City.

Buckley, William F., Jr. "Mayor Lindsay and the Jewish Community." NATIONAL REVIEW 21 (28 January 1969): 88.

"The toleration of black racism in Ocean Hill-Brownsville is only a few steps away from the toleration of the raucous racism of Adam Clayton Powell, Jr."

Cruse, Harold. "Jews and Negroes in the Communist Party." In his THE CRISIS OF THE NEGRO INTELLECTUAL, pp. 147-70. New York: William Morrow, 1967.

"The expansion in scope and quality of the Negro civil rights movement has brought to the surface the residual anti-Semitism that has always existed among Negroes, a group attitude which the Jews themselves are at least partially responsible for fostering."

_____. "My Jewish Problem and Theirs." In BLACK ANTI-SEMITISM AND JEWISH RACISM, edited by Nat Hentoff, pp. 143-88. New York: Richard W. Baron, 1969.

Argues that the Jewish experience is European while the black American's experience is uniquely his own.

_____. "Negroes and Jews--The Two Nationalisms and the Bloc(ked) Plurality." In his THE CRISIS OF THE NEGRO INTELLECTUAL, pp. 476-97. New York: William Morrow, 1967.

The path to more power is through cultural nationalism, a lesson blacks can learn from the Jews.

Featherstone, Joseph. "Inflating the Threat of Black Anti-Semitism." NEW REPUBLIC 160 (8 March 1969): 14-15.

Featherstone argues that reliable evidence indicates that there's
less anti-Semitism among blacks than among whites: "The anti-
Semitism of some black intellectuals, and the anti-Zionism of
black Marxist, Third World and Moslem groups does not find much
of a response among black people generally."

Friedman, Murray. "Is White Racism the Problem?" COMMENTARY, January
1969, pp. 61-65.

"One of the less fortunate results of the black revolution has been
the development of a by now familiar ritual in which the white
liberal is accused of racism and responds by proclaiming himself
guilty as charged." Friedman feels that "the time has come to
dispense with the 'liberal rhetoric of race relations,'" for there
can be no effective bargaining "unless due regard is paid to the
interests of both groups."

Fuller, Hoyt. "The Alien Message of the Wind." BLACK WORLD 19 (October
1970): 49-50, 78-79.

Fuller's response to an appeal for the United States to support
Israel, and his attitude toward Jewish liberals.

_____. "James Baldwin and the Black-Jewish Conflict." BLACK WORLD
20 (September 1971): 83.

An examination of the controversy between James Baldwin and
Shlomo Katz occasioned by the publication of Baldwin's "An Open
Letter to My Sister, Miss Angela Davis" and Katz's "An Open
Letter to James Baldwin."

Glazer, Nathan. "Negroes and Jews: The New Challenges to Pluralism."
COMMENTARY, December 1964, pp. 29-34.

Jews have found "their interests and those of formally less liberal
neighbors becoming similar: they both have an interest in main-
taining an area restricted to their own kind; an interest in managing the friendship and educational experiences of their children;
an interest in passing on advantages in money and skills to them."

Goldbloom, Maurice J. "The New York School Crisis." COMMENTARY,
January 1969, pp. 43-58.

The New York school strike was given constant stress by the news
media as a Jewish-Negro confrontation. The striking UFT union
was always called "Jewish," the Ocean Hill-Brownsville area was
always referred to as a black ghetto.

Hentoff, Nat, ed. BLACK ANTI-SEMITISM AND JEWISH RACISM. New York:
Richard W. Baron, 1969. 237 p.

An anthology of essays, concerned with black-Jewish relationships
by James Baldwin, Earl Raab, Harold Cruse, Julius Lester, and
others.

"How Free the Air? Increasing Anti-Semitism among New York's Militant Black
Community." NEWSWEEK, 10 February 1969, pp. 25-26.

A report on the controversy which arose over the reading of a
reputedly anti-Jewish poem over the air by Leslie Campbell, a
black militant leader during the New York school strike.

Karp, Walter, and Shapiro, H.R. "Exploding the Myth of Black Anti-Semitism."
In BLACK ANTI-SEMITISM AND JEWISH RACISM, edited by Nat Hentoff,
pp. 129-41. New York: Richard W. Baron, 1969.

The reports of wide-spread black anti-Semitism are a "political
lie" and Albert Shanker "and every other petty tyrant protecting
his power" benefits from such lies.

Katz, Shlomo, ed. NEGRO AND JEW: AN ENCOUNTER IN AMERICA.
New York: Macmillan, 1967. 141 p.

A collection of essays, originally published in the Jewish review
MIDSTREAM, concerned with black anti-Semitism. Most of the
essayists are Jewish.

Kaufman, Rabbi Jay. "Thou Shalt Surely Rebuke Thy Neighbor." In BLACK
ANTI-SEMITISM AND JEWISH RACISM, edited by Nat Hentoff, pp. 43-76.
New York: Richard W. Baron, 1969.

"White passivity in the face of the growing incidence of black
anti-Semitism is a betrayal of the ideals upon which this country
has been bred and without which it will perish."

Leo, John. "Black Anti-Semitism." COMMONWEAL, February 1969, pp. 618-
20.

"The insecurity of New York Jews, as revealed in the current
furor, bears no relation to their social or economic status today."
Shanker has manipulated Jewish insecurity "by turning a labor
question into one of anti-Semitism."

Lester, Julius. "A Response." In BLACK ANTI-SEMITISM AND JEWISH RAC-
ISM, edited by Nat Hentoff, pp. 229-37. New York: Richard W. Baron,
1969.

Argues that the problem in New York is not black anti-Semitism,
but racism.

Logan, Jomo. "A Resolution by African-Americans Condemning the Appeal by

So-called Black Leaders Calling for United States Support to Israel." BLACK WORLD 19 (October 1970): 39-42.

A response to a full-page "Appeal" in the NEW YORK TIMES of 28 June 1970, sponsored by the A. Philip Randolph Institute and signed by a number of prominent Afro-Americans. The response is signed by Jomo Logan, Chairman of A.F.R.I.C.A. (African Americans for Friendship and Retainment of Our Image, Culture and Arts).

Mayer, Martin. THE TEACHERS STRIKE: NEW YORK, 1968. New York: Harper & Row, 1968. 122 p.

A chronological review of the teachers' strike in the Ocean Hill-Brownsville school district.

Miller, Rabbi Alan W. "Black Anti-Semitism—Jewish Racism." In BLACK ANTI-SEMITISM AND JEWISH RACISM, edited by Nat Hentoff, pp. 79-114. New York: Richard W. Baron, 1969.

Concludes that "black and Jew have a community of American interest which vastly overrides black anti-Semitism and Jewish racism."

Raab, Earl. "The Black Revolution and the Jewish Question." In BLACK ANTI-SEMITISM AND JEWISH RACISM, edited by Nat Hentoff, pp. 15-41. New York: Richard W. Baron, 1969. Reprinted from COMMENTARY, January 1969, pp. 23-33.

Attributes the conflict between blacks and Jews to the fact that the "American political structure and its traditional coalitions are in naked transition."

Vorspan, Albert. "Blacks and Jews." In BLACK ANTI-SEMITISM AND JEWISH RACISM, edited by Nat Hentoff, pp. 191-226. New York: Richard W. Baron, 1969.

Feels that while some blacks are anti-Semitic, "there is no such thing as black anti-Semitism."

MOVIES

Baldwin, James. "Life Straight in de Eye." COMMENTARY 19 (January 1955): 74-77. Reprinted in his NOTES OF A NATIVE SON as "Carmen Jones," pp. 46-54. Boston: Beacon Press, 1955.

An appraisal of the 1955 Hollywood production of CARMEN JONES. Baldwin objects to the image of the blacks projected in the film (a stereotypic white view of the Negro's carnality).

———. "The Precarious Vogue of Ingmar Bergman." ESQUIRE, April 1960, pp. 128-32. Reprinted in his NOBODY KNOWS MY NAME as "The Northern Protestant," pp. 163-80. New York: Dial Press, 1961.

Although the essay is not about black filmmakers, it is interesting as film criticism by a leading black writer concerning one of Europe's foremost filmmakers.

Bennett, Lerone Jr. "The Emancipation Orgasm: Sweetback in Wonderland." EBONY, September 1971, pp. 106-18.

Bennett sees Van Peebles' portrayal of the black hero as reactionary, stereotypic, and counterrevolutionary.

Bogle, Donald. TOMS, COONS, MULATTOES, MAMMIES, AND BUCKS. New York: Viking Press, 1973. 260 p.

An interpretive history of blacks in American films. Chapters 5, 6, 7, and the epilogue deal with blacks in films since the 1940s.

Ellison, Ralph. "The Shadow and the Act." REPORTER 1 (December 1949): 17-19. Reprinted in his SHADOW AND ACT, pp. 273-81. New York: Random House, 1964.

Concerned with the portrayal of the Negro in PINKY, LOST BOUNDARIES, THE BIRTH OF A NATION, and INTRUDER IN THE DUST.

Kagan, Norman. "The Dark Horse Operas: A Film Article." NEGRO HIS-
TORY BULLETIN 36 (January 1973): 13-14.

Concerned with black ghetto films.

Lee, Don L. "The Bittersweet of Sweetback, or, Shake Yo Money Maker."
BLACK WORLD 21 (November 1971): 43-48.

Attacks the film on aesthetic grounds because of its exploitation
of sex and violence and on political grounds because it is counterrevolutionary and against the best interests of the black populace.

McBride, Joseph. "Stepin Fetchit Talks Back." FILM QUARTERLY 24 (Summer
1971): 20-26.

Stepin Fetchit (Lincoln Theodore Monroe Andrew Perry) reminisces
in an interview in a Madison, Wisconsin, night club. Stepin talks
about his association with black boxers Jack Johnson and Cassius
Clay, how he got his stage name, his career in Hollywood, and
about how his art was actually a caricature of the white man's
vision of the black and thus a secret weapon in the early race
struggle.

Manchel, Frank. "Film Images of the Negro." TEACHERS GUIDE TO MEDIA
AND METHODS 3 (April 1967): 19-23, 48.

A discussion of the stereotyping of Negro characters in cinema.

Mapp, Edward. BLACKS IN AMERICAN FILMS: TODAY AND YESTERDAY.
Metuchen, N.J.: Scarecrow Press, 1972. 278 p.

Covers period 1905 to 1971, but concentration is on the years 1962
to the release of SHAFT in 1971. Purpose is to analyze portrayal
of the "Negro as a major character in recent American films."
Black films made by black producers are not considered because
they are "aimed at black audiences, denied wide distribution and
therefore atypical."

_____. "Black Women in Films." BLACK SCHOLAR 4 (March-April 1973):
42-46.

Argues that "the sexual dimension of American racism is reflected
in the motion picture portrayal of the black woman."

Moss, Carlton. "The Negro in American Films." FREEDOMWAYS 3 (Spring
1963): 134-42.

An analysis of the extent to which black Americans are integrated
into the motion picture industry.

Murray, James P. "William Greaves: Documentaries Are Not Dead." BLACK
CREATION 4 (Fall 1972): 10-11.

Interview with black filmmaker and television producer William
Greaves.

Parks, Gordon. A CHOICE OF WEAPONS. New York: Harper & Row, 1966.
274 p.

Black photographer and writer examines his early ghetto life and
the prejudice he had to overcome in order to be a success.

Patterson, Lindsay, ed. BLACK FILMS AND FILM MAKERS: A COMPREHEN-
SIVE ANTHOLOGY FROM STEREOTYPE TO SUPERHERO. New York: Dodd,
Mead, 1975. 298 p.

A comprehensive selection of articles and essays that trace the
history of black cinema through the mid-1970s.

Peavy, Charles D. "An Afro-American in Paris: The Films of Melvin Van
Peebles." CINEASTE 3 (Summer 1969): 2-3, 31.

A review of Van Peebles' first three films: SUNLIGHT, THREE
PICKUP MEN FOR HERRICK, and THE STORY OF A THREE-DAY
PASS.

_____. "Black Film Makers (Part I): The Films of Richard Mason." CINEASTE
2 (Spring 1969): 4-5, 31.

Review of two films by a young ghetto-bred black: YOU DIG IT?
and GHETTO.

_____. "Cinema from the Slums." CINEASTE 3 (Fall 1969): 11-12, 36.

Concerned with the rehabilitation of a Philadelphia black ghetto
gang through the creation of a filmmakers' corporation and the
making of the film THE JUNGLE, about gang warfare.

_____. "Through a Lens Darkly: America's Emerging Black Film Makers."
JOURNAL OF POPULAR CULTURE 4 (Winter 1971): 674-81. Also in REMUS,
RASTUS, REVOLUTION!, edited by Marshall Fishwick, pp. 155-64. Bowling
Green, Ohio: Bowling Green University Popular Press, n.d.; and CRISES ON
CAMPUS, edited by Russel B. Nye, Ray B. Browne, and Michael Marsden,
pp. 67-75. Bowling Green, Ohio: Bowling Green University Popular Press,
1971.

Sedlack, Robert P. "Joustling with Rats: Charles Wright's 'The Wig.'" SATIRE
NEWSLETTER 7 (Fall 1969): 37-39.

Discusses Wright's use of the conventions of the mock epic to ridi-
cule the protagonist, Lester Jefferson.

Van Peebles, Melvin. SWEET SWEETBACK'S BAADASSSSS SONG. New York: Lancer Books, 1971. 192 p.

Contains details on the production of the controversial film, SWEET SWEETBACK'S BAADASSSSS SONG, stills from the movie, and the script for the film.

MUSIC

Allen, William. "The Barrier: A Critique." PHYLON 11 (1950): 134-36.

    A critical review of Jan Meyerowitz opera THE BARRIER, an
adaptation of Langston Hughes's play MULATTO.

Armstrong, Louis. SATCHMO: MY LIFE IN NEW ORLEANS. Englewood Cliffs,
N.J.: Prentice-Hall, 1954. 240 p.

    An autobiography of the great jazz musician.

Baraka, Imamu Amiri. "The Ban on Black Music." BLACK WORLD 20 (July
1971): 4-11.

    Sees the new black music as a weapon in the cultural-spiritual
revolution to provide new revolutionary consciousness.

Bechet, Sidney. TREAT IT GENTLE. New York: Hill and Wang, 1960.
245 p.

    The book is based on tape-recorded recollections made before his
death in 1959. Bechet recalls his early childhood in New Orleans
and his musical career.

Carawan, Candie, and Carawan, John. FREEDOM IS A CONSTANT STRUGGLE:
SONGS OF THE FREEDOM MOVEMENT. New York: Oak Publications, 1968.
224 p.

    A documentary with photographs and musical transcriptions.

Charters, Samuel. THE POETRY OF THE BLUES. New York: Oak Publications,
1963. 111 p.

    An analysis of the blues as an expression of Afro-American civiliza-
tion, with emphasis on the poetic devices employed by the blues-
men.

Crouch, Stanley. "Black Song West." CRICKET 2 (n.d.): 2-8.

Review of the New Art Jazz Ensemble and the jazz scene in Los Angeles.

Davis, Sammy, Jr. YES I CAN: THE STORY OF SAMMY DAVIS, JR. New York: Farrar, Straus & Giroux, 1965. 612 p.

Davis traces his life from his childhood in vaudeville, to his experience with racism in the army, his loss of an eye in an automobile accident, his conversion to Judaism, his marriage and divorce, and his second marriage, to a white woman, May Britt. Covers the first thirty-five years of Davis' life.

Eaton, Jeanette. TRUMPETER'S TALE: THE STORY OF YOUNG LOUIS ARMSTRONG. New York: William Morrow, 1955. 191 p.

A biography of Louis Armstrong written for children ages eleven to fourteen. A good book for young readers who are also interested in the history of jazz.

Ellison, Ralph. "As the Spirit Moves Mahalia." SATURDAY REVIEW 41 (September 1958): 41-43. Reprinted in his SHADOW AND ACT, pp. 213-20. New York: Random House, 1964.

A discussion of the relationship between jazz music and the gospel singing of Mahalia Jackson.

_____. "Blues People." In his SHADOW AND ACT, pp. 247-58. New York: Random House, 1964. Reprint of "The Blues," which appeared in the NEW YORK REVIEW 1 (February 6, 1964).

Objects to LeRoi Jones's treatment of the blues as sociology rather than lyrics in Jones's BLUES PEOPLE: NEGRO MUSIC IN WHITE AMERICA (see page 81).

_____. "The Charlie Christian Story." SATURDAY REVIEW, 17 May 1958, pp. 42-43, 46. Reprinted in his SHADOW AND ACT, pp. 233-40. New York: Random House, 1964.

Ellison writes that with Christian "the guitar found its jazz voice."

_____. "On Bird, Bird-Watching, and Jazz." SATURDAY REVIEW, July 1962, pp. 47-49, 62. Reprinted in his SHADOW AND ACT, pp. 221-32. New York: Random House, 1964.

A review-essay of Robert George Reisner's BIRD: THE LEGEND OF CHARLIE PARKER.

_____. "Remembering Jimmy." SATURDAY REVIEW, July 1958, pp. 36-37.

Reprinted in his SHADOW AND ACT, pp. 241-46. New York: Random House, 1964.

An essay on the ballad and blues singer, Jimmy Rushing.

Fiofori, Tom. "The Music of Sun Ra: Space Age Music." NEGRO DIGEST 19 (January 1970): 23-28.

A review of the music of Sun Ra and his Arkestra from the 1950s. Includes the various phases of Myth-Science Arkestra and Astro-Infinity Arkestra to the latest developments in the 1970s.

Garland, Phyl. "Nina Simone, High Priestess of Soul." EBONY, August 1969, pp. 156-59.

An excerpt from Garland's book, THE SOUND OF SOUL (see below), the article discusses Simone's role as a singer of the black protest movement.

_____. THE SOUND OF SOUL. Chicago: Henry Regnery, 1969. 246 p.

An examination of "soul" music and its development from earlier roots in the blues, jazz, and gospel music of the black populace.

Hendricks, Jon. "Jazz and Its Critics." LIBERATOR 9 (November 1969): 14-17.

No one can write about Afro-American musical culture with authority while ignoring Afro-American history entirely.

Horne, Lena, and Schickel, Richard. LENA. New York: Doubleday, 1965. 300 p.

An autobiographical account of Horne's career from her initial appearance at the Cotton Club in New York to her success on national television.

Hughes, Langston. FAMOUS NEGRO MUSIC MAKERS. New York: Dodd, Mead, 1955. 179 p.

Brief biographies of Afro-American musicians written primarily for juvenile readers.

_____. FIRST BOOK OF JAZZ. New York: Franklin Watts, 1955. 65 p.

Lists the "ten basic elements of jazz," famous jazz musicians, and Hughes's one hundred favorite jazz and blues records.

Jones, LeRoi. BLACK MUSIC. New York: William Morrow, 1968. 221 p.

A collection of essays primarily concerned with the black music of the 1960s. Many of the selections originally appeared in the magazine DOWNBEAT.

_____. BLUES PEOPLE: NEGRO MUSIC IN WHITE AMERICA. New York: William Morrow, 1963. 244 p.

A study of the blues tradition in America and the condition which produced it.

Keil, Charles. URBAN BLUES. Chicago: University of Chicago Press, 1966. 231 p.

Keil concentrates on "the blues singer as culture hero." The connection between church music and the blues and other popular secular music of the Negro is examined. The bluesman, feels Keil, represents the Negro male and the voice of the male-female conflict in a ghetto environment.

Labrie, Peter. "The Flame That Died: The Legacy of Otis Redding." NEGRO DIGEST 17 (April 1968): 37-40.

An appreciation of Redding's role in reviving the blues tradition for a contemporary generation.

McFarlane, Al. "The Black Scholar Interviews: McCoy Tyner." BLACK SCHOLAR 2 (October 1970): 40-46.

Interview with McCoy Tyner, jazz pianist formerly in John Coltrane's quartet.

Metcalfe, Ralph H. "The Western African Roots of Afro-American Music." BLACK SCHOLAR 1 (June 1970): 16-25.

Traces the Afro-American bluesman from his forerunner, the African griot.

Mtume, James. "Trippin'--A Need for Change." CRICKET 1 (n.d.): 1-2.

Argues that the black musician must be a "revolutionary artist."

Neal, Larry. "Further Comment on THE EMPTY FOXHOLE." CRICKET 2 (n.d.): 17-18.

A rejoinder to Shelley Manne's hostile review of Ornette Coleman's EMPTY FOXHOLE recording in the 2 November 1967 issue of DOWNBEAT.

_____. "The Sound of Soul." NEGRO DIGEST 19 (January 1970): 43-47.

Although primarily a review-essay of Phyl Garland's book, THE

SOUND OF SOUL, the essay is also a call for the expression of the black aesthetic in music: "black art must be the reincarnated accumulation of all the world's positive values; all that is useful and that moves toward concrete human liberation."

"The New Thing." TIME, 6 April 1970, pp. 87-88.

Drawing on African primitivism, Mediterranean and Asian folk music, and sounding at times like Viennese atonalists, "The New Thing" is the music of a specific time and place--the time, that of a black revolution, the place, white America.

Nicholas, A.X., ed. POETRY OF SOUL. New York: Bantam Books, 1971. 103 p.

In his introduction to this collection Nicholas objects to the "dope-infested lyrics of the drug-oriented Rock singers which distort the soul of soul with psychedelic effects."

Reisner, Robert George. BIRD: THE LEGEND OF CHARLIE PARKER. New York: Citadel Press, 1962. 256 p.

Collection of memories and anecdotes by eighty-three observers of the life and music of the black jazzman. Also included are poems, photographs, a chronology of Parker's life, and a discography of his music.

Rivelli, Pauline, and Levin, Robert. THE BLACK GIANTS. New York: World Publishing Co., 1970. 126 p.

Articles from the magazine JAZZ & POP concerning important black jazz musicians, such as John Coltrane, Ornette Coleman, and Cecil Taylor.

Rockmore, Noel; Borenstein, Larry; and Russell, Bill. PRESERVATION HALL PORTRAITS. Baton Rouge: Louisiana State University Press, 1968. Unpaged.

Seventy-five reproductions of paintings by Rockmore of jazz musicians who have played in Preservation Hall, New Orleans. Brief history of Preservation Hall and biographies of the pictured musicians are supplied by Borenstein.

Rout, Leslie B. "Reflections on the Evolution of Post-War Jazz." NEGRO DIGEST 18 (February 1969): 32-34, 92-97. Reprinted in THE BLACK AESTHETIC, edited by Addison Gayle, Jr., pp. 15-160. Garden City, N.Y.: Doubleday, 1971.

A survey of postwar developments in jazz: "The Time of Boppers, 1945-50," "The Socio-Economic Origins of the Be-Bop Revolution," "The New Thing--1959."

Shapiro, Nat, and Hentoff, Nat, eds. THE JAZZ MAKERS. New York: Rinehart and Co., 1953. 429 p. Reprinted as HEAR ME TALKIN' TO YA: THE STORY OF JAZZ AS TOLD BY THE MEN WHO MADE IT. New York: Dover Publications, 1966. 445 p.

    Contains biographies of twenty-one jazzmen.

Southern, Eileen. THE MUSIC OF BLACK AMERICANS. New York: W.W. Norton, 1971. 532 p.

    Good reference source. Contains extensive bibliography, discography, and index.

Spellman, A.B. "Revolution in Sound." In THE BLACK REVOLUTION, pp. 81-96. Chicago: Johnson Publishing Co., 1970.

    A study of the music of John Coltrane.

_____. "Revolution in Sound." EBONY, August 1969, pp. 84-89.

    An essay on the "revolution in sound" which John Coltrane helped to create. Examines, from a historical perspective, the evolution of the new music from its origins in jazz through bebop, East Coast jazz or hard bop, and the work of such musicians as Miles Davis, Thelonious Monk, Yusef Lateef, Sun Ra, Archie Shepp, the Ayler brothers.

Stewart, Jimmy. "Introduction to Black Aesthetics in Music." In THE BLACK AESTHETIC, edited by Addison Gayle, Jr., pp. 81-91. Garden City, N.Y.: Doubleday, 1971.

    A discussion of the revolutionary black music of the 1960s and a demonstration of how it breaks with the established aesthetics of the dominant white culture.

Ulanov, Barry. A HISTORY OF JAZZ IN AMERICA. New York: Viking Press, 1952. 382 p.

    Traces the history of jazz from its origin in the Storyville red light district of New Orleans to its growth in Chicago, New York, and the West Coast, and ultimately its acceptance in Europe. Covers such aspects as swing, bop, cool jazz, and blues.

Walden, Daniel. "Black Music and Cultural Nationalism: The Maturation of Archie Shepp." NEGRO AMERICAN LITERATURE FORUM 5 (Winter 1971): 150-53.

    Analysis of Shepp's role in the new black music of the 1960s.

Wellborn, Ron. "The Black Aesthetic Imperative." In THE BLACK AESTHETIC, edited by Addison Gayle, Jr., pp. 132-49. Garden City, N.Y.: Doubleday, 1971.

> A discussion of Charles Mingus, James Brown, Cecil Taylor, Sun Ra, Ornette Coleman, and John Coltrane from the perspective of the black aesthetic.

Williams, Martin T., ed. THE ART OF JAZZ: ESSAY ON THE NATURE AND DEVELOPMENT OF JAZZ. New York: Grove Press, 1959. 248 p.

> An anthology of critical essays on jazz, historical essays of the origins and development of jazz, and biographical essays on significant jazzmen.

Wilson, John Stewart. JAZZ: THE TRANSITION YEARS, 1940-1960. New York: Appleton-Century-Crofts, 1966. 185 p.

> An examination of developments in postwar jazz by the jazz critic for the NEW YORK TIMES and HIGH FIDELITY.

NOVELS

Bennett, Stephen B., and Nichols, William W. "Violence in Afro-American Fiction: An Hypothesis." MODERN FICTION STUDIES 17 (Summer 1971): 221-28.

> Study of violence in the fiction of Arna Bontemps, Richard Wright, Ralph Ellison, Chester Himes, and James Baldwin.

Bone, Robert. THE NEGRO NOVEL IN AMERICA. Rev. ed. New Haven, Conn.: Yale University Press, 1965. 289 p.

> The last three sections deal with post-World War II black novelists (pp. 153-254).

Fass, Barbara F. "Rejection of Paternalism: Hawthorne's 'My Kinsman Major Molineux' and Ellison's INVISIBLE MAN." CLA JOURNAL 14 (March 1971): 317-23.

> Hawthorne's "My Kinsman Major Molineux" and Ellison's INVISIBLE MAN involve the archetypal motif of the youth who journeys to the city, losing innocence but gaining his identity.

Fleming, Robert E. "The Novels of Ronald L. Fair." CLA JOURNAL 15 (June 1972): 477-87.

> Study of MANY THOUSAND GONE and HOG BUTCHER.

Ford, Nick Aaron. "Battle of the Books: A Critical Survey of Significant Books by and about Negroes Published in 1960." PHYLON 22 (Summer 1961): 119-34.

> Brief reviews of Gwendolyn Brooks's THE BEAN EATERS, Langston Hughes's AN AFRICAN TREASURY, Carl T. Rowan's WAIT TILL NEXT YEAR, and Richard Wright's EIGHT MEN.

_____. "Four Popular Negro Novelists." PHYLON 15 (March 1954): 196-212.

Compares Wright, Ellison, Motley, and Yerby.

_____. "A Note on Ishmael Reed: Revolutionary Novelist." STUDIES IN THE NOVEL 3 (Summer 1971): 216-18.

Reed's novels are "revolutionary" not only in their philosophy but in their innovative style. Emphasis is on THE FREE-LANCE PALL-BEARERS and YELLOW BACK RADIO BROKE DOWN.

Foster, Frances. "Charles Wright: Black Humorist." CLA JOURNAL 15 (September 1971): 44-53.

A study of Wright's THE WIG.

Fuller, Hoyt. "Black Writers' Views on Literary Lions and Values." NEGRO DIGEST 17 (January 1968): 10-48, 81-89.

The response of thirty-eight black writers to a questionnaire (twenty-five questions) sent to them by NEGRO DIGEST. An important source for black critical thinking in the late sixties.

Gayle, Addison, Jr. "Cultural Nationalism: The Black Novel and the City." LIBERATOR 9 (July 1969): 14-17.

Young black urban writers are attempting to create a literature which moves beyond Richard Wright.

Gerard, Albert. "The Sons of Ham." STUDIES IN THE NOVEL 3 (Summer 1971): 148-64.

Study of James Baldwin's GO TELL IT ON THE MOUNTAIN and ANOTHER COUNTRY. Unlike previous black fictional heroes who are alienated both from the white society which rejects them and from the black community which they reject, Baldwin's heroes accept their color and thus recover their sense of unity with their black group.

Gibson, Donald B., ed. FIVE BLACK WRITERS. New York: New York University Press, 1970. 338 p.

Essays by various authors on Wright, Ellison, Hughes, Baldwin, and LeRoi Jones. Contains useful biography of secondary sources.

Glicksberg, Charles I. "The Alienation of Negro Literature." PHYLON 11 (1950): 49-58.

Glicksberg argues that the term "Negro literature" indicates the cultural segregation in which Negro writers are confined. White critics praise Negro writers for possessing talent that is essentially "Negroid"; only those elements of their work which differentiate it _racially_ from "white" art are praised and encouraged.

    . "Race and Revolution in Negro Literature." FORUM 58 (November 1947): 300–308.

    Glicksberg explains "why there are no revolutionary writers" (i.e., Communist propagandists) among Negro writers. "It would be grotesquely false," he says, "to portray the Negro people as the black proletariat marching to battle against the Moloch-hosts of capitalism."

Hemenway, Robert, ed. THE BLACK NOVELIST. Columbus, Ohio: Charles E. Merrill, 1970. 255 p.

    Contains essays on Frank Yerby, Richard Wright, James Baldwin, and Ralph Ellison.

Hughes, John Milton Charles [Carl Milton Hughes]. THE NEGRO NOVELIST. New York: Citadel Press, 1953. Reprint. Freeport, N.Y.: Books for Libraries Press, 1967. 288 p.

    A discussion of black novelists from 1940 to 1950.

Jackson, Blyden. "The Continuing Strain: Resume of Negro Literature, 1955." PHYLON 17 (1956): 35–40.

    Includes very brief statements on James Baldwin's NOTES OF A NATIVE SON, Frank Yerby's BENTON'S ROW and THE TREASURE OF PLEASANT VALLEY.

    . "The Negro's Image of the Universe as Reflected in His Fiction." COLLEGE LANGUAGE ASSOCIATION JOURNAL 4 (September 1960): 22–31.

    Sees the "universe" of Negro literature as limited, with a quality of stasis. The writers view their universe either from the ghetto or from the color caste.

Kent, George [E.]. BLACKNESS AND THE ADVENTURE OF WESTERN CULTURE. Chicago: Third World Press, 1972. 210 p.

    Kent's book is primarily concerned with "double-consciousness" and what he terms the "sensibility" of the black writer.

Lash, John S. "Expostulation and Reply: A Critical Summary of Literature by and about Negroes in 1959." PHYLON 21 (1960): 111–23.

    Brief reviews of Alston Anderson's LOVER MAN, Charles Beaumont's THE INTRUDER, Frank L. Brown's TRUMBULL PARK, Paule Marshall's BROWN GIRL, BROWNSTONES, as well as SELECTED POEMS by Langston Hughes.

Novels

Lawson, Lewis A. "Cross Damon: Kierkegaardian Man of Dread." CLA JOURNAL 14 (March 1971): 298-316.

The positive nature of the conclusion of THE OUTSIDER can be understood only when Wright's reliance upon Kierkegaard is noted.

Lee, Robert A. "James Baldwin and Mathew Arnold: Thoughts on 'Relevance.'" CLA JOURNAL 14 (March 1971): 324-30.

The decline in James Baldwin's literary reputation is connected with demands made upon black writers to adopt certain political positions.

Margolies, Edward. NATIVE SONS: A CRITICAL STUDY OF TWENTIETH-CENTURY NEGRO AMERICAN AUTHORS. Philadelphia: J.B. Lippincott, 1968. 210 p.

The bulk of the book is concerned with black fiction since 1940, containing chapter-length studies of Richard Wright, Chester Himes, James Baldwin, Ralph Ellison, and William Demby.

_____. "The Thrillers of Chester Himes." STUDIES IN BLACK LITERATURE 1 (Summer 1970): 1-11.

A study of Himes's Harlem detective novels.

Peavy, Charles D. "The Black Revolutionary Novel, 1899-1969." STUDIES IN THE NOVEL 3 (Summer 1971): 18-189.

One aspect of the militant mood of the black writers of the late 1960s is the revival, after a seventy-year hiatus, of the genre of the black revolutionary novel such as J. Denis Jackson's [Julian Moreau] THE BLACK COMMANDOS, John A. Williams' SONS OF DARKNESS, SONS OF LIGHT, and Sam Greenlee's THE SPOOK WHO SAT BY THE DOOR.

_____. "Pop Art and the Black Revolution: Julian Moreau's THE BLACK COMMANDOS." JOURNAL OF POPULAR CULTURE 3 (Fall 1969): 205-14.

Moreau's novel represents the first attempt to incorporate the standard devices of pop culture manifested in comic books, television, science fiction, and spy thrillers as a vehicle for black consciousness.

Rosenblatt, Roger. "Black as the Color of Chaos." HARVARD ENGLISH STUDIES 1 (1970): 249-61.

Every black American writer has been forced to contend with an inherited aesthetic conception in which the color black represents all the varieties of vice, and white represents all the virtues.

Scobie, Stephen A.C. "Different Mazes: Mythology in Samuel R. Delaney's THE EINSTEIN INTERSECTION." RIVERSIDE QUARTERLY 6 (1971): 12-18.

The many times and layers of reference in THE EINSTEIN INTER-SECTION are related to Delaney's central subject of mythology.

Shands, Annette Oliver. "Gwendolyn Brooks as Novelist." BLACK WORLD 22 (June 1973): 22-30.

An analysis of MAUD MARTHA, a novel not "to inspire social advancement on the part of fellow blacks" but to "accept the challenge of being human and assert humanness with urgency."

Stoelting, Winifred L. "Human Dignity and Pride in the Novels of Ernest Gaines." CLA JOURNAL 14 (March 1971): 340-58.

A study of CATHERINE CARMIER and OF LOVE AND DUST. In the face of society's polarization, Gaines's characters demonstrate a human dignity and pride.

Walcott, Ronald. "The Novels of Hal Bennett." BLACK WORLD 23 (June 1974): 36-48, 89-97.

A discussion of Bennett's A WILDERNESS OF VINES, LORD OF DARK PLACES, and THE DARK WINE.

POETRY

Barksdale, Richard K. "Urban Crisis and the Black Poetic Avant-Garde." NEGRO AMERICAN LITERATURE FORUM 3 (Summer 1969): 40-44.

The black avant-garde poet is inevitably entangled in what Barksdale describes as a "cobweb of creative insecurity."

Bell, Bernard W. "Contemporary Afro-American Poetry as Folk Art." BLACK WORLD 22 (March 1973): 17-23, 74-87.

A discussion of the role folk ballads, sermons, spirituals, gospels, blues, and jazz have played in the development of a distinctive Afro-American literature.

Bontemps, Arna, ed. AMERICAN NEGRO POETRY. New York: Hill and Wang, 1963. 197 p.

Edited with an introduction by Bontemps, this anthology includes work of fifty-six poets. Among the post-World War II poets represented are Langston Hughes, Arna Bontemps, Richard Wright, Frank Yerby, Margaret Walker, LeRoi Jones, Gwendolyn Brooks. Also includes biographical notes.

Brooks, A. Russell. "The Motif of Dynamic Change in Black Revolutionary Poetry." CLA JOURNAL 15 (September 1971): 7-17.

Concentrates on the poetry of Don L. Lee, Sonia Sanchez, LeRoi Jones, Nikki Giovanni, Larry Neal, Carolyn Rodgers, A.B. Spelman.

Burroughs, Margaret T.G. WHAT SHALL I TELL MY CHILDREN WHO ARE BLACK? Introduction by Don L. Lee. Chicago: M.A.A.H. Press, 1968. 32 p.

Collection of poetry, one speech ("Message to Soul Sisters") and an open letter "To Black Youth of Alabama and Other Places."

Chapman, Abraham. "Black Poetry Today." ARTS IN SOCIETY 5 (Winter 1968): 401-8.

Emanuel, James A. "The Future of Negro Poetry: A Challenge for Critics." In BLACK EXPRESSION, edited by Addison Gayle, Jr., pp. 100-109. New York: Weybright and Talley, 1969.

> Black scholars and critics should focus their "professional and racial sensitivities" on the examination of the black poetic expression of their "unique fusion of the human, the American, and the individual."

Fitnah, Nazzam Al [Marvin X]. "The Black Revolutionary Poet and The Primitive Man." San Francisco: JOURNAL OF BLACK POETRY, n.d. 4 p.

> Two poems printed as a broadside and limited to one thousand copies.

Flasch, Jay. "Humor and Satire in the Poetry of M.B. Tolson." SATIRE NEWS-LETTER 7 (Fall 1969): 29-39.

> An examination of Tolson's work as satire "in the modern vein."

Gallagher, Kathleen. "The Art(s) of Poetry: Jones and MacLeish." MIDWEST QUARTERLY 12 (Summer 1971): 383-92.

> Jones's "Black Art" might have been written as a deliberate contradiction of MacLeish's "Ars Poetica."

Giddings, Paula. "A Shoulder Humped against a Sharp Concern: Some Themes in the Poetry of Margaret Walker." BLACK WORLD 21 (December 1971): 20-25.

> An examination of the themes in Margaret Walker's works.

Henderson, Stephen E. "Saturation: Progress Report on a Theory of Black Poetry." BLACK WORLD 24 (June 1975): 4-17.

> "Blackness" can be "a value in the creation, in the description, and in the criticism of Black poetry."

_____. UNDERSTANDING THE NEW BLACK POETRY: BLACK SPEECH AND BLACK MUSIC AS POETIC REFERENCES. New York: William Morrow, 1973. 394 p.

> Anthology of black poetry with emphasis on the 1960s; introduction examines such questions as what makes poetry "black," who decides, and what criteria does one use.

Kent, George E. "The Poetry of Gwendolyn Brooks." BLACK WORLD 20 (September 1971): 3-43.

> Brooks shares with Margaret Fuller the achievement of summing up the black mood of the 1940s. Her poem, "Rider To The Blood Red Wrath" (SELECTED POEMS, 1963), more than any other poem, renders the black mood of the 1950s and early 1960s.

King, Woodie, Jr., ed. BLACK SPIRITS, A FESTIVAL OF NEW BLACK POETS IN AMERICA. Foreword by Nikki Giovanni. Introduction by Don L. Lee. New York: Random House, 1972. 280 p.

> An anthology of black poetry read at a poetry festival in 1971 at New York's Apollo Theater and the Brooklyn Academy of Music.

Miller, Adam David, comp. DICES OR BLACK BONES: BLACK VOICES OF THE SEVENTIES. New York: Houghton Mifflin Co., 1970. 142 p.

> An anthology of seventeen young black poets writing in the late 1960s.

Nicholas, A.X. "A Conversation with Dudley Randall." BLACK WORLD 21 (December 1971): 26-34.

> An interview with Dudley Randall, poet and publisher of Broadside Press, conducted in Randall's home on 25 May 1971.

Otten, Charlotte F. "LeRoi Jones: Napalm Poet." CONCERNING POETRY 3 (1970): 5-11.

> Jones's poetry progresses from optimism to painful self-analysis and ultimately, nihilism.

Palmer, R. Roderick. "The Poetry of Three Revolutionists: Don L. Lee, Sonia Sanchez, and Nikki Giovanni." CLA JOURNAL 15 (September 1971): 25-36.

> The poetry of these three poets promulgates the black aesthetic, revitalizes black values, and delineates the national spirit of black people.

Randall, Dudley. "Black Poetry." In BLACK EXPRESSION, edited by Addison Gayle, Jr., pp. 109-14. New York: Weybright and Talley, 1969.

> Randall writes of the new generation of black poets and how they differ from their predecessors.

Rodgers, Carolyn M. "Black Poetry--Where It's At." NEGRO DIGEST 18 (September 1969): 7-16.

> A young black poet looks at the new black poetry which utilizes the typical black street traditions of "signifying," "rappin," "hipto," and "coatpulling."

Rowell, Charles H. "Poetry, History, and Humanism." BLACK WORLD 25 (December 1975): 4-17.

An interview with Margaret Walker recorded in May 1973. In the interview Walker stresses the importance in emphasizing humanism in a technological age.

Sedlack, Robert P. "Mari Evans: Consciousness and Craft." CLA JOURNAL 15 (September 1971): 465-76.

Concerned with Evans' I AM A BLACK WOMAN.

Sheffey, Ruthe. "The Sardonic Vision: Wit and Irony in Militant Black Poetry." BLACK WORLD 22 (June 1973): 14-21.

Satiric aspects of the poetry of Mari Evans, Dudley Randall, Don L. Lee, Nikki Giovanni.

Toure, Askia Muhammad. "Black Magic! (A Statement on the Tasks of the New Poetry)." JOURNAL OF BLACK POETRY 1 (Fall 1968): 63-64.

Essay warning against "rage poetry"--"shrill screams of hatred and rage" and "total negativity."

POLITICS

Bailey, Harry, Jr., ed. NEGRO POLITICS IN AMERICA. Columbus, Ohio:
Charles E. Merrill, 1967. 455 p.

A collection of readings concerning the role of the Negro in
American politics. The individual selections are drawn from the
better books and journal articles on the subject.

Boulware, Marcus H. THE ORATORY OF NEGRO LEADERS: 1900-1968.
Westport, Conn.: Negro Universities Press, 1969. 312 p.

Excellent discussion of the rhetoric of black preachers, politicians,
statesmen, scholars, and militant leaders. Chapter 14, "The Vessels
of God," discusses the Black Muslims. Chapter 15, "The New
Revolt Period, 1954-1965," evaluates the oratory of Robert Williams,
James Farmer, Medgar Evers, and others. Chapter 16 contrasts
Malcolm X and Whitney Young, and chapter 17 is a study of
Martin Luther King, Jr.

Cheatwood, Kiarri. "Stokely Speaks (On Young African Warriors, Domestic
Power, and World Political Economic Struggle)." BLACK WORLD 24 (November 1974): 76-83.

An overview and assessment of Carmichael's political analysis for
African people.

Chisholm, Shirley. "The Politics of Coalition." BLACK SCHOLAR 4 (September 1972): 30-32.

"Blacks must realize that there are other groups who face discrimina-
tion, and who, for reasons of their own self-interest, are willing
to join forces in breaking down petty and arbitrary barriers against
fully productive careers within the mainstream of American life."

Dymally, Mervyn M., comp. THE BLACK POLITICIAN: HIS STRUGGLE FOR
POWER. Boston: Duxbury Press, 1971. 144 p.

An anthology of the views of various black politicans. Important
source of information about the biographies, perceptions, and aspirations of black leaders.

Hatcher, Richard G. "Black Politics in the 70's." BLACK SCHOLAR 4
(September 1972): 17-22.

Hatcher was the convention host and cochairman of the National
Black Political Convention held in Gary, Indiana. This essay was
read as the keynote address at that convention.

Holloway, Harry. THE POLITICS OF THE SOUTHERN NEGRO: FROM EXCLU-
SION TO BIG CITY ORGANIZATION. New York: Random House, 1969.
374 p.

Examines the reasons why Negroes have been excluded from politics
and what factors may lead to Negro participation in politics. Data
derived from interviews with two hundred persons, reports of the
U.S. Commission on Civil Rights, and newspapers.

Ladd, Everett C. NEGRO POLITICAL LEADERSHIP IN THE SOUTH. Ithaca,
N.Y.: Cornell University Press, 1966. 348 p.

Study concentrates on leadership in Greenville, South Carolina,
and Winston-Salem, North Carolina, and is based on NAACP
files, interviews with political leaders, and attendance at political
party gatherings.

Lomax, Louis E. THE NEGRO REVOLT. New York: Harper and Bros., 1962.
271 p.

A commentary on organizations concerned with the civil rights and
equal opportunities for Afro-Americans.

Powell, Adam C., Jr. MARCHING BLACKS. New York: Dial Press, 1973.
216 p.

Important to the understanding of Powell's philosophy, this work
outlines the four steps Negroes must take to gain freedom: (1)
disciplining their resentment, (2) sustaining their indignation, (3)
developing militant leadership, and (4) utilizing only collective
social action.

Silverman, Sondra, ed. THE BLACK REVOLT AND DEMOCRATIC POLITICS.
Boston: D.C. Heath, 1970. 109 p.

A selection of readings on the political implications of the black
revolt, including articles by Harold Cruse, Stokely Carmichael,
Charles V. Hamilton, and Eldridge Cleaver.

Stone, Chuck. BLACK POLITICAL POWER IN AMERICA. Indianapolis: Bobbs-Merrill, 1968. 261 p.

Stone's tracing of "the history and development of the Negro's role in the American political system" is sometimes humorous, as in his portrait of "The Ceremonial Negro" and "The Revolving Door Negro."

Thompson, Daniel C. THE NEGRO LEADERSHIP CLASS. Englewood Cliffs, N.J.: Prentice-Hall, 1963. 174 p.

A "case study of the tactics and strategy of a subordinate group in its efforts to exact basic concessions from the powerful decision makers." The study is based on seventy-five Negro leaders in New Orleans.

Walton, Hanes, Jr. THE STUDY OF ANALYSIS OF BLACK POLITICS. Metuchen, N.J.: Scarecrow Press, 1973. 161 p.

The best bibliography on every aspect of the Negro in American politics. Lists books, articles, and dissertations on the subject.

Wilson, James G. NEGRO POLITICS: THE SEARCH FOR LEADERSHIP. Glencoe, Ill.: Free Press, 1960. 342 p.

This study is based primarily on ninety-five interviews with Chicago political leaders, but interviews were also conducted in New York, Detroit, and Los Angeles. A useful study of the role of black leaders in urban politics.

Wynn, Daniel. THE NAACP VERSUS NEGRO PROTEST. New York: Exposition Press, 1955. 115 p.

Heavily documented comparison and contrast of the two rival philosophies of black civil rights in the 1950s.

PRISON WRITING

Aswadu, Ahmad Al. "A Black View of Prison." BLACK SCHOLAR 2 (April–
May 1971): 28-31.

Impressions of various penal institutions by Aswadu, who writes,
"I have spent five years of my 21 years of existence in various
penal institutions in Illinois. I'm presently serving a 17-year-term
for a murder I had nothing to do with."

Dale, Le Afrique. "A Day's Work." BLACK SCHOLAR 2 (April–May 1971):
47-49.

A black prisoner's reflections on the plight of black Americans as
he swings an axe in a California work camp.

Davis, Angela. "The Soledad Brothers." BLACK SCHOLAR 2 (April–May
1971): 2-7.

Davis' call for action to free the "Soledad Brothers," written
while she was being held in the Marin County Jail in San Rafael,
California.

Harvey, William, and Daniels, George. BLACK MARINES AGAINST THE
BRASS. Introduction by Shirley Jolls. New York: American Servicemen's
Union, 1969. 19 p.

An interview with Harvey and Daniels, who had served two years
on six- and ten-year sentences respectively for their opposition to
the war in Vietnam. Interview conducted by Andy Stapp.

Jackson, George. SOLEDAD BROTHER. Introduction by Jean Genet. New
York: Coward-McCann, 1970. 330 p.

Letters written by Jackson in Soledad Prison before he was killed
in an attempt to escape. At the time of the book's publication
Jackson had spent ten years in prison, seven and a half of them
in solitary confinement.

Karenga, Maulana Ron. "Ideology and Struggle: Some Preliminary Notes."
BLACK SCHOLAR 6 (January–February 1975): 23–30.

Another of Karenga's continuing treatises on cultural revolution,
written during his fourth year of imprisonment.

————. "Overturning Ourselves: From Mystification to Meaningful Struggle."
BLACK SCHOLAR 4 (October 1972): 6–14.

"We must constantly reassess our position and postures, eliminate
our weaknesses and reinforce our strengths. . . . If we can over-
turn ourselves, we can overcome our collective weaknesses . . .
and defeat the enemy." Karenga wrote this while in prison following a conviction for felonious assault.

————. "A Strategy for Struggle." BLACK SCHOLAR 5 (November 1973):
8–21.

Written while Karenga was spending his third year in prison, this
essay argues that blacks should no longer "take refuge in rhetoric,
symbolic associations with the Movement's saints, traditional dress
and hair styles and social withdrawal into mysticism," but seek a
viable strategy for true liberation.

Knight, Etheridge. BLACK VOICES FROM PRISON. Introduction by Roberto
Giammanco. New York: Pathfinder Press, 1970. 288 p.

Poems, essays, and interviews by Knight and other inmates of
Indiana State Prison.

————. POEMS FROM PRISON. Preface by Gwendolyn Brooks. Detroit:
Broadside Press, 1968. 31 p.

Poems written by Knight while an inmate at Indiana State Prison.

Prisoners Solidarity Committee. FROM BEHIND THE WALLS OF AUBURN CON-
CENTRATION CAMP PRISONERS CALL OUT: FREEDOM. New York: Prisoners
Solidarity Committee, 1971. 52 p.

Concerned with the black prisoners at Auburn.

————. FROM SOLEDAD TO SAN QUENTIN. San Francisco: Prisoners
Solidarity Committee, 1971. 27 p.

Prison writing from Soledad Prison in California.

Spain, Johnny. "The Black Family and the Prisons." BLACK SCHOLAR 4
(October 1972): 18–31.

As long as society "permits any man to be locked behind walls
and bars for unjustified reasons, that man will resist; first against

the imprisonment, and then against the social order which created the imprisonment, and then against the society." Spain, a member of the Black Panther party, was one of the "San Quentin Six" involved in the escape attempt during which George Jackson was killed.

Wade, Wendell. "The Politics of Prisons." BLACK SCHOLAR 2 (April-May 1971): 12-18.

Wade's thesis is that "the incarcerated of North America, i.e., the black, the politically active (in opposition to the power structure), and the poor are either political prisoners and/or prisoners of war." Wade was a prisoner in California at the time of the composition of this piece.

PSYCHOLOGY

Banks, James A., and Grambs, Jean Dresden, eds. BLACK SELF-CONCEPT: IMPLICATIONS FOR EDUCATION AND SOCIAL SCIENCE. New York: Mc-Graw-Hill, 1972. 234 p.

> Collection of essays by various authors which explore the school's role in improving the self-perceptions and identities of black youth.

Bennett, Lerone, Jr. THE NEGRO MOOD AND OTHER ESSAYS. Chicago: Johnson Publishing Co., 1964. 104 p.

> In five essays centered on the theme of the "Negro Mood," Bennett uses the tools of social psychology to examine the "psychic mechanisms" of "Black Fury."

Clark, Kenneth B. PREJUDICE AND YOUR CHILD. Boston: Beacon Press, 1963. 247 p.

> An examination of the psychic damage that can be done to young minds—whether they be the aggressors or victims—by racial prejudice.

Cross, William E., Jr. "The Negro-to-Black Conversion Experience." BLACK WORLD 20 (July 1971): 13-27.

> Presents a five-stage model as a step toward the establishment of a "psychology of Black liberation" and a plan to create "socialization models" and child-rearing techniques that will demonstrate to black parents how to raise their children to emulate black heroes.

Glicksberg, Charles I. "Psychoanalysis and the Negro Problem." PHYLON 17 (1956): 41-51.

> "Psychoanalysis, despite its fanciful theoretical constructions, offers a cogent and empirically verifiable diagnosis of the damage wrought by the curse of caste oppression, but it cannot, and makes no effort to, provide a cure."

Grier, William H., and Cobbs, Price M. BLACK RAGE. New York: Basic Books, 1968. 219 p.

Controversial study of the psychopathology of blacks.

Grossack, Martin M., ed. MENTAL HEALTH AND SEGREGATION. New York: Springer Publishing Co., 1963. 247 p.

A collection of essays by several authors who study the psychic consequences of segregation.

Halsell, Grace. BLACK/WHITE SEX. New York: Fawcett, 1973. 192 p.

Halsell is the author of SOUL SISTER and once darkened her skin in order to live among black people. BLACK/WHITE SEX is based on a number of interviews with men and women from all walks of life who have been involved in interracial sexual relationships. Also included is a history of American attitudes toward black/white sex from Jefferson to the present.

Hendin, Herbert. BLACK SUICIDE. New York: Basic Books, 1969. 176 p.

"The high frequency of suicide among older whites has led to the misconception that suicide is a 'white' problem, obscuring the fact that among young adults of both sexes, particularly in urban areas, it is actually more of a black problem."

Hernton, Calvin C. COMING TOGETHER: BLACK POWER, WHITE HATRED AND SEXUAL HANG-UPS. New York: Random House, 1971. 192 p.

The purpose of this study is "to identify and analyze the nature of black sexuality and the character of interpersonal relations between black men and women in the historical context of American racism and oppression."

_____. SEX AND RACISM. London: Deutsch, 1969. 159 p.

An examination of the sexual implications of the race problem.

Howard, Joseph Hannibal. "How to End Colonial Domination of Black America." NEGRO DIGEST 19 (January 1970): 4-10, 66-69.

A challenge to black psychologists to reflect a world view different from that of their white counterparts.

Jones, Martin H., and Jones, Martin C. "The Neglected Client." BLACK SCHOLAR 1 (March 1970): 35-42.

"Meaningful knowledge of blackness does not exist because the great majority of student and academic personnel are from the white middle class."

Kardiner, Abram, and Ovesey, Lionel. THE MARK OF OPPRESSION: EXPLO-RATIONS IN THE PERSONALITY OF THE AMERICAN NEGRO. Cleveland: World Publishing Co., 1962. 415 p.

An examination of the acquired personality of the black as a result of his exposure to adverse social conditioning.

Karon, Bertram P. THE NEGRO PERSONALITY: A RIGOROUS INVESTIGA-TION OF THE EFFECTS OF CULTURE. New York: Springer Publishing Co., 1958. 184 p.

The American caste system is reflected in eleven black personality characteristics, six of which are directly concerned with aggression and defense mechanism of denial of aggression.

Lincoln, Charles Eric. MY FACE IS BLACK. Boston: Beacon Press, 1964. 137 p.

A prominent black sociologist explains what it is like to be a black man in America.

Meriwether, Louise M. "The Negro: Half a Man in a White World." NEGRO DIGEST 14 (October 1965): 4-13.

An examination of the psychological emasculation of the black male by two centuries of white racism.

Musgrave, Marion E. "Triangles in Black and White: Interracial Sex and Hostility in Black Literature." CLA JOURNAL 14 (June 1971): 444-51.

Examines the relationship between sex and aggression in works by Richard Wright, John A. Williams, Chester Himes, Ishmael Reed, and LeRoi Jones.

Poussaint, Alvin F. "A Psychiatrist Looks at Black Power." EBONY, March 1969, pp. 142-52.

A by-product of the black power movement is a shift from an integration-oriented mentality to self-determination and black consciousness.

Poussaint, Alvin F., and Atkinson, Carolyn. "Black Youth and Motivation." BLACK SCHOLAR 1 (March 1970): 43-51.

An analysis of the internal and external motivating factors for the militant black youth of the 1960s.

Poussaint, Alvin F., and Ladner, Joyce. "Black Power: A Failure for Racial Integration within the Civil Rights Movement." ARCHIVES OF GENERAL PSY-CHIATRY 18 (April 1968): 385-91.

Examines the reasons why black civil rights workers developed a fear that whites would "take over our movement."

Poussaint, Alvin F., and McLean, Linda R. "Black Roadblocks to Black Unity." NEGRO DIGEST 18 (November 1968): 11-18, 63-64.

An examination of the psychological difficulties hampering certain black groups because of the effects on blacks of a white racist heritage.

Pugh, Roderick W. PSYCHOLOGY AND THE BLACK EXPERIENCE. Monterey, Calif.: Brooks/Cole Publishing Co., 1972. 118 p.

A psychological assessment of black revolt and black student activism and an exploration of various methods for devising an effective community psychology program for urban blacks.

Saunders, Charles. "Assessing Race Relations Research." BLACK SCHOLAR 1 (March 1970): 17-25.

An examination of race attitudes research.

Saxe, Janet. "Review of BLACK RAGE." BLACK SCHOLAR 1 (March 1970): 58-62.

An attack on the premise of Grier and Cobbs's study (see above) of black psychology.

Sundiata, Phaon Goldman. "The White Reaction to the Black Assertion." BLACK SCHOLAR 1 (March 1970): 11-16.

Predicts that the white man's reaction to the black assertion will be psychologically determined and will be "bloody."

Thomas, Alexander, and Sillen, Samuel. RACISM AND PSYCHIATRY. New York: Bruner/Mazel, 1972. 189 p.

Illustrates the myriad ways "white racism has influenced the theory and practice in psychiatry and allied fields."

Thomas, Charles, ed. BOYS NO MORE: A BLACK PSYCHOLOGIST'S VIEW OF COMMUNITY. Beverly Hills, Calif.: Glencoe Press, 1971. 125 p.

Selections by various authors which indicate that "the concept of blackness and related matters is best handled by black social scientists."

Vontress, Clemont E. "The Black Male Personality." BLACK SCHOLAR 2 (June 1971): 10-16.

The basic and most debilitating variable of the black personality is self-hatred.

Walton, Sid. "Census 70: Blueprint for Repression." BLACK SCHOLAR 1 (March 1970): 28-34.

Census 70 will strike a blow at one of the few effective defenses an oppressed people have--secrecy about their population, size, and location.

Washington, Joseph R., Jr. MARRIAGE IN BLACK AND WHITE. Boston: Beacon Press, 1970. 358 p.

A prominent black theologian argues that there can be no end to the racial conflict until there is an acceptance of intermarriage.

Watkins, Charles A. "Simple: The Alter-Ego of Langston Hughes." BLACK SCHOLAR 2 (June 1971): 18-26.

"What emerges from the Simple stories is Hughes dramatically work-ing out his own confusion of identity, wrestling with his own name-lessness and invisibility, and doing so to liberate that special audi-ence for whom he writes."

Weaver, Edward K. "Racial Sensitivity among Negro Children." PHYLON 17 (1956): 52-60.

Indicates how the caste system has functioned to cause the Negro child to develop feelings of guilt and withdrawal and thus to work against his own interests.

White, Joseph. "Guidelines for Black Psychologists." BLACK SCHOLAR 1 (March 1970): 52-57.

The danger of black psychologists operating on the assumptions de-veloped by white psychologists primarily for white people.

Wilcox, Roger, ed. THE PSYCHOLOGICAL CONSEQUENCES OF BEING A BLACK AMERICAN. New York: John Wiley & Sons, 1971. 492 p.

A compilation of the published work of black psychologists. Con-tains useful bibliographies.

RELIGION

Barrett, Leonard E. SOUL-FORCE: AFRICAN HERITAGE IN AFRO-AMERICAN RELIGION. Garden City, N.Y.: Doubleday, 1974. 251 p.

An examination of the religious cults developed by Africans in America. Barrett argues that the Africans' racial inheritance sustained them through the hostile environment encountered in the New World.

"The Black Church: Three Views." TIME, 6 April 1970, pp. 71-73.

Three "views from the pulpit" by black religious leaders on the subject of the church and its relevancy to the black struggle for civil rights: Calvin Marshall, Samuel W. Williams, and Joseph H. Jackson.

Cleage, Albert B., Jr. THE BLACK MESSIAH. New York: Sheed and Ward, 1968. 278 p.

Presents a black nationalist theology. Biblical Jews were a black people, Jesus a black Messiah, Romans ancient honkies, Judas an Uncle Tom.

Collins, Herbert. "Store Front Churches." NEGRO AMERICAN LITERATURE FORUM 4 (July 1970): 61-68.

"Storefront churches are possibly more revolutionary and socially functional stances than they have ever been credited for."

Cone, James H. BLACK THEOLOGY AND BLACK POWER. New York: Seaburg Press, 1969. 176 p.

An attempt "to show that the goal and message of Black Power . . . is consistent with the gospel of Jesus Christ."

_____. "Failure of the Black Chruch." LIBERATOR 9 (May 1969): 14-17, 22.

"If the black church is to be relevant, it must no longer admonish
its people to be 'nice' to white society . . . . it must make an un-
qualified identification with the 'looters' and the 'rioters.'"

deCoy, Robert H. THE NIGGER BIBLE. Los Angeles: Holloway House, 1967.
304 p.

An alternative to the Old Testament in which traditional Judeo-
Christian concepts are rejected for a "Black Concept-of-God."

Frazier, E. Franklin. THE NEGRO CHURCH IN AMERICA. New York: Schoc-
ken Books, 1964. 92 p.

An examination of the black church in America from the beginning
to 1953. Frazier's thesis is that the black church in America is
not a continuation of the African tradition but is a result of the
sense of social cohesion given to uprooted slaves by the Christian
church.

Goodman, George. "Harlem's Yoruba." LOOK, 7 January 1969, pp. 32-33.

The practice of the African Yoruba rites has been revived in a
cult in Harlem.

Hamilton, Charles V. BLACK PREACHER IN AMERICA. San Diego: Morrow
Publications, 1972. 246 p.

An examination of the black preacher's role in the black church
and in the black community.

Philpot, William M., ed. BEST BLACK SERMONS. Valley Forge, Pa.: Judson
Press, 1972. 96 p.

A collection of sermons by William Holmes Borders, Sr., D.E.
King, Martin Luther King, Jr., Benjamin Mays, Hosea Williams,
and others.

Robeson, Paul. HERE I STAND. Introduction by Lloyd I. Brown. Boston:
Beacon Press, 1972. 121 p.

Published during Robeson's eight-year fight to retain his passport
when the U.S. State Department acted against his efforts to aid
the movement for African independence.

Schucter, Arnold. REPARATIONS: THE BLACK MANIFESTO AND ITS CHAL-
LENGE TO WHITE AMERICA. Philadelphia: J.B. Lippincott, 1970. 280 p.

Includes the "Black Manifesto" adopted by the National Black
Economics Development Conference (pp. 191-202), and bibliographies.

Washington, Joseph R., Jr. BLACK RELIGION: THE NEGRO AND CHRIS-
TIANITY IN THE UNITED STATES. Boston: Beacon Press, 1964. 308 p.

> A critical examination of black religion in America and the forces
> that produced it. Reviews the similarities and differences between
> black religion and white Protestantism.

_____. BLACK SECTS AND CULTS. New York: Doubleday, 1972. 176 p.

> An examination of the African roots of Afro-American religion and
> of black pentecostal sects, holiness cults, and evangelical groups,
> as well as such major figures as Daddy Grace, Prophet Cherry,
> Father Divine, Marcus Garvey, Elijah Muhammed.

_____. THE POLITICS OF GOD: THE FUTURE OF THE BLACK CHURCHES.
Boston: Beacon Press, 1970. 234 p.

> Argues that there is a theological basis for the black revolution
> ("blacks have a sacred mission to free white souls from the sins
> of racism").

Williams, Ethel L., and Brown, Clifton L. AFRO-AMERICAN RELIGIOUS
STUDIES: A COMPREHENSIVE BIBLIOGRAPHY WITH LOCATIONS IN AMERI-
CAN LIBRARIES. Metuchen, N.J.: Scarecrow Press, 1972. 454 p.

> A useful listing of sources.

Wilmore, Gayrand S. BLACK RELIGION AND BLACK RADICALISM. New
York: Doubleday, 1972. 344 p.

> An examination of the paradox of the black church, which is at
> once steeped in the values of white America and in the more inde-
> pendent and powerful institution in the black community.

RIOTS

Anderson, Jervis. "The Voices of Newark." COMMENTARY 44 (October 1967): 85-90.

An analysis of the implications of the rioting in Newark, New Jersey, on 12 July 1967.

Aptheker, Herbert. "The Watts Ghetto Uprising." POLITICAL AFFAIRS 44 (October 1965): 16-29; 44 (November 1965): 28-44.

Aptheker reviews the reasons for the Watts riot and objects to "the ruling class' denuciation of the Watts violence--especially since it was the police and the Guardsmen who killed and who wounded."

Blauner, Robert. "Whitewash over Watts." TRANSACTION 3 (March-April 1966): 2-9, 54-56.

A critique of the McCone Commission report on the riot in Watts. Blauner finds the report invalid.

Boskin, Joseph, and Krinsky, Fred. URBAN RACIAL VIOLENCE IN THE TWENTIETH CENTURY. Beverly Hills, Calif.: Glencoe Press, 1969. 148 p.

"The race riots that raged from 1906 to 1943 occurred because whites felt the license to prove their domination and superiority over Blacks. The protest riots of the 1960's occurred because Negroes were eager to overthrow that domination and to prove their equality and dignity."

Caplan, Nathan S., and Paige, J.M. "Study of Ghetto Rioters." SCIENTIFIC AMERICAN 219 (August 1968): 15-21.

An analysis of surveys made after the riots of 1967 in Detroit and Newark indicates that some of the usual hypotheses for the reasons why Negroes riot are invalid.

Cohen, Jerry, and Murphy, William S. BURN BABY BURN! THE LOS ANGELES RACE RIOT: AUGUST 1965. New York: E.P. Dutton, 1966. 318 p.

> Written by "two members of the Pulitzer Prize-winning LOS AN-GELES TIMES team," this work is an "hour by hour reconstruction" of the events during the riot.

Cohen, Nathan. THE LOS ANGELES RIOTS, A SOCIO-PSYCHOLOGICAL STUDY. New York: Praeger, 1970. 742 p.

> "Researchers found the basic cause of discontent among Negroes to be economic dependency on the white community, inadequate hous-ing, unemployment, lack of strong family structure, lack of vehicles for political expression, and poor educational facilities."

Conot, Robert E. RIVERS OF BLOOD, YEARS OF DARKNESS: THE UNFOR-GETTABLE CLASSIC ACCOUNT OF THE WATTS RACE RIOT. New York: William Morrow, 1967. 507 p.

> An account of the Watts riot.

Feagin, Joe R., and Sheatsley, Paul B. "Ghetto Resident Appraisals of a Riot." PUBLIC OPINION QUARTERLY 32 (Fall 1968): 352-62.

> An assessment of the causes for the riot which began in Harlem in July 1964, and spread to Brooklyn's Bedford-Stuyvesant section. The analysis is based on assessments made by the residents in the area.

Fogelson, Robert M. "White on Black: A Critique of the McCone Commission Report on the Los Angeles Riot." POLITICAL SCIENCE QUARTERLY 82 (September 1967): 337-67.

> A critique of the McCone Commission findings which "offered in-adequate recommendations based on erroneous analyses derived from untenable assumptions."

Hayden, Tom. REBELLION IN NEWARK. New York: Random House, 1967. 102 p.

> The story of the Newark riots from the blacks' point of view. Most of the material in the book appeared earlier in the NEW YORK REVIEW OF BOOKS.

Hersey, John. THE ALGIERS MOTEL INCIDENT. New York: Alfred A. Knopf, 1968. 397 p.

> An investigation of the killing of three blacks in the Algiers Motel on the fourth day of the 1967 Detroit riot. Hersey gives what he feels to be a psychosociological explanation of the incident.

Komorowski, Conrad. "The Detroit Ghetto Uprisings." POLITICAL AFFAIRS 46 (September 1967): 12-24.

A Communist coverage of the Detroit riot which concludes that "in addition to the dehumanized, racist brutality of the police, every major constitutional guarantee of civil and democratic rights was brutally violated."

Lachman, Sheldon J., and Waters, Thomas F. "Psycho-Social Profile of Riot Arrestees." PSYCHOLOGICAL REPORT 24 (February 1969): 171-81.

A study based on interviews with one hundred male Negroes charged with participation in the Detroit riot of July 1967.

Lincoln, James H. THE ANATOMY OF A RIOT: A DETROIT JUDGE'S RE-PORT. New York: McGraw-Hill, 1968. 206 p.

Lincoln, a juvenile court judge, examines the handling of youths by authorities during the riot, and suggests the need for more law enforcement, fewer unwanted children, a more intensive birth control and family planning procedure.

Locke, Herbert G. THE DETROIT RIOT OF 1967. Detroit: Wayne State University Press, 1969. 160 p.

An examination of the riots and violence that wracked Detroit in 1967, with maps and illustrations.

Masotti, Louis H., and Bowen, Dan R., eds. RIOT AND REBELLION: CIVIL VIOLENCE IN THE URBAN COMMUNITY. Beverly Hills, Calif.: Sage Publications, 1968. 459 p.

A selection of twenty cases for examination as an index to the nature and causes of riots in American urban areas.

Masotti, Louis H., and Corsi, Jerome R. SHOOT-OUT IN CLEVELAND: BLACK MILITANTS AND THE POLICE, JULY 23, 1968. New York: Praeger, 1969. 126 p.

An analysis of the first major "shoot-out" between police and heavily armed blacks. The incidents occurred in the summer of 1968 in Cleveland, Ohio.

Morris, Richard T., and Jeffries, Vincent. "Violence Next Door." SOCIAL FORCES 46 (March 1968): 352-58.

A report on white reactions to the riots in Watts in 1965. Report makes several conclusions about white antagonism toward Negroes: egoism is related to high antagonism, altruism to low antagonism; lack of intimate social contact with blacks is related to high antagonism, and egoism and lack of social contact combine to produce a very high antagonism.

Oberschall, Anthony. "The Los Angeles Riot of August 1965." SOCIAL PROB-
LEMS 15 (Winter 1968): 322-41.

> A sociological analysis of the causes of the Watts riot in 1965.
> "The riot is seen as a massive, violent, lower-class, Negro out-
> burst which stopped short of being an insurrection."

Ransford, H. Edward. "Isolation, Powerlessness, and Violence: A Study of
Attitudes and Participation in the Watts Riots." AMERICAN JOURNAL OF
SOCIOLOGY 73 (March 1968): 581-91.

> "Racial isolation (low degrees of intimate white contact) is strongly
> associated with a willingness to use violence when under two sub-
> jective conditions: (a) when isolated individuals feel a sense of
> powerlessness in the society and (b) when isolated individuals are
> highly dissatisfied with their treatment as Negroes."

Ritchie, Barbara, ed. THE RIOT REPORT: A SHORTENED VERSION OF THE
REPORT OF THE NATIONAL ADVISORY COMMISSION ON CIVIL DISORDERS.
New York: Viking Press, 1969. 254 p.

> A useful condensation of the commission's report on the causes for
> the civil unrest in 1967.

Rossa, Della. WHY WATTS EXPLODED. New York: Merit Publishers, 1966.
21 p.

> Sees the basic cause of the Watts riot as "the constant abuse by
> the police, symbol of the white power structure, and the prevailing
> unemployment that continued generation after generation."

Rustin, Bayard. "The Watts 'Manifesto' and the McCone Report." COMMEN-
TARY 5 (March 1966): 29-35.

> Rustin discusses the errors and misconceptions of the McCone Com-
> mission report.

Shapiro, Fred C., and Sullivan, James W. RACE RIOTS NEW YORK 1964.
New York: Thomas Y. Crowell, 1964. 222 p.

> A report of the rioting that followed the shooting of a fifteen-year-
> old black by an off-duty police lieutenant in July. Also contains
> the district attorney's report on the incident.

Tucker, Sterling. BEYOND THE BURNING: LIFE AND DEATH OF THE GHET-
TO. New York: Association Press, 1968. 160 p.

> Tucker concludes that "we are faced with only two alternatives:
> either we decide to eliminate the ghettos ourselves, or they will
> be eliminated for us. We no longer have the luxury of a third
> choice."

"The Violence." NATION 205 (August 1967): 101-7, 126.

An examination of the riots and civil unrest across the nation by several writers: Paul Good, "Nothing Worth Saving" (pp. 101-2); B.J. Widick, "Motown Blues" (pp. 102-4); Phil Kerby, "Western Justice" (pp. 104-5); Lewis M. Moroze, "Lethal Indifference" (pp. 105-6); Bennett Kremen, "Do Not Cross, Flatfoot" (pp. 107, 126).

Young, Michael. "The Liberal Approach: Its Weakness and Strengths--A Comment on the U.S. Riot Commission Report." DAEDALUS 97 (Fall 1968): 1379-89.

An objective and balanced analysis of the report of the Kerner Commission.

SOCIOLOGY

Broderick, Francis L., and Meir, August. BLACK PROTEST THOUGHT IN THE TWENTIETH CENTURY. Indianapolis: Bobbs-Merrill, 1971. 648 p.

A good review of the contemporary struggle for black power in America.

Carson, Josephine. SILENT VOICES (THE SOUTHERN NEGRO WOMAN) TO-DAY. New York: Dell, 1969. 273 p.

A portrait of the southern black woman from all levels of society. Based on extensive interviews.

Clark, Kenneth B. DARK GHETTO: DILEMMAS OF SOCIAL POWER. New York: Harper & Row, 1965. 253 p.

Using Harlem as a symbol of the ghetto, a psychologist analyzes the Negro power structure--political, religious, economic, and intellectual.

Coles, Robert. CHILDREN OF CRISIS. New York: Dell, 1967. 401 p.

Examines the psychological meaning of race and the effects of the civil rights struggle on individuals. Includes case studies of children and adults involved in the desegregation programs in the South.

Gayle, Addison, Jr. THE BLACK SITUATION. New York: Horizon Press, 1969. 221 p.

The full range of the black experience in America and its consequences for the modern age. Examines black history, philosophy, and literature.

Hare, Nathan. THE BLACK ANGLO-SAXONS. Introduction by Oliver C. Cox. New York: Marzani and Munsell, 1965. 124 p.

A penetrating analysis of motivations in middle-class black communities. Hare's contention is that the middle-class blacks have adopted the values of the white, Anglo-Saxon populace because of their own sense of social inferiority.

Hentoff, Nat. THE NEW EQUALITY. New ed. New York: Viking Press, 1965. 243 p.

Basic social and economic change is essential if a "new equality" is to exist, and this change must be "radical" in the denotative sense of word-getting at the root of problems and power.

Marx, Gary T. PROTEST AND PREJUDICE (A STUDY OF BELIEF IN THE BLACK COMMUNITY). New York: Harper & Row, 1967. 228 p.

Nationwide survey of the black man's attitude toward himself and his condition in the 1960s.

Mead, Margaret, and Baldwin, James. A RAP ON RACE. Philadelphia: J.B. Lippincott, 1971. 256 p.

Transcript of three tape-recorded conversations between Mead and Baldwin on race, sex, politics, and violence.

Moody, Anne. COMING OF AGE IN MISSISSIPPI. New York: Dial Press, 1968. 348 p.

Autobiography of a black girl growing up in the Deep South.

Parks, David. G. I. DIARY. New York: Harper and Bros., 1968. 133 p.

A black draftee's tour of duty in the army; concerned with the Vietnam war and America's racial crisis.

Staples, Robert. "The Myth of the Impotent Black Male." BLACK SCHOLAR 2 (June 1971): 2-9.

A rejoinder to the argument that the black male has been "socially castrated."

Stone, Chuck. BLACK POLITICAL POWER. Indianapolis: Bobbs-Merrill, 1968. 261 p.

An examination of the Afro-American's past, present, and future in American politics.

TELEVISION

Bond, Jean Carey. "The Media Image of Black Women." FREEDOMWAYS 15 (1975): 34-37.

An attack on the stereotyping of black women in such network productions as "Good Times," "That's My Mama," and "Get Christy Love."

Collier, Eugenia. "'Black' Shows for White Viewers." FREEDOMWAYS 14 (1974): 209-17.

A critical view of "The Autobiography of Miss Jane Pittman," "Sanford and Son," "Shaft," "Love Thy Neighbor," and "Good Times."

Haskins, James. "New Black Images in the Mass Media. How Educational Is Educational TV?" FREEDOMWAYS 14 (1974): 200-208.

Argues for a need for blacks to exercise more control over the image of blacks in PBS and commercial television.

Hobson, Sheila Smith. "The Rise and Fall of Blacks in Serious Television." FREEDOMWAYS 14 (1974): 185-99.

Observations on television shows such as "Amos and Andy," "Beulah," "Walk in My Shoes," "Of Black America," "Black Journal," "Like It Is," and "Black Perspective on the News."

Ramsey, Alvin. "Through a Glass Whitely. The Televised Rape of MISS JANE PITTMAN." BLACK WORLD 23 (August 1974): 31-36.

Ramsey sees the televised production of Ernest Gaines's novel as not only unfaithful to the novel but as an extension of white establishment propaganda through its manipulation of the black image.

Taylor, Jeanne A. "On Being Black and Writing for Television." NEGRO

AMERICAN LITERATURE FORUM   4 (Fall 1970):   79-82.

A former script writer for the television program "Soul" discusses the difficulties of blacks writing for TV.

THEATER

Bailey, Peter. "Is the Negro Ensemble Company Really Black Theater?" NEGRO DIGEST 17 (April 1968): 16-19.

Argues that the Negro Ensemble Company is not genuine "black theater" because there is "no consistent philosophy of cultural nationalism" directing its leadership.

_____. "Woodie King, Jr.: Renaissance Man of Black Theater." BLACK WORLD 26 (April 1975): 4-10.

An overview of Woodie King's career from his early work in black community theater in Detroit to national prominence in black theater and film.

Campbell, Dick. "Is There a Conspiracy against Black Playwrights?" NEGRO DIGEST 17 (April 1968): 11-15.

A black actor and producer surveys black theater and discovers that the white establishment has not let it advance beyond where it was thirty years earlier.

Coleman, Mike. "What Is Black Theater?" BLACK WORLD 20 (April 1971): 32-36.

An interview with LeRoi Jones in which Jones defines "black" theater and distinguishes it from "show business."

Cosby, John, Jr. "Open Letter to James Earl Jones." LIBERATOR 9 (June 1969): 18-19.

An attack on actor James Earl Jones, star of THE GREAT WHITE HOPE, for his decision to play the role of Malcolm X.

Dodson, Owen. "Playwrights in Dark Glasses." NEGRO DIGEST 17 (April 1968): 31-36.

Black poet, novelist, and Howard University professor argues that black playwrights should emulate recognized masters and pursue established aesthetic values.

Fuller, Hoyt W. "Black Theater in America." NEGRO DIGEST 17 (April 1968): 83-93.

A survey of black theater groups in Newark, Harlem, and Detroit.

_____. "Stage, Screen, and Black Hegemony: BLACK WORLD Interviews Woodie King, Jr." BLACK WORLD 26 (April 1975): 12-17.

King discusses the Black Theatre Alliance and makes predictions about the future of the black theater movement in America.

Hay, Samuel A. "African-American Drama, 1950-1970." NEGRO HISTORY BULLETIN 36 (January 1973): 5-8.

A discussion of what Hay calls "drama of accusation," "drama of celebration," and "cultural nationalist drama."

Jones, Martha M. "Theater Southern Style: The FST." BLACK CREATION 4 (Fall 1972): 12-13.

A brief history of the activities of the Free Southern Theater in New Orleans.

King, Woodie, Jr. "Ghetto Art and Energy." ROCKEFELLER FOUNDATION QUARTERLY 3 (1968): 18-26.

Traces the activities of the cultural Arts Program of Mobilization for Youth from its beginning in the summer of 1965.

Milner, Ronald. "Black Theater--Go Home!" NEGRO DIGEST 17 (April 1968): 5-10.

Argues that black theater must become "an organic, functioning part" of black communities.

Mitchell, Loften. "For Langston Hughes and Stella Holt." NEGRO DIGEST 17 (April 1968): 41-43, 74-77.

Black playwright and author's personal memoir of Hughes and Holt and their importance to black theater.

Riley, Clayton. "On Black Theater." In THE BLACK AESTHETIC, edited by Addison Gayle, Jr., pp. 313-30. Garden City, N.Y.: Doubleday, 1971.

A discussion of the new black drama produced since 1945. Contains extended commentary on LeRoi Jones's DUTCHMAN and THE

TOILET, as well as works by Ed Bullins and Ron Milner.

Teer, Barbara Ann. "The Great White Way Is Not Our Way—Not Yet." NEGRO DIGEST 17 (April 1968): 21-29.

Argues that the healthiest context for the development of black theater is in the black community.

Turner, Douglas. "Needed: A Theater for Black Themes." NEGRO DIGEST 17 (December 1967): 34-39.

Discusses the need for "a theater of permanence, continuity and consistency" as a necessary home base for the Negro artist.

WOMEN

Bond, Jean Carey. "The Media Image of Black Women." FREEDOMWAYS
15 (1975): 34-37.

> An attack on the stereotypes projected in "Good Times" and "That's
> My Mama," the "sexploitation" in "Get Christy Love," and the
> white male in "The Autobiography of Miss Jane Pittman."

Cade, Toni, ed. THE BLACK WOMAN: AN ANTHOLOGY. New York:
New American Library, 1970. 256 p.

> An anthology of poems, essays, and short fiction by black women
> such as Abbey Lincoln, Paule Marshall, Nikki Giovanni, and many
> others.

Chisholm, Shirley. "Race, Revolution and Women." BLACK SCHOLAR 3
(December 1971): 17-21.

> "Women must do more than sacrifice husbands and sons in the pres-
> ent Social Revolution. They must all sacrifice themselves."

_____. "Racism and Anti-Feminism." BLACK SCHOLAR 1 (January-February
1970): 40-45.

> Chisholm feels that woman's place in politics is declining.

_____. UNBOUGHT AND UNBOSSED. New York: Avon Books, 1970.
177 p.

> An autobiographical account of Chisholm's life and career, and her
> personal opinions on militant young people and the oppression of
> women.

Cornwell, Anita R. "The Negro Woman: America's Unsung Heroine." NEGRO
DIGEST 14 (October 1965): 15-18.

> "In a nation that is largely anti-female and totally anti-Negro,

the Negro woman has almost singlehandedly kept her family together on "coolie" wages and in most instances has brought her
children up to be hard-working, law-abiding citizens."

Foster, Frances S. "Changing Concepts of the Black Woman." JOURNAL OF
BLACK STUDIES 3 (June 1973): 433-54.

The emergence of the new black woman from the traditional stereotyped images: "Topsy, Peaches, Caldonia, and Aunt Chloe."

Giovanni, Nikki. BLACK FEELING, BLACK TALK. Privately printed, 1968.
19 p.

Poetry.

Hare, Nathan, and Hare, Julia. "Black Women 1970." In BLACK EXPERIENCE:
SOUL, edited by Lee Rainwater, pp. 93-105. New Brunswick, N.J.: Transaction
Books, 1973.

A discussion of the triple exploitation of black women: "black,
female, and in most cases, poor."

Jeffers, Trellie. "The Black Woman and the Black Middle Class." BLACK
SCHOLAR 4 (March-April 1973): 37-41.

A call upon black women to assume explicit moral leadership in
the struggle of the black masses.

King, Helen H. "The Black Woman and Women's Lib." EBONY, March 1971,
pp. 68-70, 74-76.

The role of the black woman is to support her man, not to oppose
him. Amina Baraka, wife of Imamu Baraka (LeRoi Jones) is quoted
as saying women's liberation is "part of America's destruction."

Noble, Jeanne. "Negro Women Today and Their Education." JOURNAL OF
NEGRO EDUCATION 26 (Winter 1957): 15-21.

Study is based on interviews with "Negro women college graduates
from six geographical sections of the country who have had an
opportunity to test out in life the results of their education."

Rushing, Andrea Benton. "Images of Black Women in Afro-American Poetry."
BLACK WORLD 24 (September 1975): 18-30.

Rushing feels that the image of black women which is projected in
Afro-American poetry closely approximates what Ralph Ellison said
about the blues: "Their attraction lies in this, that they at once
express the agony of life and the possibility of conquering it through
sheer toughness of spirit."

Sisters of B.C.D. BLACK WOMAN'S ROLE IN THE REVOLUTION. Newark, N.J.: Jihad Productions, 1969. 18 p.

Essays on what the revolutionary black woman should wear; instructions on make-up, hair, the use of alcohol.

Washington, Mary Helen. "Black Women Image Makers." BLACK WORLD 23 (August 1974): 10-18.

An examination of the stereotyping of black women in the media and in literature and a discussion of the desirable myth- and image-making roles played by Maya Angelou, Alice Walker, Gwendolyn Brooks, Paule Marshall, Toni Cade Williams.

Williams, Ora. AMERICAN BLACK WOMEN IN THE ARTS AND SOCIAL SCIENCES. Metuchen, N.J.: Scarecrow Press, 1973. 141 p.

A bibliography prepared by a black woman to serve "as a consciousness-raising device" and to refute certain myths about the black woman.

Part 2

INDIVIDUAL AUTHORS

JAMES BALDWIN

Alexander, Charlotte. "The 'Stink' of Reality: Mothers and Whores in James Baldwin's Fiction." LITERATURE AND PSYCHOLOGY 18 (1968): 9-26. Reprinted in JAMES BALDWIN: A COLLECTION OF CRITICAL ESSAYS by Keneth Kinnamon, pp. 77-95. Englewood Cliffs, N.J.: Prentice-Hall, 1974.

> Alexander contends that Baldwin "envisions a state in which men co-exist harmoniously with women who are neither 'mothers' nor 'whores.'"

Baldwin, James. "The American Dream and the American Negro." NEW YORK TIMES MAGAZINE, 7 March 1965, pp. 32-33.

> A condensed transcript of the debate held at Cambridge University between James Baldwin and William F. Buckley, Jr., on the issue "The American Dream is at the expense of the American Negro." Baldwin spoke for the proposition; Buckley opposed it.

_____. "Among the Recent Letters to the Editor." NEW YORK TIMES BOOK REVIEW, 26 February 1961, pp. 52-53.

> Baldwin points out in a letter to the editor the errors in a book review entitled "Revolt in the South."

_____. ANOTHER COUNTRY. New York: Dial Press, 1962. 436 p.

> Concerned with the fate of Rufus, a rootless black musician, his mistress, Leona, his sister, Ida, and Ida's lover, Vivaldo. Emphasis is upon the disintegration of the characters' personalities.

_____. "As Much Truth As One Can Bare." NEW YORK TIMES BOOK REVIEW, 14 January 1962, pp. 1, 38.

> Baldwin stresses the writer's role in the future of America: "It is the writer who must always remember that morality, if it is to remain or become morality, must be perpetually examined, cracked, changed, made new."

——— . "'At The Root Of The Negro Problem . . .'" TIME, 17 May 1963, pp. 26-27.

A review of Baldwin's speaking tour at California universities, his views on white liberals, and the stereotypic image of blacks.

——— . "The Black Boy Looks at the White Boy." ESQUIRE, May 1961, pp. 102-6. Reprinted in his NOBODY KNOWS MY NAME, pp. 216-41. New York: Dial Press, 1961.

Baldwin's appraisal of Norman Mailer.

——— . BLUES FOR MR. CHARLIE. New York: Dial Press, 1964. 121 p.

Using device of a testimony service in a black church, the play reconstructs the murder of Richard Henry, a twenty-year-old black, and examines how both the whites and the blacks contributed to his death.

——— . "Color." ESQUIRE, December 1962, pp. 225-52.

It is because blacks are so shackled in chains, "and because the world looks on them with such guilt, that they seem freer in their pleasures" than do white people: "white people know very little about pleasure because they are so afraid of pain."

——— . "The Creative Dilemma." SATURDAY REVIEW, 8 February 1964, pp. 14-15, 58.

Baldwin argues that "the war of an artist with his society is a lover's war, and he does, at his best, what lovers do, which is to reveal the beloved to himself and, with that revelation, to make freedom real."

——— . "The Dangerous Road before Martin Luther King." HARPER'S, February 1961, pp. 33-42.

A personal, intimate, and sometimes controversial view of Martin Luther King, Jr.

——— . "The Discovery of What It Means to Be an American." NEW YORK TIMES BOOK REVIEW, 25 January 1949, pp. 4, 22. Reprinted in his NOBODY KNOWS MY NAME, pp. 3-12. New York: Dial Press, 1961.

"Europe has what we do not have yet, a sense of the inexorable limits of life, a sense, in a word, of tragedy. And we have what they sorely need: a new sense of life's possibilities."

——— . "Equal in Paris." COMMENTARY 19 (March 1955): 251-59.

An "autobiographical story" of a young American and his experience with French justice.

_____. "Everybody's Protest Novel." PARTISAN REVIEW 16 (June 1949): 578-85.

Baldwin's controversial analysis of the character of Bigger Thomas in Richard Wright's NATIVE SON.

_____. "Faulkner and Desegregation." PARTISAN REVIEW 23 (Fall 1956): 568-73. Reprinted in his NOBODY KNOWS MY NAME, pp. 117-26. New York: Dial Press, 1961.

Baldwin's response to William Faulkner's "Letter to the North" in which he warns the North to "go slow" in the matter of desegregation in the South. The time that Faulkner asks for, says Baldwin, simply does not exist: the Negro cannot wait any longer.

_____. "Fifth Avenue Uptown: A Letter from Harlem." ESQUIRE, July 1960, pp. 126-30. Reprinted in his NOBODY KNOWS MY NAME, pp. 56-71. New York: Dial Press, 1961.

A personal view of Harlem, its people, its slums, its housing projects. Baldwin also draws comparisons between northern and southern attitudes toward blacks. He concludes that there are but two sides to the same coin and that the "South will not change--cannot change--until the North changes."

_____. THE FIRE NEXT TIME. New York: Dial Press, 1963. 120 p.

Literary and political essays describing the black's disillusionment with the white man. Contains two sections, "My Dungeon Shook," a letter to his nephew on the occasion of the centennial of the emancipation, and "Down at the Cross," reflections on contemporary black leaders.

_____. GIOVANNI'S ROOM. New York: Dial Press, 1956. 248 p.

Concerned with an intensive homosexual relationship between a young American and Giovanni in France.

_____. GOING TO MEET THE MAN. New York: Dial Press, 1965. 249 p.

First collection of Baldwin's short stories, including three works not previously printed.

_____. GO TELL IT ON THE MOUNTAIN. New York: Alfred A. Knopf, 1953. 303 p.

Novel, set in Harlem, is concerned with the conversion of a black boy on his fourteenth birthday and flashbacks to the lives of three generations of his family.

_____ . "The Hard Kind of Courage." HARPER'S, October 1958, pp. 61-65. Reprinted in his NOBODY KNOWS MY NAME, as "A Fly in Buttermilk," pp. 83-97. New York: Dial Press, 1961.

Baldwin interviews an "integrated" school boy, his mother, and his school principal.

_____ . "The Harlem Ghetto: Winter 1948." COMMENTARY 5 (February 1948): 165-70. Reprinted in his NOTES OF A NATIVE SON, pp. 57-72. Boston: Beacon Press, 1955.

Traces the psychological and economic basis for the Negro's hostility toward the Jew.

_____ . IF BEALE STREET COULD TALK. New York: Dial Press, 1974. 197 p.

Novel of social realism about a black family's efforts to get a young man out of jail before his wife has a baby.

_____ . "Image: Three Views." OPERA NEWS 27 (8 December 1962): 8-12.

Transcription of a discussion of man's images in the arts today, a symposium at Hofstra College, Hempstead, Long Island in May 1961. The moderator was Malcolm Preston, the three creative artists were James Baldwin, Ben Shahn, and Darius Milhaud.

_____ . JAMES BALDWIN, NIKKI GIOVANNI: A DIALOGUE. Foreword by Ida Lewis. Afterword by Orde Coombs. Philadelphia: J.B. Lippincott, 1973. 112 p.

Slightly revised transcription of a taped conversation between Nikki Giovanni and Baldwin. The conversation was taped in London for the television program "Soul."

_____ . "James Baldwin Breaks His Silence: An Interview." ATLAS 13 (March 1967): 47-49.

An interview conducted by CEP DERGISI, a Turkish journal. Baldwin's views on civil rights, the reason for his living in Istanbul, the Negro and Communism, the Negro and Christianity.

_____ . "Journey to Atlanta." NEW LEADER 31 (9 October 1948): 8-9. Reprinted in his NOTES OF A NATIVE SON. Boston: Beacon Press, 1955.

Impressions of the Progressive party and the Atlanta black community gathered when the Melodeers, a black singing group, accepted an invitation to sing on tour with the George Wallace party in the South.

_____. "Letter from a Region in My Mind." NEW YORKER, 17 November
1962, pp. 59-144.

Baldwin writes of Malcolm X, the Black Muslims, and Elijah
Muhammad. Also appears in THE FIRE NEXT TIME as "Down at
the Cross: Letter from a Region in My Mind," as the second
section of the book.

_____. "Letter from the South: Nobody Knows My Name." PARTISAN RE-
VIEW 26 (Winter 1959): 72-82. Reprinted in his NOBODY KNOWS MY
NAME, pp. 98-116. New York: Dial Press, 1961.

Baldwin's impressions gathered from a trip to the South. Baldwin
says that "The South imagines that it 'knows' the Negro, the North
imagines that it has set him free. Both camps are deluded."

_____. "Letters from a Journey." HARPER'S, May 1963, pp. 48-52.

Observations sent back to New York during a trip to write a series
of articles and a book on Africa. The selections from these com-
munications reveal the pressures and anxieties of being a writer.

_____. "A Letter to My Nephew." PROGRESSIVE 26 (December 1962):
19-20.

Reprinted as the first section of THE FIRE NEXT TIME under the
title "My Dungeon Shook: Letter to My Nephew on the One
Hundredth Anniversary of the Emancipation." Baldwin ends the
letter by observing that America is celebrating emancipation "one
hundred years too early."

_____. "Liberalism and the Negro." COMMENTARY 37 (March 1964):
25-42.

The edited transcript of a three-hour discussion, moderated by
Norman Podhoretz. Discussants include James Baldwin, Nathan
Glazer, Sidney Hook, and Gunnar Myrdal.

_____. "Life Straight in de Eye." COMMENTARY 19 (January 1955): 74-
77. Reprinted in his NOTES OF A NATIVE SON, as "Carmen Jones," pp. 46-
54. Boston: Beacon Press, 1955.

A review of the 1955 motion picture production, CARMEN JONES.
Baldwin finds the rampant sexuality of the movie, which accounted
for its popularity, an ultimately "sterile and depressing eroticism."

_____. "Many Thousands Gone." PARTISAN REVIEW 17 (November-December
1951): 665-80. Reprinted in his NOTES OF A NATIVE SON, pp. 24-45.
Boston: Beacon Press, 1955.

Baldwin believes that no American Negro exists who does not have "his private Bigger Thomas living in the skull." Essay traces the role the Negro has played in the obliteration of his own personality.

. "Mass Culture ,and the Creative Artist: Some Personal Notes." DAEDALUS 89 (Spring 1960): 371-76.

Baldwin feels that we are undergoing a metamorphosis which will "rob us of our myths and give us our history." Meanwhile, mass culture "can only reflect our chaos: and perhaps we had better remember that this chaos contains life--and a great transforming energy."

. "Me and My House." HARPER'S, November 1955, pp. 54-61. Reprinted in his NOTES OF A NATIVE SON, as "Notes of a Native Son," pp. 85-114. Boston: Beacon Press, 1955.

An autobiographical essay recalling the death and funeral of Baldwin's father and the riots in Harlem in 1943.

. "A Negro Assays the Negro Mood." NEW YORK TIMES MAGAZINE, 12 March 1961, pp. 25, 103-4. Reprinted in his NOBODY KNOWS MY NAME, as "East River, Downtown: Postscript to a Letter from Harlem," pp. 72-82. New York: Dial Press, 1961.

Baldwin comments on the blacks who rioted in the United Nations while Adlai Stevenson was addressing the General Assembly, on the Black Muslims, and on the increasing discontent of black people in America.

. "Negroes Are Anti-Semitic Because They're Anti-White." NEW YORK TIMES MAGAZINE, 9 April 1967, pp. 26-27.

"The Jew is singled out by Negroes not because he acts differently from other white men, but because he doesn't."

. "The Negro in American Culture." CROSS CURRENTS 11 (Summer 1961): 204-24.

Transcription of a radio broadcast on WBAI-FM, concerning the Civil War commemorations then taking place. Moderator was Nat Hentoff; participants were James Baldwin, Alfred Kazin, Lorraine Hansberry, Langston Hughes, and Emile Capouya.

. "The Negro in Paris." REPORTER, 6 June 1950, pp. 34-36. Reprinted in his NOTES OF A NATIVE SON, as "Encounter on the Seine: Black Meets Brown," pp. 117-23. Boston: Beacon Press, 1955.

The confrontation of the African and the American Negro in Paris is "over a gulf of three hundred years--an alienation too vast to be conquered in an evening's goodwill, too heavy and too double-edged ever to be trapped in speech."

_____. NOBODY KNOWS MY NAME. New York: Dial Press, 1961. 241 p.

Thirteen essays recording the last months of Baldwin's self-exile to
Europe, his return to America and Harlem, and his first trip South
at the time of the school integration troubles.

_____. NO NAME IN THE STREET. New York: Dial Press, 1972. 172 p.

Baldwin's statement on what has happened to America through the
political and social agonies of her recent history. An indictment
of white civilization in general and the United States in particular.

_____. "On Catfish Row." COMMENTARY 28 (September 1959): 246-48.

A criticism of the film version of George Gershwin's opera, PORGY
AND BESS. Sees the image projected in the film as unreal.

_____. ONE DAY, WHEN I WAS LOST: A SCENARIO. BASED ON ALEX
HALEY'S "THE AUTOBIOGRAPHY OF MALCOLM X." New York: Dial Press,
1973. 280 p.

Baldwin's dramatization of the life and death of Malcolm X.

_____. "The Precarious Vogue of Ingmar Bergman." ESQUIRE, April 1960,
pp. 128-32. Reprinted in his NOBODY KNOWS MY NAME, as "The Northern
Protestant," pp. 163-80. New York: Dial Press, 1961.

A recounting of a meeting with Bergman in Sweden. Baldwin gives
his views on many of Bergman's films.

_____. "Princes and Powers." ENCOUNTER 8 (January 1957): 52-60.
Reprinted in his NOBODY KNOWS MY NAME, pp. 13-55. New York:
Dial Press, 1961.

Baldwin's review of the Conference of Negro-African writers and
artists held at the Sorbonne in Paris, September 1956.

_____. "A Question of Identity." PARTISAN REVIEW 21 (July-August 1954):
402-10. Reprinted in his NOTES OF A NATIVE SON, pp. 124-37. Boston:
Beacon Press, 1955.

Baldwin feels that the American student abroad can "discover his
own country" from the vantage point of Europe.

_____. "Race, Hate, Sex, and Colour: A Conversation." ENCOUNTER 25
(July 1965): 55-60.

Transcription of a recorded and televised interview with James
Baldwin and Colin McInnes. Interviewer was James Mossman.
Interview was conducted by the B.B.C. in its Encounter Series.

_____. "Richard Wright." ENCOUNTER 16 (April 1961): 58-60. Reprinted in his NOBODY KNOWS MY NAME, as "The Exile," pp. 190-99. New York: Dial Press, 1961.

A personal memoir written after Wright's death. Baldwin feels that at least part of the trouble between him and Wright was that he was "nearly twenty years younger than Wright and had never been in the South."

_____. "The Search for Identity." In AMERICAN PRINCIPLES AND ISSUES: THE NATIONAL PURPOSE, edited by Oscar Handlin, pp. 459-67. New York: Holt, Rinehart and Winston, 1961.

Published in HARPER'S (October 1953) as "Stranger in the Village" (see below).

_____. "Stranger in the Village." HARPER'S, October 1953, pp. 42-48. Reprinted in his NOTES OF A NATIVE SON, pp. 159-75. Boston: Beacon Press, 1955.

Baldwin's experience as the only black in a small Swiss village.

_____. "The Survival of Richard Wright." REPORTER, 16 March 1961, pp. 52-55.

A review of Richard Wright's EIGHT MEN. Baldwin finds the violence in Wright's works "gratuitous and compulsive."

_____. "Sweet Lorraine." ESQUIRE, November 1969, pp. 140-41. Also published as the introduction to Hansberry's TO BE YOUNG, GIFTED AND BLACK, pp. ix-xii. Englewood Cliffs, N.J.: Prentice-Hall, 1969.

Baldwin's recollections of Hansberry shortly after her death from cancer.

_____. "A Talk To Teachers." SATURDAY REVIEW, 21 December 1963, pp. 42-44.

A transcription of a tape-recorded talk, delivered extemporaneously, to a special in-service course for teachers, titled "The Negro: His Role in The Culture and Life of the United States." Baldwin's topic was "The Negro Child--His Self Image."

_____. TELL ME HOW LONG THE TRAIN'S BEEN GONE. New York: Dial Press, 1968. 484 p.

Concerned with the differing responses of three generations of Afro-Americans to their experience.

_____. "Theatre: The Negro In and Out." In BEYOND THE ANGRY

BLACK by John A. Williams, pp. 2-101. New York: Cooper Square Publishers, 1966.

> Baldwin views the use of Negro actors in the American theater ("I have rarely seen a Negro actor really well used on the American stage or screen, or on television") and then makes extended comments on Edward Albee's plays.

———. "There's a Bill Due That Has to Be Paid." LIFE, 24 May 1963, pp. 81-84.

> Excerpts from speeches made by Baldwin on tour. Reflects his increasing anger and militancy.

———. "To Whom It May Concern: Report from Occupied Territory." NATION 203 (11 July 1966): 39-43.

> Baldwin's report on police brutality in Harlem.

———. "A Word from Writer Directly to Reader." In FICTION OF THE FIFTIES by Herbert Gold, pp. 18-19. New York: Doubleday, 1959.

> Baldwin's response to the question "In what way--if any--do you feel that the problem of writing for the Fifties has differed from the problems of writing in other times?"

"Baldwin: Gray Flannel Muslim." CHRISTIAN CENTURY 80 (12 June 1963): 791.

> Contends that Baldwin has won popularity on the lecture circuit by catering to his audiences' guilt and masochism and that he offers no real plan for the betterment of race relations.

Bigsby, C.W.E. "Committed Writer: James Baldwin as Dramatist." TWENTIETH CENTURY LITERATURE 13 (April 1967): 39-48.

> "Baldwin's chief fault lies . . . not so much in his dehumanization of the whites as in his sentimentalising of the Negroes."

———. "James Baldwin." In his CONFRONTATION AND COMMITMENT: A STUDY OF THEMES AND TRENDS IN CONTEMPORARY AMERICAN DRAMA, 1959-1966, pp. 126-37. Columbia: University of Missouri Press, 1968.

> Baldwin dehumanizes the whites and sentimentalizes the Negroes in his drama. Baldwin's BLUES FOR MR. CHARLIE also indicates his inability to master the dramatic form.

Bluefarb, Sam. "James Baldwin's 'Previous Condition.'" NEGRO AMERICAN LITERATURE FORUM 3 (Spring 1969): 26-29.

> A critique of Baldwin's short story "Previous Condition," identifying Peter with Baldwin himself.

Bone, Robert. "The Novels of James Baldwin." TRI-QUARTERLY 2 (Winter 1965): 3-20.

> Bone finds Baldwin "strongest as an essayist, weakest as a play-wright, and successful in the novel from on only one occasion."

Boyle, Kay. "Introducing James Baldwin." In CONTEMPORARY AMERICAN NOVELISTS, edited by Harry T. Moore, pp. 155-57. Carbondale: Southern Illinois University Press, 1964.

> An introduction to a personal appearance by James Baldwin in which Boyle says that Baldwin's art offers us "a far better national reality than any we have ever known."

Bradford, Melvin E. "Faulkner, Baldwin, and the South." GEORGIA REVIEW 20 (1965): 431-43.

> A response to Baldwin's stand in his essay entitled "Faulkner and Desegregation." Argues that Baldwin has no "sense of community" and as a result cannot appreciate Faulkner's complex position on the race question.

Buckley, W[illiam]. F., Jr. "The Call to Color Blindness." NATIONAL RE-VIEW 14 (18 June 1963): 488.

> "What is important about Baldwin is that he is a great artist, not that he is an evangelist of racial reconciliation. In the latter capacity he will, pursuing his present course, do great harm."

_____. "The Negro and the American Dream." NATIONAL REVIEW 17 (6 April 1965): 273.

> A response to Baldwin's remarks made before the Cambridge Union on the subject "The American Dream is at the expense of the American Negro."

Cartey, Wilfred. "The Realities of Four Negro Writers." COLUMBIA UNI-VERSITY FORUM 9 (Summer 1966): 34-42.

> A discussion of Baldwin's GO TELL IT ON THE MOUNTAIN, George Lamming's IN THE CASTLE OF MY SKIN, Carolina Marie de Jesus' CHILD OF THE DARK, and Ezekiel Mphahlele's DOWN SECOND AVENUE. Cartey's thesis is that the four books represent "four personal hells, concomitant in time but in four separate cor-ners of the world," where the heroes of the novels "live, move, and have their being--or, sometimes, nonbeing."

Charney, Maurice. "James Baldwin's Quarrel with Richard Wright." AMERI-CAN QUARTERLY 15 (Spring 1963): 65-75.

> Charney contends: "Baldwin's central beliefs about man and the

purpose of the novel are surprisingly close to those of Faulkner's Nobel Prize Acceptance Speech." He also contends that Baldwin "resolutely affirms his concern with man, black or white, in all of his complexity. The hard deterministic world of NATIVE SON denies this complexity and must be rejected."

Ciardi, John. "Black Man in America." SATURDAY REVIEW, 6 July 1963, p. 13.

Ciardi's reflections on a phonographic recording of James Baldwin's BLACK MAN IN AMERICA. The recording is an interview with James Baldwin "as a man, as an artist, and as a Negro" by Studs Terkel.

Cleaver, Eldridge. "Notes On A Native Son." In his SOUL ON ICE, pp. 97-111. 1968. Reprinted in JAMES BALDWIN: A COLLECTION OF CRITICAL ESSAYS, edited by Keneth Kinnamon, pp. 66-76. Englewood Cliffs, N.J.: Prentice-Hall, 1974.

Cleaver contends that there is a hatred of blacks permeating Baldwin's writings. "Baldwin's essay on Richard Wright," says Cleaver, "reveals that he despised--not Richard Wright, but his masculinity."

Coles, R. "Baldwin's Burden." PARTISAN REVIEW 31 (Summer 1964): 409-16.

"Baldwin translates his own adolescent agony into the hate in all Negroes for whites and then predicts the white man's inevitable doom unless he learns a radically new way of getting along with the Negro."

Collier, Eugenia W. "The Phrase Unbearably Repeated." PHYLON 25 (1964): 288-96.

The phrase "unbearably repeated" is "Do you love me?" Baldwin's ANOTHER COUNTRY, argues Collier, is a brutal, violent book, but underneath the brutality and violence the book is primarily not about sex or race but about "the individual's lonely and futile quest for love."

_____. "Thematic Patterns in Baldwin's Essays." BLACK WORLD 21 (June 1972): 28-34.

Baldwin's essays unravel "the complexities of our times--and since time is three dimensional, these complexities involve our history and our projected future as well as our turbulent present."

Cox, C.B., and Jones, A.R. "After the Tranquilized Fifties: Notes on Sylvia Plath and James Baldwin." CRITICAL QUARTERLY 6 (Summer 1964): 107-22.

"Novelists such as James Baldwin or David Storey or William
Burroughs mirror an age in which the predominant feeling is one
of being overwhelmed by irrational forces which are properly
imaged in violence, terror and perversity."

Dupee, F.W.   "James Baldwin and the 'Man.'"   NEW YORK REVIEW OF
BOOKS 1 (1963): 1-2. Reprinted in JAMES BALDWIN AND THE CRITIC by
Keneth Kinnamon, pp. 11-15.   Englewood Cliffs, N.J.: Prentice-Hall, 1974.

Dupee feels that "when Baldwin replaces criticism with prophecy
he manifestly weakens his grasp of his role, his style, and his
great theme itself."

Dwyer, R.J.   "I Know about the Negroes and the Poor."   NATIONAL REVIEW
15 (17 December 1963): 517-18.

Argues that Baldwin does not know the typical Negro and his
problems. "His experience is conspicuously atypical; his personality so unusual, his development so early, his success so complete,
that he can have no idea of the hopelessness of the poor, or of
the typical Negro. The only hopelessness he could possibly know
is the hopelessness of the successful."

Eckman, Fern Marja.   THE FURIOUS PASSAGE OF JAMES BALDWIN.   New
York: M. Evans, 1966.   245 p.

The first published biography of James Baldwin.

Elkoff, Marvin.   "Everybody Knows His Name."   ESQUIRE, August 1964,
pp. 59-64, 120-23.

Baldwin is correct when he describes himself as "disreputable,"
for he "inveighs against the grain of every American standard
except Success--culturally, sexually, politically; he is a bohemian,
an outsider, an unorthodox and unofficial man in his whole style
of life."

Finn, J.   "The Identity of James Baldwin."   COMMONWEAL 77 (26 October
1962): 113-16.

A commentary on Baldwin's writing career, with particular emphasis
on ANOTHER COUNTRY, NOTES OF A NATIVE SON, and NO-
BODY KNOWS MY NAME.

Fischer, Russell G.   "James Baldwin: A Bibliography, 1947-1962."   BULLETIN
OF BIBLIOGRAPHY 24 (January-April 1965): 127-30.

Foster, David E.   "'Cause My House Fell Down': The Theme of the Fall in
Baldwin's Novels."   CRITIQUE 13 (1971): 50-62.

Argues that "the theme of man's fall from innocence--his 'loss of Eden'--forms a significant part of each of James Baldwin's first three novels: GO TELL IT ON THE MOUNTAIN (1952), GIO-VANNI'S ROOM (1956) and ANOTHER COUNTRY (1962)."

Gayle, Addison, Jr. "A Defense of James Baldwin." CLA JOURNAL 10 (March 1967): 201-8.

Defends Baldwin against attacks made upon his writing by Robert Bone in THE NEGRO NOVEL IN AMERICA and on his character by Eldridge Cleaver in "Notes On A Native Son."

Gross, Barry. "The 'Uninhabitable Darkness' of Baldwin's ANOTHER COUNTRY: Image and Theme." NEGRO AMERICAN LITERATURE FORUM 6 (Winter 1972): 113-21.

Much of Baldwin's subject matter is "based on color--specifically, black and white--and light and dark."

Hagopian, John V. "James Baldwin: The Black and the Red-White-and-Blue." CLA JOURNAL 7 (December 1963): 133-40.

An analysis of Baldwin's short story, "This Morning, This Evening, So Soon."

Harper, Howard M. DESPERATE FAITH: A STUDY OF BELLOW, SALINGER, MAILER, BALDWIN, AND UPDIKE. Chapel Hill: University of North Carolina Press, 1967. 200 p.

The material dealing exclusively with Baldwin is on pages 137-61. A discussion of literary techniques and Baldwin's view of man as seen through his art.

Howe, Irving. "Black Boys and Native Sons." In his A WORLD MORE AT-TRACTIVE, pp. 98-122. New York: Horizon Press, 1963.

Concerned with Baldwin's attack on his famous "literary elder," Richard Wright.

_____. "James Baldwin: At Ease in Apocalypse." HARPER'S, September 1968, pp. 92, 95-100. Reprinted in JAMES BALDWIN: A COLLECTION OF CRITICAL ESSAYS, edited by Keneth Kinnamon, pp. 96-108. Englewood Cliffs, N.J.: Prentice-Hall, 1974.

Howe sees Baldwin as suffering from "the most disastrous of psychic conditions--a separation between his feelings and his voice."

Kent, George [E.]. "Baldwin and the Problem of Being." CLA JOURNAL 7 (1964): 202-14. Reprinted in JAMES BALDWIN: A COLLECTION OF CRITI-CAL ESSAYS, edited by Keneth Kinnamon, pp. 16-27. Englewood Cliffs,

N.J.: Prentice-Hall, 1974.

Kent concludes that since the publication of his first novel Baldwin "has not evolved the artistic form that will fully release and articulate his obviously complex awareness."

Kindt, Kathleen A. "James Baldwin: A Checklist, 1949-1962." BULLETIN OF BIBLIOGRAPHY 24 (January-April 1965): 123-27.

Kinnamon, Keneth, ed. JAMES BALDWIN: A COLLECTION OF CRITICAL ESSAYS. Englewood Cliffs, N.J.: Prentice-Hall, 1974. 169 p.

An anthology of thirteen critical essays about Baldwin. In the introduction, Kinnamon states that "Baldwin has always been concerned with the most personal and intimate areas of experience and also with the broadest questions of national and global destiny."

Levin, David. "Baldwin's Autobiographical Essays: The Problem of Negro Identity." MASSACHUSETTS REVIEW 5 (Winter 1964): 239-47.

"The word 'identity' recurs over and over again in Baldwin's autobiographical essays. The essential question, for himself and for the American Audience that he assumes is white, is: Who am I? or: How Can I be myself."

Macebuh, Stanley. JAMES BALDWIN: A CRITICAL STUDY. New York: Third Press, 1973. 194 p.

According to the author's preface, this study is "as much a personal testament as it is an analysis of the writings of this most annoying of writers." Macebuh feels that once Baldwin left the "theological terror" that had preoccupied him at first and "began to make his fiction and essays the vehicle for the expression of his own sense of moral disgust and passionate fury, he attained a place in the history of American letters that few so far can claim in this century."

Margolies, Edward. "The Negro Church: James Baldwin and the Christian Vision." In his NATIVE SONS, pp. 102-26. Philadelphia: J.B. Lippincott, 1969.

A discussion of the role the black church plays in Baldwin's short fiction: "The Outing," "Sonny's Blues," "Going to Meet the Man," and in GO TELL IT ON THE MOUNTAIN, ANOTHER COUNTRY, BLUES FOR MR. CHARLIE, and THE FIRE NEXT TIME.

Mead, Margaret, and Baldwin, James. A RAP ON RACE. Philadelphia: J.B. Lippincott, 1971. 256 p.

A transcript of seven-and-one-half hours of taped conversation

between Margaret Mead and James Baldwin on race and society.
The dialogue was taped in August 1970.

Newman, Charles. "The Lesson of the Master: Henry James and James Baldwin." YALE REVIEW 56 (October 1966): 45-59. Reprinted in JAMES BALD-
WIN: A COLLECTION OF CRITICAL ESSAYS, edited by Keneth Kinnamon,
pp. 52-65. Englewood Cliffs, N.J.: Prentice-Hall, 1974.

> Newman contends that since Baldwin has gained a reputation "by
> exploiting social paradoxes" it should not be surprising that his
> literary antecedents should be traced not to "Richard Wright or
> Harriet B. Stowe, but to the Brahmin, Henry James."

O'Daniel, Therman B. "James Baldwin: An Interpretative Study." CLA JOUR-
NAL 7 (September 1963): 37-47.

> An overview of Baldwin's first three novels and three volumes of
> essays. O'Daniel sees Baldwin as an excellent writer.

Standley, Fred J. "James Baldwin: A Checklist, 1963-1967." BULLETIN OF
BIBLIOGRAPHY 25 (May-August 1968): 135-37.

> A useful index to the works of James Baldwin.

GWENDOLYN BROOKS

Brooks, Gwendolyn. ANNIE ALLEN. New York: Harper & Row, 1949. 60 p.
Poems.

_____. THE BEAN EATERS. New York: Harper & Row, 1960. 71 p.
Poems.

_____. BRONZEVILLE BOYS AND GIRLS. New York: Harper & Row, 1956.
40 p.
Poems.

_____. FAMILY PICTURES. Detroit: Broadside Press, 1970. 23 p.
Poems.

_____. Foreword to NEW NEGRO POETS: U.S.A., edited by Langston Hughes,
pp. 13-14. Bloomington: Indiana University Press, 1964.
The "poet laureate of Chicago" expresses her views on the new
generation of black poets.

_____. IN THE MECCA: POEMS. New York: Harper & Row, 1968. 54 p.
Poems.

_____. MAUD MARTHA, A NOVEL. New York: Harper & Row, 1953. 180 p.
Portrait of the youth, marriage, and motherhood of a Chicago
woman.

_____. A PORTION OF THAT FIELD: THE CENTENNIAL OF THE BURIAL
OF LINCOLN. Urbana: University of Illinois Press, 1967. 97 p.
Papers delivered in May 1965, in Springfield, Illinois, by Brooks
and others.

_____. REPORT FROM PART ONE. Prefaces by Don L. Lee and George [E.] Kent. Detroit: Broadside Press, 1972. 215 p.

An autobiography which uses family pictures and poems to contribute to a new format for autobiographical writing. Brooks has written seven volumes of poetry: A STREET IN BRONZEVILLE, ANNIE ALLEN, THE BEAN EATERS, SELECTED POEMS, IN THE MECCA, RIOT, and FAMILY PICTURES; one novel: MAUD MARTHA; and an anthology of work by young Chicago poets, JUMP BAD.

_____. RIOT. Detroit: Broadside Press, 1969. 22 p.

Poems.

_____. SELECTED POEMS. New York: Harper & Row, 1963. 127 p.

Selected poems written between 1944 and 1963.

_____. A STREET IN BRONZEVILLE. New York: Harper and Bros., 1945. 57 p.

Poems.

_____. THE WORLD OF GWENDOLYN BROOKS. New York: Harper & Row, 1971. 426 p.

Contains A STREET IN BRONZEVILLE, ANNIE ALLEN, MAUD MARTHA, THE BEAN EATERS, and IN THE MECCA.

Davis, Arthur P. "The Black and Tan Motif in the Poetry of Gwendolyn Brooks." CLA JOURNAL 6 (December 1962): 90-97.

A study of the theme of rejection based on color--not the rejection of the blacks by the whites, but the rejection of darker Negroes by lighter-skinned Negroes.

_____. "Gwendolyn Brooks: A Poet of the Unheroic." CLA JOURNAL 7 (December 1963): 108-25.

Davis contends that, to Brooks, twentieth-century men "lack bigness": "We are little creatures contented with little things and little moments."

Furman, Mava R. "Gwendolyn Brooks: The Unconditioned Poet." CLA JOURNAL 17 (September 1973): 1-10.

Brooks has discarded the "conditioned" poems that were "exhortations to whites for equality" and has explored new and significant ways to bring about change.

Hansell, William H. "Aestheticism versus Politics: Militancy in Gwendolyn Brooks 'The Chicago Picasso' and 'The Wall.'" CLA JOURNAL 17 (September 1973): 11-15.

Hudson, Clenora F. "Racial Themes in the Poetry of Gwendolyn Brooks." CLA JOURNAL 17 (September 1973): 16-20.

> An examination of Brooks's SELECTED POEMS as a commentary on the "nature of racism and the suffering of Black people in a racist society."

Kent, George E. "The Poetry of Gwendolyn Brooks, Part I." BLACK WORLD 20 (September 1971): 30 ff.

> An appreciation of the poetic achievement of the black Chicago poet.

_____. "The Poetry of Gwendolyn Brooks, Part II." BLACK WORLD 20 (October 1971): 36-48, 68-71.

> An analysis of the shorter poems of Brooks. Kent divides these works into "light" and "complex" poems.

Loff, Jon N. "Gwendolyn Brooks: A Bibliography." CLA JOURNAL 17 (September 1973): 21-32.

> A helpful bibliography which lists secondary sources as well as the prose and poetry of Brooks.

McCluskey, John. "In the Mecca." STUDIES IN BLACK LITERATURE 4 (Autumn 1973): 25-30.

> An analysis of Brooks's poetry, with particular attention to her long poem, "In the Mecca."

Shands, Annette Oliver. "Gwendolyn Brooks as Novelist." BLACK WORLD 22 (June 1973): 22-30.

> The message of Brooks's MAUD MARTHA is "to accept the challenge of being human and to assert humanness with urgency."

ED BULLINS

Bullins, Ed. "Black Theatre Groups: A Directory." DRAMA REVIEW 12 (Summer 1968): 172-73.

A select list of black community theater groups active in 1968 compiled by Ed Bullins, guest editor for the special black theater issue of the DRAMA REVIEW.

_____. "The Corner." In BLACK DRAMA ANTHOLOGY, edited by Woodie King, Jr., and Ron Milner, pp. 77-88. New York: New American Library, 1971.

A group of black males and one female drink wine and "rap" on a corner before going to an abandoned car for group sex.

_____. DUPLEX: A BLACK LOVE FABLE IN FOUR MOVEMENTS. New York: William Morrow, 1971. 166 p.

The effect of ghetto-induced spiritual and material poverty on black tenants in the slum.

_____. FIVE PLAYS. Indianapolis: Bobbs-Merrill, 1968. 282 p.

Contains GOIN' A BUFFALO; IN THE WINE TIME; A SON COME HOME; THE ELECTRONIC NIGGER; and CLARA'S OLE MAN. Five plays concerned with the poverty, both physical and emotional, of ghetto life.

_____. "The Harlem Mice." BLACK WORLD 24 (June 1975): 54-55.

An allegorical fable concerning three mice who live in the heart of Harlem.

_____. THE HUNGERED ONE: EARLY WRITINGS. New York: William Morrow, 1971. 160 p.

A collection of short fiction, mostly brief sketches. At least two of the sketches have the same titles as Bullins' later plays, IN

THE WINE TIME and IN NEW ENGLAND WINTER.

_____. THE RELUCTANT RAPIST. New York: Harper & Row, 1973. 166 p.

Bullins' first novel, concerned with Steven Benson's early life in north Philadelphia and the eastern shore of Maryland, to adult life in Los Angeles and later Philadelphia.

_____. "A Short Statement on Street Theatre." DRAMA REVIEW 12 (Summer 1968): 93.

An outline of "black revolutionary agit-prop" or street theater, its purpose, its method, and the types of drama utilized.

_____. "The So-Called Western Avant-garde Drama." In BLACK EXPRESSION, edited by Addison Gayle, Jr., pp. 143-46. New York: Weybright and Talley, 1969.

Bullins states that "it is the white man's vision of reality that is most identifiable in his drama, and Black dramatists are not heir to that type of madness."

_____. "A SON COME HOME." NEGRO DIGEST 17 (April 1968): 54-73.

A one-act play by Bullins which opened in February 1968, at the Off-Broadway American Place Theater.

_____. THE THEME IS BLACKNESS: 'THE CORNER,' OTHER PLAYS. New York: William Morrow, 1972. 183 p.

Contains introduction examining the development of black drama in the 1960s and early 1970s, explaining the use of non-Western symbolism in black drama of this period. Fifteen plays written from 1965 to 1970 are included in the collection.

_____. "Travel from Home." BLACK REVIEW 1 (1971): 40-45.

A short story about the vicious beating of a white stranger by two black youths in the ghetto.

_____, ed. THE NEW LAFAYETTE THEATRE PRESENTS; PLAYS WITH AESTHETIC COMMENTS BY 6 BLACK PLAYWRIGHTS. Garden City, N.Y.: Doubleday, 1974. 301 p.

Contains selections by Ed Bullins, J.E. Gaines, Clay Goss, Oyamo, Sonia Sanchez, Richard Wesley.

_____. NEW PLAYS FROM THE BLACK THEATRE. New York: Bantam Books, 1969.

A collection of plays typical of those produced in the black community theaters in the late 1960s. Included are plays by LeRoi Jones, Kingsley Bass, Sonia Sanchez, Marvin X, Herbert Stokes, Ed Bullins, Ben Caldwell, Salimu, N.R. Davidson, Charles H. Fuller, Jr.

Evans, Don. "The Theatre of Confrontation: Ed Bullins, Up against the Wall." BLACK WORLD 23 (April 1974): 14-18.

Evans feels that Bullins is not negative in his drama but is concerned with the factors that render the black man impotent in his struggle to reach revolutionary goals.

Hay, Samuel A. "Structural Elements in Ed Bullins' Plays." BLACK WORLD 23 (April 1974): 21-26.

An indictment against Walter Kerr and other white critics for refusing to see that Bullins has successfully used structural innovations-- notably In DUPLEX.

Marvin X. "An Interview with Ed Bullins." NEGRO DIGEST 18 (April 1969): 9-16.

An interview with Ed Bullins, playwright-in-residence at the New Lafayette Theater in Harlem and editor of the journal BLACK THEATRE. Bullins discusses dramatists active in the new black drama, including Sonia Sanchez, LeRoi Jones, Sister Salimu.

Mason, Clifford; Macbeth, Robert; and Bullins, Ed. "The Electronic Nigger Meets the Gold Dust Twins." BLACK THEATRE 1 (n.d.): 24-29.

Transcription of a "suppressed" taped interview of Robert Macbeth and Ed Bullins by Mason for station WBAI theater program.

O'Brien, John. "Interview with Ed Bullins." NEGRO AMERICAN LITERATURE FORUM 7 (Fall 1973): 108-12.

Bullins discusses the black writers who have influenced his work, his drama, and his fiction in THE HUNGERED ONES.

"Purlie Victorious." EBONY, March 1962, pp. 55-56.

A review of the Broadway production of PURLIE VICTORIOUS, starring Ossie Davis as the Reverend Purlie Victorious and Ruby Dee as Gussie Mae Jenkins. The play was a broad satire on segregation in the South.

Smitherman, Geneva. "Ed Bullins, State One: Everybody Wants to Know Why I Sing the Blues." BLACK WORLD 23 (April 1974): 4-13.

"Stage One" of Bullins' work consists of plays such as GOIN'
A BUFFALO, IN THE WINE TIME, IN NEW ENGLAND WINTER,
THE CORNER, and DUPLEX. Smitherman says of this work, "Por-
traying what he calls the 'realities and contradictions' of black
life, Bullins uses the blues motif as the central mechanism for con-
veying his message."

Steele, Shelby. "White Port and Lemon Juice: Notes on Ritual in the New
Black Theater." BLACK WORLD 22 (June 1973): 4-13, 78-83.

Black dramatists use symbols, characterizations, themes, and language to reaffirm values and commitment of their audiences. Discusses examples in the plays of Ed Bullins, Ben Caldwell, and
others.

GEORGE CAIN

Billingsley, Ronald G.   "The Burden of the Hero in Modern Afro-American Fiction."   BLACK WORLD   25 (December 1975):   38-45, 66-73.

The hero of Cain's semiautobiographical novel, BLUESCHILD BABY, is "isolated not only by his society but by the futile way in which he attempts to cope with it."

Cain, George. BLUESCHILD BABY. New York: McGraw-Hill, 1972. 201 p.

Semiautobiographical novel about a young man who becomes addicted to drugs but who regains his self-respect because of a woman.

ELDRIDGE CLEAVER

Cleaver, Eldridge. "An Address Given at a Rally in His Honor a Few Days before He Was Scheduled to Return to Jail." RAMPARTS 7 (November 1968): 6-10.

> Cleaver speaks of the impending hearing concerning the revocation of his parole, his collaboration with Bobby Seale in writing a biography of Huey P. Newton, and white politicians, such as Mayor Alioto and President Lyndon B. Johnson.

_____. "The Crisis of the Black Bourgeoisie." BLACK SCHOLAR 4 (January 1973): 2-11.

> Cleaver inveighs against the black middle class for their counterproductive activities against revolutionary actions of more militant blacks.

_____. "Education and Revolution." BLACK SCHOLAR 1 (November 1969): 44-52.

> A revolutionary treatise on how to destroy the power structure in America.

_____. ELDRIDGE CLEAVER: POST PRISON WRITINGS AND SPEECHES. Edited with an appraisal by Robert Scheer. New York: Random House, 1969. 211 p.

> A sequel to Cleaver's SOUL ON ICE, the book is concerned with Cleaver's activities after his release from prison on parole.

_____. "The Fire Now: Field Nigger Power Takes Over the Black Movement." COMMONWEAL 88 (14 June 1968): 375-77.

> Cleaver's assessment of the black leadership in America since the assassination of Martin Luther King, Jr., and his advocacy of the Black Panther party nomination for president of the United States, Robert F. Williams, a black leader in exile in the People's Republic of China.

_____. "The Flashlight." PLAYBOY, December 1969, pp. 120-24, 287-302.

Cleaver's first excursion into fiction, a short tale of suspense.

_____. "A Letter from Jail." RAMPARTS 6 (May 1968): 18-21.

An article smuggled out of prison and published for the first time in RAMPARTS magazine. Cleaver calls for black revolutionary action.

_____. "On Lumpen Ideology." BLACK SCHOLAR 4 (November-December 1972): 2-10.

"The basic task confronting revolutionaries today is to further define the Lumpen condition, to refine Lumpen Ideology, spread Lumpen Consciousness, and lead the struggle, through righteous practice, to seize physical control of the machines, of technology, and destroy, forever, hegemony of the usurpers over the social heritage of humanity."

_____. SOUL ON ICE. New York: McGraw-Hill, 1968. 210 p.

Collection of essays and letters written in Folsom State Prison in California about the forces shaping Cleaver's life.

Cleaver, Kathleen. "On Eldridge Cleaver." RAMPARTS 7 (June 1969): 4-11.

A personal account by Kathleen Cleaver of her experiences with her husband in the Black Panther party and an appeal for contributions to the Cleaver Bail Fund.

Leary, Mary Ellen. "The Uproar over Cleaver." NEW REPUBLIC 159 (30 November 1968): 21-24.

An analysis of the conditions that caused Bobby Seale, Eldridge Cleaver, and other Black Panthers to be sought out as public speakers--as a kind of "guest star" on college campuses and public assemblies.

Lockwood, Lee. CONVERSATION WITH ELDRIDGE CLEAVER. New York: McGraw-Hill, 1970. 129 p.

Transcription of four tape-recorded interviews with Cleaver in June 1969, while Cleaver was in exile from the United States.

_____. CONVERSATIONS WITH ELDRIDGE CLEAVER: ALGIERS. New York: McGraw-Hill, 1970. 131 p. Paperback reprint. New York: Dell, 1970. 129 p.

Transcriptions of taped conversations in Havana and later in Algiers.

Cleaver talks about revolutionary tactics and the condition of the revolutionary in exile.

Marine, Gene. "Getting Eldridge Cleaver." RAMPARTS 6 (May 1968): 49-50.

A defense of Cleaver while he was imprisoned. Marine sees Cleaver's imprisonment as a form of political punishment.

Nower, Joyce. "Cleaver's Vision of America and the New White Radical: A Legacy of Malcolm X." NEGRO AMERICAN LITERATURE FORUM 4 (March 1970): 12-21.

Influence of Cleaver and Malcolm X on the young white radicals.

CYRUS COLTER

Colter, Cyrus. THE RIVERS OF EROS. Chicago: Swallow Press, 1972. 219 p.

A novel about Clotilda, an aging and widowed black woman who runs a rooming house in the Chicago ghetto and tries to hold her family together.

O'Brien, John. "Forms of Determinism in the Fiction of Cyrus Colter." STUDIES IN BLACK LITERATURE 4 (Summer 1973): 24-28.

A study of Colter's THE BEACH UMBRELLA (1970), a collection of short stories, and his first published novel, THE RIVERS OF EROS.

HAROLD CRUSE

Cruse, Harold. THE CRISIS OF THE NEGRO INTELLECTUAL. New York: William Morrow, 1967. 594 p.

The varied reasons for the contemporary crisis of the Negro intellectual are examined, such as integrationism, civil-rightsism, socialism, communism. Sections 4-6 are concerned with the 1960s.

_____. "Harold Cruse Looks Back on Black Art and Politics in Harlem." NEGRO DIGEST 18 (November 1968): 19-25, 65-69.

A defense of Cruse's controversial book THE CRISIS OF THE NEGRO INTELLECTUAL, against the attacks of Julian Mayfield.

Mayfield, Julian. "Childe Harold." NEGRO DIGEST 18 (November 1968): 26-27.

A rejoinder to Cruse's defense against Mayfield's earlier attack on THE CRISIS OF THE NEGRO INTELLECTUAL.

MARGARET DANNER

Danner, Margaret. IMPRESSIONS OF AFRICAN ART FORMS IN THE POETRY OF MARGARET DANNER. Detroit: Broadside Press, 1969. 19 p.

_____. IRON LACE. Milbrook, N.Y.: Kriya Press, 1968. 32 p.
Poetry.

_____. TO FLOWER: POEMS. Nashville, Tenn.: Hemphill Press, 1963. 30 p.
Poetry.

Danner, Margaret, and Randall, Dudley. POEM COUNTERPOEM. Detroit: Broadside Press, 1966. 24 p.
Poetry.

WILLIAM DEMBY

Demby, William. BEETLECREEK. New York: Rinehart, 1950. 223 p.

Deterministic novel about people in a small American town. Emphasis on social and environmental problems.

_____. THE CATACOMBS. New York: Pantheon, 1965. 244 p.

Experimental novel concerned with the question of survival in an increasingly technological world.

OWEN DODSON

Dodson, Owen. THE CONFESSION STONE: SONG CYCLES. London: Paul Bremen, 1970. 28 p.

    Poetry.

_____. POWERFUL LONG LADDER. New York: Farrar, 1946. 103 p.
    Poetry.

W.E.B. DUBOIS

Broderick, Francis L. W.E.B. DUBOIS: NEGRO LEADER IN A TIME OF CRISIS. Stanford, Calif.: Stanford University Press, 1959. 259 p.

A well-documented biography of a key figure in race leadership. Contains useful bibliography.

Clarke, John Henrik, et al., eds. BLACK TITAN: W.E.B. DUBOIS. Boston: Beacon Press, 1970. 333 p.

An anthology compiled by the editors of FREEDOMWAYS. Langston Hughes, Paul Robeson, Kwame Nkrumah, Martin Luther King, Jr., Roy Wilkins, and others recall the work of DuBois. Also contains selections from the works of DuBois.

DuBois, W.E.B. "American Negroes and Africa's Rise To Freedom." NATIONAL GUARDIAN 13 (13 February 1961):

Concerned with Afro-Americans and their role in Pan-Africanism.

_____. THE AUTOBIOGRAPHY OF W.E.B. DUBOIS. A SOLILOQUY ON VIEWING MY LIFE FROM THE LAST DECADE OF ITS FIRST CENTURY. Introduction by Herbert Aptheker. New York: International Publishers Co., 1968. 448 p.

Contains selected bibliography, a biographical calendar, and helpful appendixes.

_____. "His Last Message to the World." JOURNAL OF NEGRO HISTORY 49 (April 1964): 145.

Written 26 June 1957, this piece was released at DuBois's death 27 August 1963.

_____. "Of the Sorrow Songs." In BLACK EXPRESSION, edited by Addison Gayle, Jr., pp. 37-47. New York: Weybright and Talley, 1969.

Reprinted from DuBois's THE SOULS OF BLACK FOLK, the selection describes the genesis of the old spirituals and hymns.

_____. SELECTED POEMS. Foreword by Kwame Nkrumah. Accra: Ghana Universities Press, 1965. 42 p.

Poetry.

_____. "The White Masters of the World." In AMISTAD 2: WRITINGS ON BLACK HISTORY & CULTURE, edited by John A. Williams and Charles F. Harris, pp. 169-200. New York: Random House, 1971.

"An attempt to show briefly what the domination of Europe over the world has meant to mankind and especially to Africans in the nineteenth and twentieth centuries." A selection from DuBois's book, THE WORLD AND AFRICA (1965).

_____. "Whither Now and Why." QUARTERLY REVIEW OF HIGHER EDUCATION AMONG NEGROES 28 (July 1960): 135-41.

An address read at the twenty-fifth conference of the Association of Social Science Teachers held at Johnson C. Smith University, Charlotte, North Carolina, 1-2 April 1960.

Fletcher, Diorita C. "W.E.B. DuBois' Arraignment and Indictment of White Civilization." BLACK WORLD 22 (May 1973): 16-22.

An analysis of the essays of DuBois. Fletcher contends that "Du Bois . . . coupled his studies of Black American and African History with the condemnation of white civilization in such a manner as to suggest that to study the one was to expose the other."

Harding, Vincent. "W.E.B. DuBois and the Black Messianic Vision." In BLACK TITAN: W.E.B. DUBOIS, edited by John Henrik Clarke et al., pp. 52-68. Boston: Beacon Press, 1970.

DuBois was obsessively concerned with "the ultimate destiny of black people in America; that dark, compelling destiny was almost always defined by him as fulfilling the national vocation."

King, Martin Luther, Jr. "Honoring Dr. DuBois." In BLACK TITAN: W.E.B. DUBOIS, edited by John Henrik Clarke et al., pp. 176-83. Boston: Beacon Press, 1970.

A memorial speech in which King concludes that DuBois's "greatest value was his committed empathy with all the oppressed and his divine dissatisfaction with all forms of injustice."

Tuttle, William M., Jr. W.E.B. DUBOIS. Englewood Cliffs, N.J.: Prentice-Hall, 1973. 186 p.

A biography of the significant black leader, with bibliographical notes and index.

Walker, S. Jay. "DuBois' Uses of History." BLACK WORLD 24 (February 1975): 4-11.

DuBois "retold" history from his own standards and ethics.

LONNE ELDER III

Elder, Lonne III. "CHARADES ON EAST FOURTH STREET." In BLACK DRAMA ANTHOLOGY, edited by Woodie King, Jr., and Ron Milner, pp. 147-66. New York: New American Library, 1971.

A police officer is kidnapped, threatened, and tortured for the supposed molestation of a young black girl.

Gant, Liz. "An Interview with Lonne Elder III." BLACK WORLD 22 (April 1973): 38-48.

Elder discusses the background for his art, with specific comments on his plays and on his work on the motion picture SOUNDER.

RALPH ELLISON

Baily, Lugene, and Moore, Frank E. "A Selected Checklist of Material by and about Ralph Ellison." BLACK WORLD 20 (April 1971): 126-30.

A useful bibliography which also lists dissertations.

Baumbach, Johnathan. "Nightmare of a Native Son: Ellison's INVISIBLE MAN." CRITIQUE 6 (Spring 1963): 48-65. Reprinted in his THE LANDSCAPE OF NIGHTMARE, pp. 196-212. New York: New York University Press, 1958.

Discussion of Ellison's Tod Clifton as a martyr-saint and of Ellison's use of satire and surrealism.

Benoit, Bernard, and Fabre, Michel. "A Bibliography of Ralph Ellison's Published Writings." STUDIES IN BLACK LITERATURE 2 (Autumn 1971): 25-28.

A useful index to Ellison's published works.

Bloch, Alice. "Sight and Imagery in INVISIBLE MAN." ENGLISH JOURNAL 55 (November 1966): 1019-21, 1024. Reprinted in A CASEBOOK ON RALPH ELLISON'S "INVISIBLE MAN," edited by Joseph F. Trimmer, pp. 264-68. New York: Thomas Y. Crowell, 1972.

The blindness motif runs through the novel and is implied in the word "invisible" of the title: most of the people the protagonist meets do not see him because the "'inner eyes' of traditions, racial barriers, and personal desires prevent them from seeing him as an individual."

Bone, Robert. "Ralph Ellison and the Uses of Imagination." TRI-QUARTERLY 6 (1966): 39-54. Reprinted in ANGER AND BEYOND: THE NEGRO WRITER IN THE UNITED STATES, edited by Herbert Hill, pp. 86-111. New York: Harper & Row, 1966; and in A CASEBOOK ON RALPH ELLISON'S "INVISIBLE MAN," edited by Joseph F. Trimmer, pp. 203-24. New York: Thomas Y. Crowell, 1972.

A discussion of the chief elements Ellison utilizes in his art: music, literature, politics, and culture.

Carson, David L. "Ralph Ellison: Twenty Years After." STUDIES IN AMERI-
CAN FICTION 1 (Spring 1973): 1-23.

An interview with Ellison conducted by Carson in the New York
City residence of Ellison on 30 September 1971.

Cash, Earl A. "The Narrators in INVISIBLE MAN and NOTES FROM THE
UNDERGROUND: Brothers in the Spirit." CLA JOURNAL 16 (June 1973):
505-7.

An examination of the kinship between the narrators in the two
works, particularly in the prologue and epilogue of INVISIBLE
MAN and part 1 of NOTES FROM THE UNDERGROUND.

Christian, Barbara. "Ralph Ellison: A Critical Study." In BLACK EXPRESSION,
edited by Addison Gayle, Jr., pp. 353-65. New York: Weybright and Talley,
1969.

An explication of Ellison's INVISIBLE MAN, which shows the
similarities as well as the differences between the novel and
Ellison's essays.

Clarke, John Henrik. "The Visible Dimensions of INVISIBLE MAN." BLACK
WORLD 20 (December 1970): 27-30.

Clarke sees Ellison's novel as falling into two categories: "A
general American novel about general American situation, and
a novel about the inability of white America to really see Black
America."

Collier, Eugenia W. "The Nightmare Truth of an Invisible Man." BLACK
WORLD 20 (December 1970): 12-19.

Collier contends that by examining the dreams of the nameless
protagonist of INVISIBLE MAN we can "trace the unfolding of
the novel's essential truth."

Corry, John. "Profile of an American Novelist." BLACK WORLD 20 (December 1970): 116-25.

An essay based on an interview in Ellison's apartment.

Covo, Jaqueline. "Ralph Ellison in France: Bibliographic Essays and Checklist
of French Criticism, 1954-1971." CLA JOURNAL 16 (June 1973): 519-26.

The best source for the French reception of Ellison.

Deutsch, Leonard J. "Ellison's Early Fiction." NEGRO AMERICAN LITERATURE

FORUM 7 (Summer 1973): 53-54.

A study of such early works as "Slick Gonna Learn," "The Birth-mark," "Afternoon," "Mister Toussan," "That I Had The Wings," "Flying Home," and "King of the Bingo Game."

Ellison, Ralph. "An American Dilemma: A Review." In his SHADOW AND ACT, pp. 303-17. New York: Random House, 1964.

Review of Gunnar Myrdal's AN AMERICAN DILEMMA.

_____. "And Hickman Arrives." NOBLE SAVAGE 1 (1956): 5-49.

A fragment of an unpublished novel.

_____. "The Art of Fiction: An Interview." PARIS REVIEW 8 (Spring 1955): 55-71. Reprinted in his SHADOW AND ACT, pp. 167-83. New York: Random House, 1964; and in WRITERS AT WORK: THE PARIS REVIEW INTERVIEWS, SECOND SERIES, by Malcolm Cowle, pp. 320-34. New York: Viking Press, 1963.

An interview with Ellison conducted by Alfred Chester and Wilma Howard in Paris in the spring of 1955. Contains statements concerning Ellison's aesthetic and his belief in the universality of good literature.

_____. "The Art of Fiction: Robert Penn Warren." PARTISAN REVIEW 25 (Spring 1958): 212-22. Part of "The Negro Writer in America," an exchange with Stanley Edgar Hyman. Reprinted in his SHADOW AND ACT as "Change the Joke and Slip the Yoke," pp. 45-59. New York: Random House, 1964.

Ellison takes issue with an essay written by Hyman.

_____. "As the Spirit Moves Mahalia." SATURDAY REVIEW, 27 September 1958, pp. 41-43. Reprinted in his SHADOW AND ACT, pp. 213-20. New York: Random House, 1964.

_____. "At Home." TIME, 2 February 1959, p. 2.

A letter to the editors of TIME protesting against being described as being "self-exiled in Rome" in an article entitled "Amid the Alien Corn," TIME, 17 November 1958.

_____. "Beating That Bay." NEW REPUBLIC 113 (22 October 1945): 535-36. Reprinted in his SHADOW AND ACT, pp. 95-101. New York: Random House, 1964.

An analysis of Bucklin Moon's PRIMER FOR WHITE FOLKS.

_____. "Blues People." In his SHADOW AND ACT, pp. 247-58. New York: Random House, 1964. A reprint of "The Blues," which originally appeared in the NEW YORK REVIEW 1 (6 February 1964): 5-7.

Intended as a corrective to Jones's overly sociological approach
to the blues in BLUES PEOPLE: NEGRO MUSIC IN WHITE AMER-
ICA (see section on LeRoi Jones, p. 204).

_____. "Brave Words for a Startling Occasion." In his SHADOW AND ACT,
pp. 102-6. New York: Random House, 1964.

Address for Presentation Ceremony, National Book Award, 27
January 1953.

_____. "The Charlie Christian Story." SATURDAY REVIEW, 17 May 1958,
pp. 42-43, 46. Reprinted in his SHADOW AND ACT, pp. 233-40.   New
York: Random House, 1964.

An essay on the great jazz guitarist, Charlie Christian.

_____. "Dialogue." In WHO SPEAKS FOR THE NEGRO?, edited by Robert
Penn Warren, pp. 347-54. New York: Random House, 1965.

Ellison speaks of his experiences and of the human condition.

. "February." SATURDAY REVIEW, 1 January 1955, p. 25.

An impressionistic reflection of an experience in country fields
shortly after his mother's death.

_____. "The Golden Age/Time Past. Manners and Morals at Minton's, 1941:
The Setting for a Revolution." ESQUIRE, October 1973, pp. 260-64, 478.
Reprinted in his SHADOW AND ACT, pp. 199-212. New York: Random House,
1964.

Reprint of part of a section in GOLDEN AGE OF JAZZ, January
1959. The article resulted from the fact that Ellison had deplored
the fact that most jazz history was romanticized and not factual.

. "Harlem America." NEW LEADER 49 (26 September 1966): 25-35.

Testimony before U.S. Senate Subcommittee on Executive Reorgan-
ization, regarding the federal role in urban problems. Questions
are asked by Chairman Jacob K. Javits and Senators Abraham Ribicoff,
Robert F. Kennedy, and Joseph M. Montoya.

_____. "Harlem Is Nowhere." HARPER'S, August 1964, pp. 53-57.

An essay on the Negro ghetto in the North: "the ruin that is
Harlem . . . the scene and symbol of the Negro's perpetual
alienation in the land of his birth."

_____. "Hidden Name and Complex Fate." In THE WRITERS EXPERIENCE, edited by Ralph Ellison and Karl Shapiro, pp. 1-15. Washington, D.C.: Library of Congress, 1964. Reprinted in Ellison's SHADOW AND ACT, pp. 144-66. New York: Random House, 1964.

Discusses early literary influence upon him during his formative period. This is an address sponsored by the Gertrude Clarke Whittall Foundation.

_____. "If the Twain Shall Meet." NEW YORK HERALD TRIBUNE BOOK WEEK, 8 November 1964, pp. 1, 20-25.

Review of THE SOUTHERN MISTIQUE by Howard Zinn.

_____. INVISIBLE MAN. New York: Random House, 1952. 439 p.

A novel which combines naturalism, expressionism, and surrealism to delineate the experience of its nameless protagonist, a black Everyman.

_____. "Invisible Man: Prologue to a Novel." PARTISAN REVIEW 19 (January-February 1952): 31-40.

An early fragment from INVISIBLE MAN.

_____. "It Always Breaks Out." PARTISAN REVIEW 30 (Spring 1963): 13-28.

A short piece on southern racism and bigotry.

_____. "Juneteenth." QUARTERLY REVIEW OF LITERATURE 13 (1965): 262-76.

An early fragment "from work in progress" about a wounded man's thoughts concerning "Juneteenth," or Emancipation Day.

_____. "Letters: No Apologies." HARPER'S, July 1967, pp. 4, 8, 12, 14, 16, 18.

A letter written in response to Norman Podhoretz, who had taken issue with Ellison in an earlier letter to the editors regarding Ellison's remarks about some writers for COMMENTARY. Podhoretz's reply to this letter is printed with Ellison's letter.

_____. "Letter to '48." MAGAZINE OF THE YEAR 2 (May 1948): 145.

Answer to reader's letter concerning autobiographical element in "Battle Royal" episode.

      . "Living with Music." In his SHADOW AND ACT, pp. 187-98. New York: Random House, 1964. Originally published in HIGH FIDELITY, December 1955.

Ellison discusses the important role music played in his life and writing career. Contains some humorous passages discussing how he used music as a "sound defense" to drown outside external distracting noises in the neighborhood.

      . "The Novel as a Function of American Democracy." WILSON LIBRARY BULLETIN 41 (June 1967): 1022-27.

A paper based on a lecture given 23 March 1967, at the Free Library of Philadelphia. Ellison says that "if there had been more novelists with the courage of Mark Twain or James or Hemingway, we would not be in the moral confusion in which we find ourselves today."

      . "On Becoming a Writer." COMMENTARY 38 (October 1964): 57-60. Included as part of introduction to his SHADOW AND ACT, pp. 11-23. New York: Random House, 1964.

Ellison discusses why he became a writer.

      . "On Bird, Bird-Watching, and Jazz." SATURDAY REVIEW, 28 July 1962, pp. 47-49, 62. Reprinted in his SHADOW AND ACT, pp. 221-32. New York: Random House, 1964.

A review-essay of Reisner's BIRD: THE LEGEND OF CHARLIE PARKER.

      . "Out of the Hospital and Under the Bar." In SOON ONE MORNING, edited by Herbert Hill, pp. 242-90. New York: Alfred A. Knopf, 1963. Preceded by "Author's Note," p. 243.

A previously unpublished section of INVISIBLE MAN, a fragment from the portion about the protagonist's attempt to get out of the hospital after an explosion at a paint factory.

      . "A Rejoinder." NEW LEADER 47 (3 February 1964): 15-22. Reprinted in his SHADOW AND ACT as "The World and the Jug," part 2, pp. 120-43. New York: Random House, 1964.

A response to Howe's reply to Ellison's original article, "The World and the Jug," published in the NEW LEADER (see below).

      . "Remembering Jimmy." SATURDAY REVIEW, 12 July 1958, pp. 36-37. Reprinted in his SHADOW AND ACT, pp. 241-46. New York: Random House, 1964.

An essay concerned with blues singer Jimmy Rushing.

. "Richard Wright's Blues." ANTIOCH REVIEW 5 (Summer 1945): 198-211. Reprinted in his SHADOW AND ACT, pp. 77-94. New York: Random House, 1964.

Wright's most important achievement, says Ellison, was that he "converted the American Negro impulse toward self-annihilation and 'going-under-ground' into a will to confront the world, to evaluate his experience honestly and throw his findings unashamedly into the guilty conscience of America."

. SHADOW AND ACT. New York: Random House, 1964. 317 p.

A collection of essays by Ellison, with an eleven-page introduction by Ellison.

. "The Shadow and the Act." REPORTER, December 1949, pp. 17-19. Reprinted in his SHADOW AND ACT, pp. 273-81. New York: Random House, 1964.

Ellison's views of four films concerning the Negro: INTRUDER IN THE DUST, THE BIRTH OF A NATION, LOST BOUNDARIES, and PINKY.

. "Sociology, Morality, and the Novel." In THE LIVING NOVEL, A SYMPOSIUM, edited by Granville Hicks, pp. 58-91. New York: Macmillan, 1957.

Poses the question, "How does one in the novel (the novel which is a work of art and not a disguised piece of sociology) persuade the American reader to identify that which is basic in man beyond all differences of class, race, wealth, or formal education?"

. "Some Questions and Some Answers." In his SHADOW AND ACT, pp. 261-72. New York: Random House, 1964.

A series of answers to questions involving the subject of "Negro culture."

. "A Song of Experience." IOWA REVIEW 1 (Spring 1970): 30-40.

An excerpt from a novel in progress.

. "Stepchild Fantasy." SATURDAY REVIEW, 8 June 1946, pp. 25-26.

A review of AMERICAN DAUGHTER, by Era Bell Thompson. Ellison says that what is "positive" in AMERICAN DAUGHTER is its "dream of an America in which all groups are united, the one irrepressible dream in which all Americans believe."

. "Stephen Crane and the Mainstream of American Fiction." Introduction to THE RED BADGE OF COURAGE AND FOUR GREAT STORIES by Stephen Crane, pp. 7-24. New York: Dell, 1960. Reprinted in Ellison's SHADOW AND ACT, pp. 60-76. New York: Random House, 1964.

An appreciation of Crane's fiction.

_____. "Tell It Like It Is, Baby." NATION 201 (20 September 1965): 129-36.

From Rome (1956): An attempt at an essay about the southern congressman's defiance of the Supreme Court concerning desegregation.

_____. "That Same Pain, That Same Pleasure: An Interview." Interview by R.G. Stern. DECEMBER 3 (Winter 1961): 30-32, 37-46. Reprinted in Ellison's SHADOW AND ACT, pp. 3-23. New York: Random House, 1964.

Ellison says in the interview that "if the writer exists for any social good, his role is that of preserving in art those human values which can endure by confronting change."

_____. "Twentieth Century Fiction and the Black Mask of Humanity." CONFLUENCE 2 (December 1953): 3-21. Reprinted in his SHADOW AND ACT, pp. 24-44. New York: Random House, 1964.

An examination of the fictional treatment of the Negro by Twain, Hemingway, and Faulkner.

_____. "A Very Stern Discipline." HARPER'S, March 1967, pp. 76-95.

An interview with Ellison by three young black writers. Ellison revised the tapes of the interview before their publication in HARPER'S.

_____. "What America Would Be Like without Blacks." TIME, 6 April 1970, pp. 54-55.

"The nation could not survive being deprived of their [the black's] presence because, by the irony implicit in the dynamics of American democracy, they symbolize both its most stringent testing and the possibility of its greatest human freedom."

_____. "The World and the Jug." NEW LEADER 46 (9 December 1963): 22-26. Reprinted in his SHADOW AND ACT as "The World and the Jug," part 1, pp. 107-20. New York: Random House, 1964.

An attack on Irving Howe's views presented in "Black Boys and Native Sons," DISSENT (Autumn 1963).

Ellison, Ralph, and McPherson, James Alan. "Indivisible Man." ATLANTIC MONTHLY, December 1970, pp. 45-60.

Ralph Ellison

A combination of dialogue and written correspondence between Ellison and McPherson.

Ford, Nick Aaron. "The Ambivalence of Ralph Ellison." BLACK WORLD 20 (December 1970): 5-9.

Ford feels that conflicting impressions left by many key sections of INVISIBLE MAN may help explain the novel's intellectual challenge.

Gvereschi, Edward. "Anticipations of INVISIBLE MAN: Ralph Ellison's 'King of the Bingo Game.'" NEGRO AMERICAN LITERATURE FORUM 6 (Winter 1972): 122-24.

Sees Ellison's early short fiction, "King of the Bingo Game," as a prototype for INVISIBLE MAN.

Hersey, John, ed. RALPH ELLISON: A COLLECTION OF CRITICAL ESSAYS. Englewood Cliffs, N.J.: Prentice-Hall, 1974. 180 p.

Thirteen essays on Ellison by Saul Bellow, Robert Penn Warren, Irving Howe, and others, as well as an interview with Ellison himself.

Horowitz, Floyd R. "Ralph Ellison's Modern Version of Brer Bear and Brer Rabbit in INVISIBLE MAN." MID-CONTINENT AMERICAN STUDIES JOURNAL 4 (Fall 1963): 21-27.

Examines Ellison's use of the bear and the fox symbol in the narrative of INVISIBLE MAN.

Howe, Irving. "Black Boys and Native Sons." In A CASEBOOK ON RALPH ELLISON'S "INVISIBLE MAN," edited by Joseph F. Trimmer, pp. 150-69. New York: Thomas Y. Crowell, 1972. Reprinted from his A WORLD MORE ATTRACTIVE, pp. 98-122. New York: Horizon Press, 1963.

Concerned with Baldwin and Ellison and their relationship to Richard Wright.

Hurowitz, Ellin. "The Rebirth of the Artist." In A CASEBOOK ON RALPH ELLISON'S "INVISIBLE MAN," edited by Joseph F. Trimmer, pp. 238-53. New York: Thomas Y. Crowell, 1972.

Argues that "INVISIBLE MAN is another kind of portrait of the artist, the making of an exile."

Jackson, Esther Merle. "The American Negro and the Image of the Absurd." PHYLON 23 (Winter 1962): 359-71.

Concerned with Faulkner's character Joe Christmas (LIGHT IN AUGUST), Bigger Thomas in Wright's NATIVE SON, and the protagonist in Ellison's INVISIBLE MAN.

Kaiser, Ernest. "A Critical Look at Ellison's Fiction and at Social and Literary Criticism by and about the Author." BLACK WORLD 20 (December 1970): 53-59, 81-97.

"Instead of using his fiction to penetrate the smooth, slick camouflages of our society . . . Ellison uses the myths and rituals of the Black people's folklore to show that Black suffering has always existed and always will exist no matter what the Blacks do."

Kent, George [E.]. "Before Ideology: Reflections on Ralph Ellison and the Sensibility of Younger Black Writers." In his BLACKNESS AND THE ADVENTURE OF WESTERN CULTURE, pp. 184-201. Chicago: Third World Press, 1972.

Kent sees the major difference between Ellison and the younger black writers lying in Ellison's "ritual affirmation of faith in the West, his emphasis on cultural blending, and his exclusion of Africa as a psychological resource."

_____. "Ralph Ellison and Afro-American Folk and Cultural Tradition." In his BLACKNESS AND THE ADVENTURE OF WESTERN CULTURE, pp. 152-63. Chicago: Third World Press, 1972.

Concerned with Ellison's belief in the value of the folk tradition.

Kostelanetz, Richard. "The Politics of Ellison's Booker: INVISIBLE MAN as Symbolic History." CHICAGO REVIEW 19 (1967): 5-26.

"Although Ellison does not have his narrator confront every known political possibility, the novel is still the most comprehensive one-volume fictional-symbolic treatment of the history of the American Negro in the twentieth century."

Lane, James B. "Underground to Manhood: Ralph Ellison's INVISIBLE MAN." NEGRO AMERICAN LITERATURE FORUM 7 (Summer 1973): 64-72.

An examination of INVISIBLE MAN as an "urban novel."

Mason, Clifford. "Ralph Ellison and the Underground Man." BLACK WORLD 20 (December 1970): 20-26.

"Ellison has personalized the masks of our culture to a degree hitherto unknown in our literature, and has given us, as a consequence, a greater insight into national hypocrisy as it exists for all groups in this country."

Menegeling, Marvin E. "Whitman and Ellison: Older Symbols in a Modern Mainstream." In A CASEBOOK ON RALPH ELLISON'S "INVISIBLE MAN," edited by Joseph F. Trimmer, pp. 269-72. New York: Thomas Y. Crowell, 1972.

Shows the indebtedness of chapter 5 of Ellison's INVISIBLE MAN to Whitman's "When Lilacs Last in the Dooryard Bloom'd."

Neal, Larry. "Ellison's Zoot Suit." BLACK WORLD 20 (December 1970):
31-52.

> Neal sees Ellison's work as being firmly rooted in the black aes-
> thetic and showing a "consistent concern for capturing the essen-
> tial truths of the Black man's experience in America."

"Ralph Ellison: His Literary Works and Status." BLACK WORLD 20 (December
1970): entire issue.

> Special issue contains eight essays concerning Ellison and his art
> and a selected bibliography of works by and about Ellison.

Rovit, Earl H. "Ralph Ellison and the American Comic Tradition." WISCONSIN
STUDIES IN CONTEMPORARY LITERATURE 1 (Fall 1960): 34-42. Reprinted
in A CASEBOOK ON RALPH ELLISON'S "INVISIBLE MAN," edited by Joseph
F. Trimmer, pp. 254-63. New York: Thomas Y. Crowell, 1972.

> Rovit considers INVISIBLE MAN a "profoundly comic work" and
> places it in the tradition of American national humor.

Schafer, William J. "Ralph Ellison and the Birth of the Anti-Hero." CRITIQUE:
STUDIES IN MODERN FICTION 10 (1968): 81-93. Reprinted in A CASEBOOK
ON RALPH ELLISON'S "INVISIBLE MAN," edited by Joseph F. Trimmer, pp. 225-
37. New York: Thomas Y. Crowell, 1972.

> "The problem of identity and existence that Ellison poses transcends
> the issues of social justice and equity; it is not a question of the
> 'Negro problem' or 'race issues.'"

Stark, John. "INVISIBLE MAN: Ellison's Black Odyssey." NEGRO AMERICAN
LITERATURE FORUM 7 (Summer 1973): 60-63.

> A discussion of THE ODYSSEY as a source for Ellison's INVISIBLE
> MAN.

Trimmer, Joseph F., ed. A CASEBOOK ON RALPH ELLISON'S "INVISIBLE
MAN." New York: Thomas Y. Crowell, 1972. 321 p.

> Contains sections on the racial and artistic heritage of the novel,
> critical essays, and a very useful bibliography.

Walling, William. "'Art' and 'Protest': Ralph Ellison's INVISIBLE MAN Twenty
Years After." PHYLON 34 (June 1973): 120-34.

> An examination of two decades of criticism of Ellison's INVISIBLE
> MAN and a defense against its more militant detractors in the late
> 60s.

_____. "Ralph Ellison's INVISIBLE MAN: 'It Goes a Long Way Back Some Twenty Years.'" PHYLON 34 (March 1973): 4-16.

> Walling finds that "while critical opinion has generally agreed that Ellison's novel is of major dimensions, specific judgments remain sharply divided." Most of the controversy is concerned with the book's fidelity to the changing problems of the black man in America.

Weinstein, Sharon Rosenburg. "Comedy and the Absurd in Ellison's INVISIBLE MAN." STUDIES IN BLACK LITERATURE 3 (Autumn 1972): 12-16.

> INVISIBLE MAN can be viewed as "the protagonist's education in laughter--and as his parallel progression in a realization of the absurd."

Williams, John A. "Ralph Ellison and INVISIBLE MAN: Their Place in American Letters." BLACK WORLD 20 (December 1970): 10-11.

> A brief appraisal of Ellison's importance to black writing and to black Americans.

JAMES EMANUEL

Emanuel, James A. "Blackness Can: A Quest For Aesthetics." In THE BLACK
AESTHETIC, edited by Addison Gayle, Jr., pp. 192-223. Garden City, N.Y.:
Doubleday, 1971.

> Emanuel sees that in the creation of the black aesthetic the "im-
> mediate issue is the question of the racial integrity and the intel-
> lectual breadth of the molders of the black aesthetic."

_____. "The Future of Negro Poetry: A Challenge for Critics." In BLACK
EXPRESSION, edited by Addison Gayle, Jr., pp. 100-109. New York: Weybright and Talley, 1969.

> Black critics must meet the need for a "sympathetic but thorough
> and high-principled estimate of the best contributions of Negro
> poets."

_____. PANTHER MEN. Detroit: Broadside Press, 1970. 32 p.

> Poetry.

_____. THE TREEHOUSE AND OTHER POEMS. Detroit: Broadside Press,
1968. 24 p.

> Poetry.

MARI EVANS

Evans, Mari. I AM A BLACK WOMAN. New York: William Morrow, 1970. 95 p.

Poetry.

_____. WHERE IS ALL THE MUSIC? London: Paul Bremen, 1968. 24 p.

Poetry.

SARAH WEBSTER FABIO

Fabio, Sarah Webster. A MIRROR: A SOUL; A TWO-PART VOLUME OF POEMS. San Francisco: J. Richardson, 1969. 44 p.

Poetry.

RONALD FAIR

Fair, Ronald. HOG BUTCHER. New York: Harcourt, Brace & World, 1966. 182 p.

Naturalistic novel of Chicago's South Side ghetto.

_____. MANY THOUSAND GONE, AN AMERICAN FABLE. New York: Harcourt, Brace & World, 1965. 114 p.

Metaphorical tale of twentieth-century blacks in a Mississippi county who do not know slaves have been freed after the Civil War.

_____. WE CAN'T BREATHE. New York: Harper & Row, 1972. 216 p.

Autobiographical novel about coming of age in the Chicago black ghetto of the 1930s and 1940s.

_____. WORLD OF NOTHING. New York: Harper & Row, 1970. 224 p.

Book contains two novellas: JEROME, which deals with the illegitimate son of a minister and a Christ archetype parishioner, and WORLD OF NOTHING, which deals with a Chicago ghetto folk-hero.

ERNEST GAINES

Beauford, Fred. "A Conversation with Ernest J. Gaines." BLACK CREATION 4 (Fall 1972): 16-18.

Interview with Gaines in which he discusses his art and the influence of Hemingway and Faulkner on his work.

Billingsley, Ronald G. "The Burden of the Hero in Modern Afro-American Fiction." BLACK WORLD 25 (December 1975): 38-45, 66-73.

Psychological health (or manhood) is far more important to Ned Douglass in Gaines's THE AUTOBIOGRAPHY OF MISS JANE PITTMAN than physical health, and he can die to prove it.

Bryant, Jerry H. "From Death to Life: The Fiction of Ernest J. Gaines." IOWA REVIEW 3 (Winter 1972): 106-20. Chapter 1 of Gaines's novel, THE HOUSE AND THE FIELD, appeared in the same issue, pp. 121-25.

An analysis of CATHERINE CARMIER, BLOODLINE, OF LOVE AND DUST, and THE AUTOBIOGRAPHY OF MISS JANE PITTMAN.

Gaines, Ernest J. THE AUTOBIOGRAPHY OF MISS JANE PITTMAN. New York: Dial Press, 1971. 245 p.

A novel concerned with the recollections of a 110-year-old exslave and her views on the black militancy of the 1960s.

_____. BLOODLINE. New York: Dial Press, 1968. 249 p.

Five long stories thematically related.

_____. CATHERINE CARMIER. New York: Atheneum, 1964. 248 p.

Novel concerned with the alienation and frustration of a young Negro college graduate when he returns to his Louisiana community.

_____. OF LOVE AND DUST. New York: Dial Press, 1967. 281 p.

A story of love, violence, and vengeance on a Louisiana plantation in the 1940s.

NIKKI GIOVANNI

Bailey, Peter. "Nikki Giovanni: 'I Am Black, Female, Polite.'" EBONY, February 1972, pp. 48-54, 56.

This illustrated review article, containing excerpts from her poetry and informative commentary by Bailey, is based on interviews with Giovanni and a close study of her art. Bailey notes Giovanni's admiration for the philosophy of Ayn Rand.

Brooks, Russell. "The Motifs of Dynamic Change in Black Revolutionary Poetry." CLA JOURNAL 15 (September 1971): 7-17.

Brooks finds in Giovanni's poetry an "ominous note of impending upheaval and of rigorous and uncompromising opposition to anyone, including even her own lover, who would seek to avert it."

Giovanni, Nikki. BLACK FEELING, BLACK TALK/BLACK JUDGEMENT. New York: William Morrow, 1970. 98 p.

Collection of poems tracing the evolution of a black girl who wanted to sing with Ray Charles to a fiery militant who asks "Can you kill, nigger, can you kill?"

_____. BLACK JUDGEMENT. Detroit: Broadside Press, 1968. 36 p.

Poetry.

_____. "Black Poems, Poseurs, and Power." NEGRO DIGEST 18 (June 1969): 30-34.

Giovanni reminds black artists that the "jews had over 100 art festivals while in the concentration camps" and warns of the danger to black people in America. She inveighs against the "militarism" of the United Brothers in Newark and black artists who "perform" militant roles for white audiences or who become token "niggers-in-residence" at white universities.

_____. BLACK TALK. 2d ed., enl. New York: The author, 1969. 26 p.

Poetry.

_____. "Convalescence--Compared to What." BLACK POWER 1 (1971): 117-28.

Although the essay is couched in revolutionary black rhetoric, the true subject is genius and individualism and shows the influence of the philosophy of Ayn Rand.

_____. EGO TRIPPING AND OTHER POEMS FOR YOUNG PEOPLE. New York: Lawrence Hill, 1973. 37 p.

Poems.

_____. GEMINI: AN EXTENDED AUTOBIOGRAPHICAL STATEMENT ON MY FIRST TWENTY-FIVE YEARS OF BEING A BLACK POET. Introduction by Barbara Crosby. New York: Viking Press, 1971. 149 p.

Contains selections formerly published in NEGRO DIGEST.

_____. MY HOUSE. New York: William Morrow, 1972. 69 p.

Poetry.

_____. "The Planet of Junior Brown." BLACK WORLD 21 (March 1972): 70-71.

A review of Virginia Hamilton's children's book, THE PLANET OF JUNIOR BROWN.

_____. RE-CREATION. Detroit: Broadside Press, 1970. 48 p.

Poetry.

_____. SPIN A SOFT BLACK SONG: POEMS FOR CHILDREN. New York: Hill and Wang, 1971. Unpaged.

Poetry.

Palmer, R. Roderick. "The Poetry of Three Revolutionists: Don L. Lee, Sonia Sanchez, and Nikki Giovanni." CLA JOURNAL 15 (September 1971): 25-36.

Palmer sees Giovanni as "the most polemic, the most incendiary; the poet most impatient for change, and who thus advocates open violence."

SAM GREENLEE

Burrell, Walter. "Rappin with Sam Greenlee--An Interview." BLACK WORLD
20 (July 1971): 42-47.

>   Greenlee talks about his first novel, THE SPOOK WHO SAT BY
>   THE DOOR, the possibility of making the novel into a film, and
>   his projected second novel, BAGHDAD BLUES.

Greenlee, Sam. BLUES FOR AN AFRICAN PRINCESS. Introduction by Nikki
Giovanni. Chicago: Third World Press, 1971. 36 p.

>   Poetry.

_____. "Sonny's Seasons." BLACK WORLD 19 (October 1970): 58-63.

>   A children's story about a young boy's initiation into the meaning
>   of "turfs" and forbidden areas in Chicago's black South Side.

_____. THE SPOOK WHO SAT BY THE DOOR. New York: Richard W.
Baron, 1969. 248 p.

>   Black C.I.A. agent returns to the ghetto, where he trains a
>   revolutionary black army recruited from ghetto gangs.

DICK GREGORY

Gregory, Dick. FROM THE BACK OF THE BUS. New York: Avon Books, 1962. 125 p.

Autobiographical and philosophical comments by a black comedian and political activist.

_____. NIGGER. New York: E.P. Dutton, 1964. 224 p.

An autobiographical account tape-recorded by Gregory and transcribed by Robert Lipsyte.

LORRAINE HANSBERRY

Brown, Lloyd W. "Lorraine Hansberry as Ironist: A Reappraisal of A RAISIN IN THE SUN." JOURNAL OF BLACK STUDIES 4 (March 1974): 237-47.

Brown sees Hansberry's play as being, ultimately, far from optimistic about the "moral malaise" and "spiritual weariness" that tarnishes any "dreams-for-change."

Hansberry, Lorraine. "The Black Revolution and the White Backlash." NATIONAL GUARDIAN 26 (4 July 1964): 5-9.

Transcript of a town hall forum with Hansberry and Ossie Davis, Ruby Dee, LeRoi Jones, John O. Killens, Paule Marshall, Charles E. Silberman, and James Wechsler, narrated by David Susskind.

_____. "A Challenge to Artists." FREEDOMWAYS 3 (Winter 1963): 31-35.

Transcription of a speech delivered at the Rally to Abolish The House Un-American Activities Committee, Manhattan Center, New York, 27 October 1962.

_____. "Congolese Patriot." NEW YORK TIMES, 26 March 1961, p. 4.

A letter to the editor in which Hansberry objects to Dr. Ralph Bunche's "apology" for the demonstrations at the United Nations after the murder of Lumumba.

_____. "The Drinking Gourd." In LES BLANCS: COLLECTED LAST PLAYS OF LORRAINE HANSBERRY, edited by Robert Nemiroff, pp. 217-310. New York: Random House, 1972.

A play about slavery which was intended for production in an NBC television series celebrating the centennial of the Civil War. The play is a corrective on the GONE WITH THE WIND view of slavery, and is published with a critical introduction (pp. 189-215) and notes by Robert Nemiroff on two songs used in the play (pp. 311-21).

_____. "Flag from a Kitchenette Window." MASSES AND MAINSTREAM 3 (September 1950): 38-40.

Poems.

_____. "For a Young Negro I Have Met, a Love Song." In her TO BE YOUNG, GIFTED AND BLACK, pp. 80-81. Englewood Cliffs, N.J.: Prentice-Hall, 1969.

Poem.

_____. "Interim." In her TO BE YOUNG, GIFTED AND BLACK, p. 90. Englewood Cliffs, N.J.: Prentice-Hall, 1969.

Poem.

_____. "The Legacy of W.E.B. DuBois." In BLACK TITAN: W.E.B. DU-BOIS, edited by John Henrik Clarke et al., pp. 17-21. Boston: Beacon Press, 1970.

One of the last speeches made by Hansberry before her terminal illness. The speech was made at a W.E.B. DuBois memorial at Carnegie Hall, New York, 23 February 1964.

_____. "LES BLANCS." In LES BLANCS: COLLECTED LAST PLAYS OF LORRAINE HANSBERRY, edited by Robert Nemiroff, pp. 47-172. New York: Random House, 1972.

Play centers on a group of people caught in the midst of a revolution in Africa. The play is published with Nemiroff's critical introduction (pp. 35-46) and postscript (pp. 173-86) concerning the critical reception of the play.

_____. LES BLANCS: COLLECTED LAST PLAYS OF LORRAINE HANSBERRY. Edited by Robert Nemiroff. Introduction by Julius Lester. New York: Random House, 1972. 381 p.

Contains three plays, LES BLANCS, THE DRINKING GOURD, and WHAT USE ARE FLOWERS? Each play is published with a critical background by Robert Nemiroff.

_____. "Lynchsong." MASSES AND MAINSTREAM 4 (July 1951): 19-20.

Poem.

_____. "Me Tink Me Hear Sounds in De Night." THEATRE ARTS 44 (October 1960): 9-11, 69-70. Reprinted in AMERICAN PLAYWRIGHTS ON DRAMA, as "The Negro in the American Theater," edited by Horst Frenz, pp. 160-67. New York: Hill and Wang, 1965.

"The role of the Negro in the American theatre is still dishearten-

ingly small—and almost everyone must share the blame, including
our leading playwrights."

_____. THE MOVEMENT: A DOCUMENTARY OF A STRUGGLE FOR EQUAL-
ITY. New York: Simon & Schuster, 1965. 127 p. Reprinted in England by
Penguin Books as A MATTER OF COLOUR.

Photo-journalism compiled in collaboration with a young white
photographer, Danny Lyon, and with the assistance of the Student
Non-Violent Coordinating Committee.

_____. "My Name Is Lorraine Hansberry, I Am a Writer." ESQUIRE, Novem-
ber 1969, pp. 140-41.

A transcript of dated notes Hansberry kept during the last months
of her life.

_____. "The Nation Needs Your Gifts." NEGRO DIGEST 13 (August 1964):
26-29.

An address delivered by Hansberry to the winners of a creative
writing contest. Hansberry says that "though it be a thrilling
and marvelous thing to be merely young and gifted in such times,
it is doubly so to be young, gifted, and black."

_____. "The Negro in American Culture." A symposium reprinted in C.W.E.
Bigsby. THE BLACK AMERICAN WRITER 1, FICTION, by C.W.E. Bigsby.
Baltimore: Pelican Books, 1971. 273 p.

A symposium with Hansberry, Langston Hughes, James Baldwin,
Nat Hentoff, Emile Capouya, and Alfred Kazin.

_____. A RAISIN IN THE SUN. New York: Random House, 1969. 146 p.

A drama concerned with a black family's attempts to leave the
ghetto and move to the white suburbs. The family is presided
over by a magnificently realized black matriarch.

_____. THE SIGN IN SIDNEY BRUSTEIN'S WINDOW. Introduction by Robert
Nemiroff. New York: Signet, 1966. 143 p.

A three-act play detailing the victims and victimizers of society.
Published with an introduction and tribute to Hansberry by her
husband, Robert Nemiroff.

_____. TO BE YOUNG, GIFTED AND BLACK: A PORTRAIT OF LORRAINE
HANSBERRY IN HER OWN WORDS. Englewood Cliffs, N.J.: Prentice-Hall,
1969. 226 p.

A dramatization of Hansberry's plays, interviews, letters, and autobiographical excerpts by her husband, Robert Nemiroff.

_____. "WHAT USE ARE FLOWERS?" In LES BLANCS: COLLECTED LAST PLAYS OF LORRAINE HANSBERRY, edited by Robert Nemiroff, pp. 323-70. New York: Random House, 1972.

MICHAEL S. HARPER

Harper, Michael S. DEAR JOHN, DEAR COLTRANE. Pittsburgh: University of Pittsburgh Press, 1970. 88 p.

Poems influenced by the intonations of black speech, the rhythm of jazz.

————. HISTORY IS YOUR HEARTBEAT. Urbana: University of Illinois Press, 1971. 95 p.

Poems influenced by the works of black musicians such as John Coltrane and McCoy Tyner, and expressive of Harper's historical and mythic interests.

————. NIGHTMARE BEGINS RESPONSIBILITY. Urbana: University of Illinois Press, 1973.

Poetry.

————. PHOTOGRAPHS, NEGATIVES, HISTORY AS APPLE TREE. San Francisco: Scarab Press, 1972. 29 p.

Limited edition of Harper's poetry.

————. SONG: I WANT A WITNESS. Pittsburgh: University of Pittsburgh Press, 1972. 63 p.

Poetry.

ROBERT HAYDEN

Hayden, Robert. A BALLAD OF REMEMBRANCE. London: Paul Bremen, 1962.
72 p.
  Poetry.

_____. FIGURE OF TIME. Nashville, Tenn.: Hemphill Press, 1955. 20 p.
  Poetry.

_____. SELECTED POEMS. New York: October House, 1970. 64 p.

DAVID HENDERSON

Henderson, David. DE MAYOR OF HARLEM. New York: E.P. Dutton, 1970. 128 p.

Poetry.

_____. FELIX OF THE SILENT FOREST. Introduction by LeRoi Jones. New York: Poets Press, 1967. 48 p.

Collection of Henderson's poetry.

_____. "THE MAN WHO CRIED I AM: A Critique." In BLACK EXPRESSION, edited by Addison Gayle, Jr., pp. 365-71. New York: Weybright and Talley, 1969.

CHESTER HIMES

Billingsley, Ronald G. "The Burden of the Hero in Modern Afro-American Fiction." BLACK WORLD 25 (December 1975): 38-45, 66-73.

"Perhaps nowhere in modern Black writing is the attempt of the hero [Bob Jones] to define and maintain himself as a positive and effective human being more poignantly revealed than in IF HE HOLLERS LET HIM GO."

Himes, Chester. ALL SHOT UP. New York: Avon Books, 1960. 160 p.

Novel concerned with black homosexuals and transvestites, the car sales racket, and political machinations.

_____. THE BIG GOLD DREAM. New York: Avon Books, 1960. 160 p.

Another violent detective novel involving the exploits of black detectives Grave Digger Jones and Coffin Ed Johnson. Also concerned with Sweet Prophet Brown and his Temple of Wonderful Prayer.

_____. BLACK ON BLACK: BABY SISTER AND SELECTED WRITINGS. New York: Doubleday, 1973. 287 p.

A collection of seventeen short stories, five essays, and a movie scenario, "Baby Sister."

_____. BLIND MAN WITH A PISTOL. New York: William Morrow, 1969. 238 p.

Coffin Ed Johnson and Grave Digger Jones look for the killer of a white film producer in a chaos of black power marches, Black Muslims, and Soul brothers.

_____. CAST THE FIRST STONE. New York: Coward-McCann, 1952. 346 p.

Psychological novel about prison life.

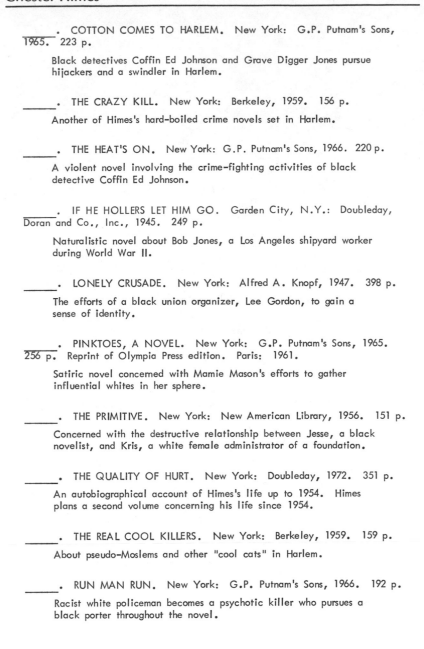

_____. COTTON COMES TO HARLEM. New York: G.P. Putnam's Sons, 1965. 223 p.

Black detectives Coffin Ed Johnson and Grave Digger Jones pursue hijackers and a swindler in Harlem.

_____. THE CRAZY KILL. New York: Berkeley, 1959. 156 p.

Another of Himes's hard-boiled crime novels set in Harlem.

_____. THE HEAT'S ON. New York: G.P. Putnam's Sons, 1966. 220 p.

A violent novel involving the crime-fighting activities of black detective Coffin Ed Johnson.

_____. IF HE HOLLERS LET HIM GO. Garden City, N.Y.: Doubleday, Doran and Co., Inc., 1945. 249 p.

Naturalistic novel about Bob Jones, a Los Angeles shipyard worker during World War II.

_____. LONELY CRUSADE. New York: Alfred A. Knopf, 1947. 398 p.

The efforts of a black union organizer, Lee Gordon, to gain a sense of identity.

_____. PINKTOES, A NOVEL. New York: G.P. Putnam's Sons, 1965. 256 p. Reprint of Olympia Press edition. Paris: 1961.

Satiric novel concerned with Mamie Mason's efforts to gather influential whites in her sphere.

_____. THE PRIMITIVE. New York: New American Library, 1956. 151 p.

Concerned with the destructive relationship between Jesse, a black novelist, and Kris, a white female administrator of a foundation.

_____. THE QUALITY OF HURT. New York: Doubleday, 1972. 351 p.

An autobiographical account of Himes's life up to 1954. Himes plans a second volume concerning his life since 1954.

_____. THE REAL COOL KILLERS. New York: Berkeley, 1959. 159 p.

About pseudo-Moslems and other "cool cats" in Harlem.

_____. RUN MAN RUN. New York: G.P. Putnam's Sons, 1966. 192 p.

Racist white policeman becomes a psychotic killer who pursues a black porter throughout the novel.

_____. THE THIRD GENERATION. Cleveland: World Publishing Co., 1954. 350 p.

Novel of three generations of a black family from slavery to free-dom and security, to degeneration and disaster.

Margolies, Edward. "Experiences of the Expatriate Writer: Chester Himes." CLA JOURNAL 15 (June 1972): 421-27.

If one reads the expatriate novels of Chester Himes "correctly," one finds that "Himes' European perspective has left him even more pessimistic."

_____. "The Thrillers of Chester Himes." STUDIES IN BLACK LITERATURE 1 (Summer 1970): 1-11.

A discussion of Himes's grim humor in his thrillers. Margolies feels that Himes's humor derives from the "pop, campy, pulp magazine character" of his stories.

Nelson, Raymond. "Domestic Harlem: The Detective Fiction of Chester Himes." VIRGINIA QUARTERLY REVIEW 48 (Spring 1972): 260-76.

Concerned with the series of novels about the adventures of Coffin Ed Johnson and Grave Digger Jones. Himes referred to the books as his "Harlem Domestic" series.

LANGSTON HUGHES

Davis, Arthur. "The Tragic Mulatto Theme in Six Works of Langston Hughes."
PHYLON 16 (1955): 195-204.

An examination of the theme of the "tragic mulatto" in THE WEARY
BLUES (1925), FINE CLOTHES TO THE JEW (1927), THE WAYS OF
WHITE FOLKS (1934), THE BARRIER (1950), and LAUGHING TO
KEEP FROM CRYING (1952).

Emanuel, James A. LANGSTON HUGHES. New York: Twayne Publishers,
1967. 192 p.

The first full-length biography of Hughes. Useful bibliography is
included.

Farrison, W. Edward. "Langston Hughes: Poet of the Negro Renaissance."
CLA JOURNAL 15 (June 1972): 401-10.

"Amid the confusion of tongues of groups who during his last twenty
years flourished from time to time as would-be saviours of the Negro,
Hughes held fast to the original and best ideals of the Negro Renaissance."

Hughes, Langston. ASK YOUR MAMA; 12 MOODS FOR JAZZ. New York:
Alfred A. Knopf, 1961. 92 p.

Twelve poems written to be read aloud to jazz music. Includes
directions for musical accompaniment.

_____. THE BEST OF SIMPLE. New York: Hill and Wang, 1961. 245 p.

The best of Hughes's short fiction concerning the comic protagonist,
Jesse B. Simple.

_____. FAMOUS AMERICAN NEGROES. New York: Dodd, 1954. 147 p.

Biographies of famous Afro-Americans from Phillis Wheatley in the colonial period to Ralph Bunche and Jackie Robinson in the twentieth century.

_____. FAMOUS NEGRO MUSIC MAKERS. New York: Dodd, 1955. 179 p.

Brief biographies of Afro-American musicians written primarily for juvenile readers.

_____. FIELDS OF WONDER. New York: Alfred A. Knopf, 1947. 114 p.

Poetry.

_____. FIGHT FOR FREEDOM: THE STORY OF THE NATIONAL ASSOCIATION FOR THE ADVANCEMENT OF COLORED PEOPLE. New York: W.W. Norton, 1962. 224 p.

Hughes's history of the organization and growth of the NAACP. Illustrated, with bibliography and index.

_____. THE FIRST BOOK OF AFRICA. New York: Franklin Watts, 1961. 82 p.

A book written for juvenile readers about modern and ancient African history, the medieval Negro kingdoms, the Moslem influence, the European civilization.

_____. FIRST BOOK OF JAZZ. New York: Franklin Watts, 1955. 65 p.

Written for readers of ages twelve to sixteen. Lists the "ten basic elements of jazz," famous jazz musicians, and Hughes's one hundred favorite jazz and blues records.

_____. FIRST BOOK OF RHYTHMS. New York: Franklin Watts, 1954. 63 p.

The "rhythms" discussed by Hughes are of music, dance, painting, sculpture, athletics, architecture, and nature.

_____. FIRST BOOK OF THE WEST INDIES. New York: Franklin Watts, 1956. 62 p.

Written for juvenile readers, this study lists famous men and women born in the West Indies, the population and capitals of the islands, and the tropical plants of the region.

_____. FIVE PLAYS. Bloomington: Indiana University Press, 1963. xvii, 258 p.

Contains three plays of the 1930s, MULATTO, SOUL GONE HOME, and LITTLE HAM as well as two post-World War II plays, SIMPLY

HEAVENLY, based on SIMPLE TAKES A WIFE, and TAMBOURINES
TO GLORY. SIMPLY HEAVENLY is the definitive folk comedy of
Harlem life; TAMBOURINES TO GLORY is a folk play which,
though technically a comedy, is also a morality play and musical
melodrama.

_____. LAMENT FOR "DARK PEOPLES," AND OTHER POEMS. Edited with
an introduction by H. Driessen. Amsterdam: H. van Krimpen, 1944. 48 p.

Poetry.

_____. LAUGHING TO KEEP FROM CRYING. New York: Henry Holt,
1952. 206 p.

Twenty-four short stories concerned with blacks and other minority
groups and their relationship with the dominant whites.

_____. MONTAGE OF A DREAM DEFERRED. New York: Henry Holt, 1951. 75 p.

Poetry.

_____. "MOTHER AND CHILD." In BLACK DRAMA ANTHOLOGY, edited by
Woodie King, Jr., and Ron Milner, pp. 399-405. New York: New American
Library, 1971.

A group of Negro church women discuss the implications of a
black man's love affair with a white woman and how it will cause
trouble in the black community.

_____. ONE WAY TICKET. New York: Alfred A. Knopf, 1949. 136 p.

Poetry.

_____. THE PANTHER AND THE LASH: POEMS OF OUR TIMES. New York:
Alfred A. Knopf, 1967. 101 p.

Poetry.

_____. SELECTED POEMS. New York: Alfred A. Knopf, 1959. 297 p.

Poetry.

_____. SIMPLE SPEAKS HIS MIND. New York: Simon & Schuster, 1950.
231 p.

A collection of the Jesse B. Simple stories which originally appeared in the Chicago DEFENDER.

_____. SIMPLE STATES A CLAIM. New York: Rinehart, 1957. 191 p.

Simple (Jesse B. Simple) gives his humorous views on racial questions and American society.

_____. SIMPLE'S UNCLE SAM. New York: Hill and Wang, 1965. 180 p.

Forty-six stories, collected here for the first time, in which Hughes's character Jesse B. Simple makes witty comments on American life.

_____. SIMPLE TAKES A WIFE. New York: Simon & Schuster, 1953. 240 p.

Stories told through conversations between the author and Jesse B. Simple.

_____. SOMETHING IN COMMON AND OTHER STORIES. New York: Hill and Wang, 1963. 236 p.

Thirty-seven stories written by Langston Hughes, eleven of them collected for the first time in book form.

_____. SWEET FLYPAPER OF LIFE. New York: Simon & Schuster, 1956. 98 p.

A combination of fiction and documentary of life in Harlem as seen by an elderly black grandmother, with photographs by Roy DeCarava.

_____. TAMBOURINES TO GLORY. New York: John Day, 1958. 188 p.

Two Harlem women found a church of their own.

_____, ed. AFRICAN TREASURY. New York: Crown, 1960. 207 p.

Forty selections of articles, essays, poems, and short fiction by contemporary black Africans collected by Hughes over a period of six years.

Hughes, Langston, and Meltzer, Milton. BLACK MAGIC: A PICTORIAL HISTORY OF THE NEGRO IN AMERICAN ENTERTAINMENT. New York: Prentice-Hall, 1968. 375 p.

A pictorial history of the black artist (dancer, actor, singer, and composer) from the time of slavery to the 1960s.

_____. PICTORIAL HISTORY OF THE NEGRO IN AMERICA. New York: Crown, 1956. 316 p.

A pictorial history of Afro-Americans from 1619 to the 1950s.

Kent, George [E.]. "Langston Hughes and the Afro-American Folk and Cultural Tradition." In his BLACKNESS AND THE ADVENTURE OF WESTERN CULTURE, pp. 53-75. Chicago: Third World Press, 1972.

Langston Hughes "chose to build his vision on the basis of the folk experience as it had occurred in the South and as it appeared modified in the modern industrial city."

Mintz, Lawrence E. "Langston Hughes's Jesse B. Simple: The Urban Negro As Wise Fool." SATIRE NEWSLETTER 7 (Fall 1969): 11-21.

Simple is an urban black "crackerbarrel philosopher" and is in the tradition of the American wise fool.

O'Daniel, Therman. LANGSTON HUGHES, BLACK GENIUS: A CRITICAL EXAMINATION. New York: William Morrow, 1971. 245 p.

Thirteen essays examining the diverse talents of Hughes: seven plays, ten volumes of poetry, nine books of fiction, seven juvenile books, two opera librettos, two autobiographies, and translations into English of a French novel and two volumes of Spanish poetry.

Presley, James. "The American Dream of Langston Hughes." SOUTHWEST REVIEW 48 (Autumn 1963): 380-86.

What Hughes's harshest right-wing critics failed to realize is that Hughes himself was a great believer in the American Dream.

KRISTIN HUNTER

Hunter, Kristin. GOD BLESS THE CHILD. New York: Charles Scribner's Sons, 1964. 307 p.

Novel about Rosie Fleming's frantic pursuit of the American Dream.

_____. THE LANDLORD. New York: Charles Scribner's Sons, 1966. 338 p.

Psychotic young man buys tenement full of nonpaying renters, most of whom are black. This action is therapeutic for him.

_____. THE SOUL BROTHERS AND SISTER LOU. New York: Charles Scribner's Sons, 1968. 248 p.

Sister Lou transcends hatred engendered by a white policeman's killing of an innocent member of her club.

YUSEF IMAN

Iman, Yusef. SOMETHING BLACK: FREEDOM POETRY. Newark, N.J.: Jihad
Productions, 1966. 40 p.

Poetry.

TED JOANS

Joans, Ted. AFRODISIA: NEW POEMS. New York: Hill and Wang, 1970. 150 p.

Poetry.

_____. ALL OF TED JOANS AND NO MORE: POEMS AND COLLAGES. New York: Excelsior Press, 1961. 93 p.

Poetry.

_____. A BLACK MANIFESTO IN JAZZ POETRY AND PROSE. London: Calder and Boyars, 1971. 92 p.

Poetry.

_____. BLACK POW-WOW: JAZZ POEMS. New York: Hill and Wang, 1969. 130 p.

Poetry.

_____. THE TRUTH: A POEM. Amsterdam: Surrealistisch Kabinet, 1968. 40 p.

Poetry.

LEROI JONES (AMIRI BARAKA)

Note: Everett LeRoi Jones has published under various names: LeRoi Jones, Amiri Baraka, Imamu Amiri Baraka, Ameer Baraka, and Imamu Ameer Baraka. Hudson's brief bibliography is useful in this context in that it includes the various names under which the titles listed in this bibliography were published. All are listed here under Jones, LeRoi.

Adams, George R. "'My Christ' in DUTCHMAN." CLA JOURNAL 15 (September 1971): 54-58.

> Jones's character Clay Williams represents several archetypes: the Old Adam tempted and expelled from Eden after he reveals his possession of forbidden knowledge (about his blackness), the New Adam, a black Messiah, and the Christ of the Second Advent coming to avenge all murdered blacks.

Alsop, Stewart. "American Sickness." SATURDAY EVENING POST, 13 July 1968, p. 6.

> An editorial on the polarities represented in riot-torn Newark, New Jersey, by LeRoi Jones and Tony Imperiale.

Bigsby, C.W.E. "LeRoi Jones." In his CONFRONTATION AND COMMITMENT: A STUDY OF THEMES AND TRENDS IN CONTEMPORARY AMERICAN DRAMA, 1959-1966, pp. 138-55. Columbia: University of Missouri Press, 1968.

> A discussion of Jones's THE TOILET, DUTCHMAN, and THE SLAVE.

Brecht, Stefan. "LeRoi Jones' Slave Ship." DRAMA REVIEW 14 (1970): 212-19.

> SLAVE SHIP seen as "national epos" and "patriotic spectacle."

Brown, Cecil. "About LeRoi Jones." EVERGREEN REVIEW 14 (February 1970): 65-70.

> An essay on Jones and his drama.

_____. "Apotheosis of a Prodigal Son." KENYON REVIEW 30 (1968): 654-61.

A general review of Jones's early drama, with some personal observations on Jones himself.

_____. "Black Literature and LeRoi Jones." BLACK WORLD 19 (June 1970): 24-31.

An assessment of Jones's "The Myth of a Negro Literature."

Brown, Lloyd W. "LeRoi Jones As Novelist: Theme and Structure in THE
SYSTEM OF DANTE'S HELL." NEGRO AMERICAN LITERATURE FORUM 7
(Winter 1973): 132-42.

An examination of three techniques employed by Jones--irony, plot,
and narrative viewpoint--in a description of the hero's descent into
the hell of self-hate.

Brustein, Robert. "Three Plays and a Protest." NEW REPUBLIC 152 (23 January
1965): 32-33.

Contains a brief review of Jones's THE SLAVE and THE TOILET.
THE TOILET, says Brustein, "is not a drama but a psycho-drama,
designed for the acting out of sado-masochistic racial fantasies."
THE SLAVE is a play "out of control," exhibiting a "raving chau-
vinism."

Coleman, Mike. "What Is Black Theater? An Interview with Imamu Amiri
Baraka." BLACK WORLD 20 (April 1971): 32-36.

In the interview Jones distinguishes between "black theater" and
"show business" and defines what he means by the expression "negro
theater pimp."

Costello, Donald P. "LeRoi Jones: Black Man As Victim." COMMONWEAL
88 (June 1968): 436-40.

An analysis of Jones's THE TOILET, DUTCHMAN, and THE SLAVE.
Jones has sacrificed his art to his hatred for the whites.

"Curtains for LeRoi Jones." TIME, 12 January 1968, p. 14.

A report on the trial of LeRoi Jones in the court of Judge Leon
Kapp after the Newark riots. The judge admitted as evidence of
Jones's complicity in the riots a poem that Jones had published in
the EVERGREEN REVIEW.

Dennison, George. "The Demagogy of LeRoi Jones." COMMENTARY 39
(February 1965): 67-70.

An examination of the "propaganda" projected by Jones in his plays, THE TOILET and THE SLAVE, and in his public addresses.

Dorn, Edward, and Jones, LeRoi. HANDS UP. New York: Corinth Books, 1964. Unpaged.

Poetry.

"Evasive Action." NEWSWEEK, 28 December 1964, pp. 56-57.

A review of Jones's THE TOILET and THE SLAVE. Reacts against the racism implicit in Jones's plays.

"Hopes, Dreams, Fantasies." NEWSWEEK, 19 February 1973, p. 75.

A theater review discussing Baraka's (Jones's) play A RECENT KILLING, an autobiographical drama based on Jones's experience in the air force.

Hudson, Theodore R. FROM LEROI JONES TO AMIRI BARAKA: THE LITERARY WORKS. Durham, N.C.: Duke University Press, 1973. 222 p.

A biographical and critical study of Jones and his art.

_____. A LEROI JONES (AMIRI BARAKA) BIBLIOGRAPHY: A KEYED RE-SEARCH GUIDE TO WORKS BY LEROI JONES AND TO WRITING ABOUT HIM AND HIS WORKS. Washington, D.C.: By the author, 1971. 18 p.

Jackson, Esther M. "LeRoi Jones: Form and the Progression of Consciousness." CLA JOURNAL 17 (September 1973): 33-56.

An examination of Jones's career as artist and thinker as "a progression from lyrical to moral consciousness."

"The Jones Boy." NEWSWEEK, 2 May 1966, p. 106.

A review of Jones's collected nonfiction, HOME: SOCIAL ESSAYS. Sees Jones as an agent provocateur.

Jones, LeRoi. "African Slaves/American Slaves: Music Of." KULCHUR 4 (Fall 1961): 45-55.

Jones traces the African background for Afro-American blues, jazz, spirituals, and work songs.

_____. "Afrikan Revolution (Conakry, Guinea, February 4, 1973, after Amilcar Cabral's Funeral)." BLACK WORLD 22 (May 1973): 44-48.

Poem.

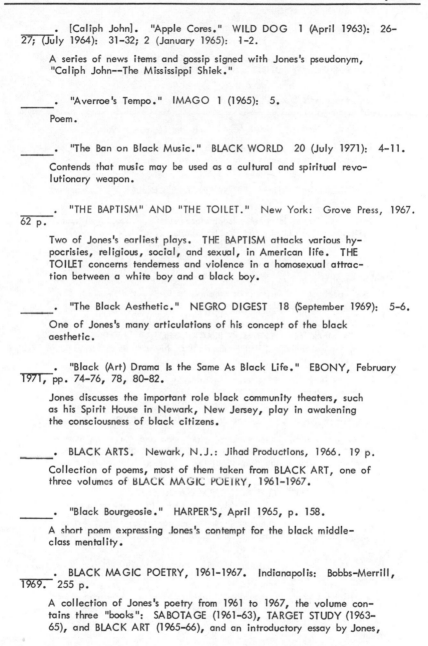

_____. [Caliph John]. "Apple Cores." WILD DOG 1 (April 1963): 26-27; (July 1964): 31-32; 2 (January 1965): 1-2.

A series of news items and gossip signed with Jones's pseudonym, "Caliph John--The Mississippi Shiek."

_____. "Averroe's Tempo." IMAGO 1 (1965): 5.

Poem.

_____. "The Ban on Black Music." BLACK WORLD 20 (July 1971): 4-11.

Contends that music may be used as a cultural and spiritual revolutionary weapon.

_____. "THE BAPTISM" AND "THE TOILET." New York: Grove Press, 1967. 62 p.

Two of Jones's earliest plays. THE BAPTISM attacks various hypocrisies, religious, social, and sexual, in American life. THE TOILET concerns tenderness and violence in a homosexual attraction between a white boy and a black boy.

_____. "The Black Aesthetic." NEGRO DIGEST 18 (September 1969): 5-6.

One of Jones's many articulations of his concept of the black aesthetic.

_____. "Black (Art) Drama Is the Same As Black Life." EBONY, February 1971, pp. 74-76, 78, 80-82.

Jones discusses the important role black community theaters, such as his Spirit House in Newark, New Jersey, play in awakening the consciousness of black citizens.

_____. BLACK ARTS. Newark, N.J.: Jihad Productions, 1966. 19 p.

Collection of poems, most of them taken from BLACK ART, one of three volumes of BLACK MAGIC POETRY, 1961-1967.

_____. "Black Bourgeosie." HARPER'S, April 1965, p. 158.

A short poem expressing Jones's contempt for the black middle-class mentality.

_____. BLACK MAGIC POETRY, 1961-1967. Indianapolis: Bobbs-Merrill, 1969. 255 p.

A collection of Jones's poetry from 1961 to 1967, the volume contains three "books": SABOTAGE (1961-63), TARGET STUDY (1963-65), and BLACK ART (1965-66), and an introductory essay by Jones,

"An Explanation of the Work."

_____. "A Black Mass." LIBERATOR 6 (June 1966): 14 ff. Also published in his FOUR BLACK REVOLUTIONARY PLAYS. Indianapolis: Bobbs-Merrill, 1969.

One of Jones's "ritual" plays of black consciousness.

_____. BLACK MUSIC. New York: William Morrow, 1968. 221 p.

A collection of essays, primarily reprinted from the magazine DOWNBEAT, concerned with black music in the 1960s.

_____. "Black Nationalism: 1972." BLACK SCHOLAR 4 (September 1972): 23-29.

Jones says "there is no total social progress for a people without institutions to maintain and develop their way of life (culture)."

_____. "Black Revolutionary Poets Should Also Be Playwrights." BLACK WORLD 22 (April 1972): 4-6.

Black poets should write skits or plays to further the creation of a national black consciousness.

_____. "A Black Value System." BLACK SCHOLAR 1 (November 1969): 54-60. Also published by Jihad Productions of Newark, New Jersey, in 1970 as a broadside.

An essay based on the seven principles of the U.S. organization headed by Maulana Ron Karenga.

_____. "Black Woman." BLACK WORLD 19 (July 1970): 7-11.

As long as anything separates the black man and the black woman from "moving together, being together, being absolutely in tune," then the spirit and the purpose of the "black nation" will not rise.

_____. BLOODRITES. In BLACK DRAMA ANTHOLOGY, edited by Woodie King, Jr., and Ron Milner, pp. 25-31. New York: New American Library, 1971.

A ritualistic drama which projects the message that "Black Art must be Collective, Committed, and Functional."

_____. BLUES PEOPLE: NEGRO MUSIC IN WHITE AMERICA. New York: William Morrow, 1963. 244 p.

A definitive study of the classic blues tradition in American society and the conditions that produced this unique musical heritage.

_____. "Brides of the Captured." NIAGARA FRONTIER REVIEW, Spring-Summer 1965, pp. 65-66.

Poem.

_____. "The Bridge." EVERGREEN REVIEW 4 (March-April 1960): 59-60.

Poem dedicated to Wieners and McClure.

_____. "The Burning General." WILD DOG 1 (May 1964): 44.

Poem.

_____. "Chapter." NIAGARA FRONTIER REVIEW, Spring-Summer 1965, pp. 57-58.

Poem.

_____. "The Colonial School of Melican Poetry." KULCHUR 3 (Summer 1963): 83-84.

An attack on issue no. 5 of the SIXTIES, edited by Robert Bly and William Dufy.

_____. "The Congress of African People." BLACK SCHOLAR 6 (January-February 1975): 2-5.

Jones was most instrumental in the formation of the Congress of African Peoples.

_____. "The Coronation of the Black Queen." BLACK SCHOLAR 1 (June 1970): 46-48.

Instead of European-oriented rites, Jones argues, black students should use the ceremony he outlines in this essay for the coronation of Campus Queens.

_____. "Corregidor." KULCHUR 5 (Spring 1965): 38.

A poem dedicated to Fred Herko, the dancer..

_____. "Correspondence." EVERGREEN REVIEW 2 (Spring 1959): 253-56.

A letter to the editors of EVERGREEN REVIEW concerning Jack Kerouac's essay, "The Essentials of Spontaneous Prose," and Kerouac's "spontaneous writing" style.

_____. "Cuba Libre." EVERGREEN REVIEW 15 (November-December 1960): 139-59. Republished by the Fair Play for Cuba Committee, New York, 1966, as a pamphlet.

Jones's impressions of a trip made with other American blacks to Cuba in July 1960. The trip was arranged by the Fair Play for Cuba Committee.

_____. THE DEAD LECTURER: POEMS. New York: Grove Press, 1974. 79 p.

Poetry.

_____. "Death Is Not As Natural As You Fags Seem to Think." IMAGO 1 (1965): 9.

Poem.

_____. "The Death of Horatio Alger." EVERGREEN REVIEW 9 (June 1965): 28-29, 92-93.

Short story about youth and racial misunderstanding.

_____. "THE DEATH OF MALCOLM X." In NEW PLAYS FROM THE BLACK THEATRE, edited by Ed Bullins, pp. 1-20. New York: Bantam Books, 1969.

A dramatic presentation of the murder of Malcolm X.

_____. "La Dolce Vita." KULCHUR 4 (Fall 1961): 85-90.

A review of Fellini's film.

_____. "THE DUTCHMAN" AND "THE SLAVE." New York: William Morrow, 1964. 88 p.

Two short plays by Jones centering on the black-white conflict. DUTCHMAN is concerned with the ritual murder of a black intellectual on a subway. THE SLAVE is about a black revolution in which a white intellectual is killed by a black revolutionary and former intellectual.

_____. "Engines." IMAGO 1 (1965): 6-8.

Poem.

_____. "The Evolver." NEGRO DIGEST 17 (September-October 1968): 58-59.

Poetry.

_____. "The Fire Must Be Permitted to Burn Full Up." JOURNAL OF BLACK POETRY 1 (Summer-Fall 1969): 62-65.

Essay calling for the revolutionary commitment of black writers.

_____. "Footnote to a Pretentious Book." FLOATING BEAR 18 (1962): 7.
Poem.

_____. Foreword to BLACK FIRE, AN ANTHOLOGY OF AFRO-AMERICAN
WRITING, edited by LeRoi Jones and Larry Neal, pp. 17-18. New York:
William Morrow, 1968.

Written in Jones's difficult latter style, the foreword states that
the anthology contains the works of the "wizards" and the "bards"
of "the constant conscious striving (jihad) of a nation coming back
into focus."

_____. "For Hettie in Her Fifth Month." BIG TABLE 1 (Spring 1960): 113-
14.

Poem.

_____. FOUR BLACK REVOLUTIONARY PLAYS. Indianapolis: Bobbs-Merrill,
1969. 89 p.

Includes EXPERIMENTAL DEATH KIT UNIT #1, A BLACK MASS,
GREAT GOODNESS OF LIFE, and MADHEART. Also contains a
two-page introduction by Jones and "Why No J-E-L-L-O," a note
by Jones stating why the publisher refused to include the play
J-E-L-L-O in this collection.

_____. "From the System of Dante's Hell: The Eighth Ditch." FLOATING
BEAR 9 (1961): 1-7.

Fragment from the novel.

_____. "Going Down Slow." EVERGREEN REVIEW 10 (October 1966): 41-
43, 93-96.

Short story about a jealous man driven to murder.

_____. "Habari Gani." BLACK WORLD 22 (May 1973): 43-44.
Poem.

_____. "The Heavy." NIAGARA FRONTIER REVIEW, Spring-Summer 1965,
p. 59.

Poem.

_____. HOME: SOCIAL ESSAYS. New York: William Morrow, 1966.
252 p.

A collection of twenty-four essays written after 1960 on such subjects as racism, politics, foreign policy, sex, literature.

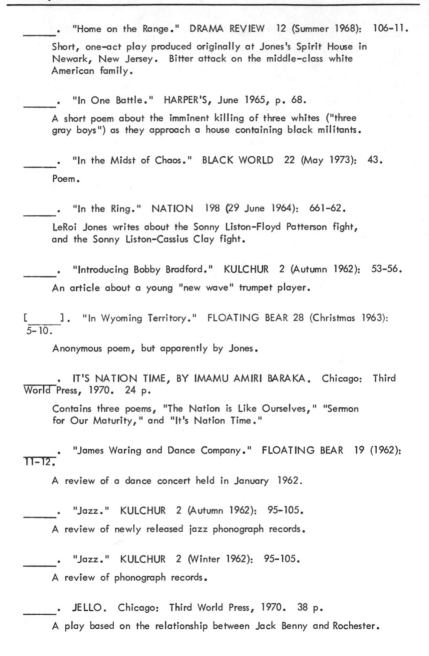

_____. "Home on the Range." DRAMA REVIEW 12 (Summer 1968): 106-11.

Short, one-act play produced originally at Jones's Spirit House in Newark, New Jersey. Bitter attack on the middle-class white American family.

_____. "In One Battle." HARPER'S, June 1965, p. 68.

A short poem about the imminent killing of three whites ("three gray boys") as they approach a house containing black militants.

_____. "In the Midst of Chaos." BLACK WORLD 22 (May 1973): 43.

Poem.

_____. "In the Ring." NATION 198 (29 June 1964): 661-62.

LeRoi Jones writes about the Sonny Liston-Floyd Patterson fight, and the Sonny Liston-Cassius Clay fight.

_____. "Introducing Bobby Bradford." KULCHUR 2 (Autumn 1962): 53-56.

An article about a young "new wave" trumpet player.

[____]. "In Wyoming Territory." FLOATING BEAR 28 (Christmas 1963): 5-10.

Anonymous poem, but apparently by Jones.

_____. IT'S NATION TIME, BY IMAMU AMIRI BARAKA. Chicago: Third World Press, 1970. 24 p.

Contains three poems, "The Nation is Like Ourselves," "Sermon for Our Maturity," and "It's Nation Time."

_____. "James Waring and Dance Company." FLOATING BEAR 19 (1962): 11-12.

A review of a dance concert held in January 1962.

_____. "Jazz." KULCHUR 2 (Autumn 1962): 95-105.

A review of newly released jazz phonograph records.

_____. "Jazz." KULCHUR 2 (Winter 1962): 95-105.

A review of phonograph records.

_____. JELLO. Chicago: Third World Press, 1970. 38 p.

A play based on the relationship between Jack Benny and Rochester.

Printed with an introduction entitled "Negro Theater Pimp Gets
Big Off Nationalism," which examines the connection between
black ideology and black theater.

_____. "Jim Brown on the Screen." BLACK THEATRE 4 (April 1970): 32;
also in BLACK WORLD 19 (June 1970): 12-13.

Poem.

_____. JUNKIES ARE FULL OF (SHHH...). In BLACK DRAMA ANTHOL-
OGY, edited by Woodie King, Jr., and Ron Milner, pp. 11-23. New York:
New American Library, 1971.

A one-act play attacking dope peddling and dope addiction among
black people.

_____. "Lady Bug." NIAGARA FRONTIER REVIEW, Spring-Summer 1965,
p. 64.

Poem.

_____. "The Largest Ocean in the World." JUGEN 8 (1962): 58-59.

Short sketch about a boy's fantasies and impressions as he moves
through a street at night.

_____. "Leadbelly Gives an Autograph." TROBAR (1964): 38-39.

A long poem from Jones's early avant-garde period.

_____. "Lefty." NIAGARA FRONTIER REVIEW, Spring-Summer 1965, pp. 64-
65.

Poem.

_____. "Letter to Diane DiPrima." FLOATING BEAR 5 (1961): 4.

A letter concerning the future editorial policies of their joint
editorship of the FLOATING BEAR.

_____. "Like Rousseau, History As a Process." POETRY 105 (December 1965):
161-62.

Two poems, the first a love poem, the second, personal and intro-
spective.

_____. "Lines to Garcia Lorca." JUGEN 1 (1958): 17-18.

Poem.

_____. "Look Inside." BLACK WORLD 22 (May 1973): 43.

Poem.

_____. "MADHEART." In BLACK FIRE, AN ANTHOLOGY OF AFRO-AMERICAN WRITING, edited by LeRoi Jones and Larry Neal, pp. 574-88. New York: William Morrow, 1968. Also published in Jones's FOUR BLACK REVOLUTIONARY PLAYS (see above).

A psycho-mythic play utilizing overt and subliminal messages to purge white consciousness and white values from the minds of the black audience.

_____. "Morning Purpose." NATION 198 (6 January 1964): 37.

A poem to the morning that sends us, "Whip shaped, to deal with romance."

_____. "The Need for a Cultural Base to Civil Rites and Bpower Mooments" [sic]. In THE BLACK POWER REVOLT, edited by Floyd Barbour, pp. 119-26. Boston: Porter Sargent, 1968.

Argues that no revolution can be successful without strong cultural underpinnings.

_____. "The Negro Middle Class Flight from Heritage." NEGRO DIGEST 13 (February 1964): 80-95.

An excerpt from Jones's book, BLUES PEOPLE: NEGRO MUSIC IN WHITE AMERICA.

_____. "The New Sheriff." EVERGREEN REVIEW 5 (July-August 1961): 96.

A short, erotic poem. Central image is white virgins.

_____. "Node." JUGEN 6 (1960): 38.

Poem.

_____. "A Note on the Twelve Poems." FLOATING BEAR 6 (1961): 7-8.

An editor's note on the twelve poems which precede it.

_____. "OK Shoot!" BLACK WORLD 22 (May 1973): 40.

Poem.

_____. "Parthenos." JUGEN 4 (1959): 23-26.

Poem.

_____. "Philistinism and the Negro Writer." In ANGER AND BEYOND: THE NEGRO WRITER IN THE UNITED STATES, edited by Herbert Hill, pp. 51-61. New York: Harper & Row, 1966.

One of Jones's many essays arguing for black aesthetic.

_____. "A Poem Some People Will Have to Understand." WILD DOG 1 (13 July 1963): 11.

Poem.

_____. "Police." DRAMA REVIEW 12 (Summer 1968): 112-15.

Short satiric one-act play about a black policeman and a white policeman in the Negro community. Police are portrayed as insane and homosexual.

_____. "The Politics of Rich Painters." FLOATING BEAR 22 (1962): 6-7.

Poem.

_____. PREFACE TO A TWENTY-VOLUME SUICIDE NOTE. New York: Totem Press in association with Corinth Books, 1961. 47 p.

Poetry.

_____. "Putdown of the Whore of Babylon." JUGEN 7 (1961): 4-5.

A comment on the granting of the National Book Award to Robert Lowell and the Pulitzer Prize for poetry to W.D. Snodgrass.

_____. RAISE, RACE, RAYS, RAZE. New York: Random House, 1971. 169 p.

Essays which were published after 1965. A collage of poetry, prose, politics, and black nationalism.

_____. "Relurk." NIAGARA FRONTIER REVIEW, Spring-Summer 1965, pp. 60-61.

Poem.

_____. "The Screamers." GENESIS WEST 2 (Fall 1963): 81-86.

A short story about ecstatic reactions to black music which is mistaken for a riot.

_____. SLAVE SHIP. Newark, N.J.: Jihad Productions, 1969. 16 p. Also in NEGRO DIGEST (April 1967): 62-74.

A one-act play by Jones, concerned with the crossing of the Atlantic of a slave ship. One of Jones's more "mythic" dramas.

_____. "Slice of Life." JUGEN 1 (1968): 16.

Poem.

_____. "Suppose Sorrow Was a Time Machine." JUGEN 2 (1958): 9-11.

A short story about a series of avatars of a person named "Tom" as he passes through the history of black American experience.

_____. THE SYSTEM OF DANTE'S HELL. New York: Grove Press, 1965. 132 p.

A narrative written in an innovative style which examines the author's childhood and youth, his experiences in a Newark slum, a small southern town, and New York City.

_____. TALES. New York: Grove Press, 1968. 132 p.

A collection of sixteen short stories, many of which were previously published in journals. Most of the stories are autobiographical.

_____. "Target Study." NIAGARA FRONTIER REVIEW, Spring-Summer 1965, pp. 54-56.

Poem.

_____. "Technology and Ethos." In AMISTAD 2: WRITINGS ON BLACK HISTORY AND CULTURE, edited by John A. Williams and Charles F. Harris, pp. 319-22. New York: Random House, 1971.

An attack on the technological West and the morality that produced it.

_____. "They Think You're an Airplane and You're Really a Bird!" EVERGREEN REVIEW 11 (December 1967): 51-53, 96-97.

An interview with LeRoi Jones conducted by Saul Gottlieb on 6 September 1967, at Spirit House after the Newark riots.

_____. "Three Poems by LeRoi Jones." EVERGREEN REVIEW 11 (December 1967): 48-49.

Three short poems, "Leroy," "Black People," and "The Black Man Is Making New Gods," which illustrate Jones's increasing militancy and anti-Semitism.

_____. "Tight Rope." NATION 197 (13 July 1963): 40.

A poem addressed to a woman whose laughter is like bright beads.

_____. "The Toilet." KULCHUR 3 (Spring 1963): 25-39.

Early printing of Jones's one-act play.

_____. "Tokenism: 300 Years for 5 Cents." KULCHUR 2 (Spring 1962):
29-39.

An essay in which Jones defines "tokenism" as "the setting up of
social stalemates or the extension of meager privilege to some few
'selected' Negroes in order that a semblance of compromise or
'progress,' or a lessening of racial repression seems to be achieved,
while actually helping to maintain the status quo just as rigidly. . . ."

_____. "Toward Ideological Clarity." BLACK WORLD 24 (November 1974):
24-33, 84-95.

A short version of a position paper by Baraka, who sees the black
liberation movement as "the vanguard of struggle within the U.S.
not only against racism but for socialism."

_____. "Toward the Creation of Political Institutions for All African Peoples."
BLACK WORLD 21 (October 1972): 54-78.

A comparison of the significance of the National Black Political
Convention, held in Gary, Indiana, and the Democratic National
Convention held in Miami.

_____. "Two Poems." KULCHUR 4 (Winter 1964-65): 2-3.

The two poems are "A Western Lady" and "Correction." These
poems are similar to his earlier poetry in that they are not militant.

_____. "Two Yale Men." KULCHUR 2 (Autumn 1962): 88-91.

A review of Alan Dugan's POEMS and Jack Gilbert's VIEWS OF
JEOPARDY.

_____. "US." BLACK WORLD 22 (May 1973): 41-42.

Poem.

_____. "'Valery As Dictator,' 'The Liar,' 'Snake Eyes.'" POETRY 103
(December 1963): 157-59.

Three short poems, apparently autobiographical.

_____. "What Does Non-Violence Mean?" NEGRO DIGEST 14 (November
1964): 4-19.

Jones's views on various aspects of the civil rights movement.

_____, ed. AFRICAN CONGRESS: A DOCUMENTARY OF THE FIRST MOD-
ERN PAN-AFRICAN CONGRESS. New York: William Morrow, 1972. 512 p.

This volume, edited with an introduction by LeRoi Jones, contains
the proceedings of this first Congress of African people held in
Atlanta in 1970. Included are both speeches and workshops.

_____. "Why I Changed My Ideology: Black Nationalism and Socialist Revo-
lution." BLACK WORLD 24 (July 1975): 30-42.

An article adapted from an address delivered by the head of the
Congress of African People in Detroit.

Jones, LeRoi, and Abernathy, Billy. IN OUR TERRIBLENESS: PICTURES OF
THE HIP WORLD. Indianapolis: Bobbs-Merrill, 1969. Unpaged.

"A poetic-photographic essay." Title of book is derived from
black slang, which ironically inverts (or subverts) the meaning of
white language. For example, "bad" is black slang for good,
"terrible" signifies splendid or superb.

Jones, LeRoi, and Neal, Larry, eds. BLACK FIRE: AN ANTHOLOGY OF
AFRO-AMERICAN WRITING. New York: William Morrow, 1968. 670 p.

An anthology of young post-World War II black writers. Expressive
of the militant anger that characterized the mood of the late 1960s.
Contains essays, poetry, fiction, and drama.

Klinkowitz, Jerome. "LeRoi Jones: DUTCHMAN as Drama." NEGRO AMERI-
CAN LITERATURE FORUM 7 (Fall 1973): 123-26.

"DUTCHMAN, written at the point in Jones' life when he abandoned his white wife and his posture as a Village intellectual in
favor of a more racial militancy, is not only substantial drama,
but is cathartic within Jones own career."

Lederer, Richard. "The Language of LeRoi Jones' 'The Slave.'" STUDIES IN
BLACK LITERATURE 4 (Spring 1973): 14-16.

Walker Vessels "knows that his single-minded hatred has caused
him his 'creative impulse,' his art, and has pulverized his language,
the badge of his identity."

Llorens, David. "Ameer (LeRoi Jones) Baraka." EBONY, August 1969, pp. 75-
83.

Jones's rise to the leadership of the black arts movement is traced
from his founding of the short-lived Black Arts Repertory Theatre-

School in Harlem to Spirit House in Newark, his activities with
the Black Community Development and Defense organization, and
his role as a minister of the Kawaida faith.

Margolies, Edward. "Prospects: LeRoi Jones?" In his NATIVE SONS, pp. 190-
99. Philadelphia: J.B. Lippincott, 1969.

Deplores Jones's "mad pronouncements" and "hysterical nonsense,"
yet admits that beneath his despair and masochism Jones is an artist.

Marvin X. See under X, Marvin.

Miller, Jeanne-Marie. "The Plays of LeRoi Jones." CLA JOURNAL 14
(March 1971): 331-39.

A study of DUTCHMAN, THE SLAVE, THE TOILET, BAPTISM,
EXPERIMENTAL DEATH KIT UNIT #1, A BLACK MASS, GREAT
GOODNESS OF LIFE, MADHEART, and SLAVE SHIP.

Mootry, Maria K. "Themes and Symbols in Two Plays by LeRoi Jones." NEGRO
DIGEST 18 (April 1969): 42-47.

An analysis of THE BAPTISM and THE TOILET. In THE BAPTISM,
Jones dramatizes a dichotomy in attitudes toward the church among
black people. THE TOILET represents a personal dilemma for a
sensitive, intelligent black man.

Munro, C. Lynn. "LeRoi Jones: A Man in Transition." CLA JOURNAL 17
(September 1973): 57-78.

Traces Jones's transition from an allegiance to white standards and
"serious" writing to an evolving, personal ideology, mythology,
and ritual in his "political art."

"New Scripts in Newark." TIME, 26 April 1968, pp. 18-19.

A report on Jones's apparent political turnabout in dealing with
white pressure groups in Newark.

O'Brien, John. "Racial Nightmares and the Search for Self: An Explication
of LeRoi Jones' 'A Chase (Alighier's Dream).'" NEGRO AMERICAN LITERATURE
FORUM 7 (Fall 1973): 89-90.

"A Chase" is more "a verbal montage or prose poem in which we
are bombarded by a series of rapid images of ghetto sounds, sights,
and smells" rather than a conventional short story.

Oliver, Edith. "Off Broadway." NEW YORKER, 26 December 1964, pp. 50-52.

A slight and superficial review of Jones's THE TOILET and THE
SLAVE.

LeRoi Jones

Peavy, Charles D. "Myth, Magic, and Manhood in LeRoi Jones' MADHEART."
STUDIES IN BLACK LITERATURE 1 (Summer 1970): 12-20.

A discussion of Jones's use of Christian, Arabic, and Hebraic
mythology combined with elements of Artaud's theater of cruelty
to form a modern morality play for black consciousness.

Pennington-Jones, Paulette. "From Brother LeRoi Jones through THE SYSTEM OF
DANTE'S HELL to Imamu Ameer Baraka." JOURNAL OF BLACK STUDIES 4
(December 1973): 195-214.

Traces Jones's growth as he moves further away from the aesthetic
and the sensibilities of the white world to a militant black consciousness.

Resnik, H.S. "Brave New Words." SATURDAY REVIEW, 9 December 1967,
pp. 28-29.

Review of Jones's TALES. "The earlier tales are done in a fre-
quently bewildering telegraphic style that is more notation than
expression." The writing fluctuates between "precision and elegance"
and "the crude strength of slang."

Rice, Julian C. "LeRoi Jones' DUTCHMAN: A Reading." CONTEMPORARY
LITERATURE 12 (Winter 1971): 42-59.

DUTCHMAN is a warning about psychic realities which could cause
whites to act upon a compulsive urge to murder blacks, who, by
their lack of consciousness, would be accomplices in their own
destruction.

Schreck, S. "LeRoi Jones, or Poetics and Policemen, or Trying Heart, Bleeding
Heart." RAMPARTS MAGAZINE 6 (29 June 1968): 14-19.

A criticism of Jones's apparent compromising of his former political
position.

"Spasms of Fury." TIME, 25 December 1964, pp. 62-63.

A review of Jones's THE TOILET and THE SLAVE. Jones's true
target in these plays is the well-intentioned white intellectual,
but his portrayal of Negroes as "semi-cretinous urban cannibals"
is offensive.

Taylor, Willene P. "The Fall of Man Theme in Imamu Amiri Baraka's DUTCH-
MAN." NEGRO AMERICAN LITERATURE FORUM 7 (Winter 1973): 127-30.

An examination of DUTCHMAN from the perspective of Christian
typology.

Tener, Robert L. "Role Playing As a Dutchman." STUDIES IN BLACK LITERA-
TURE 3 (Autumn 1972): 17-21.

Tener argues that DUTCHMAN should be examined as "part of that
body of literature that treats with the duel of the sexes." The
play's immediate dramatic ancestors, says Tener, are Strindberg's
MISS JULIE, Ionesco's THE LESSON, and Albee's WHO'S AFRAID
OF VIRGINIA WOOLF?

Toure, Askia Muhammad (Roland Snellings). "Open Black Dialogue: A Letter
to Ed Spriggs concerning LeRoi Jones and Others." BLACK DIALOGUE 3
(Winter 1967-68): 3-4, 16.

A critical appraisal of Jones's obsession with black-white sexual
relations and his unconcern with the black masses, and a negative
response to Jones's play, SLAVESHIP.

Velde, Paul. "Pursued by the Furies." COMMONWEAL 88 (June 1968):
440-41.

A review of Jones's play HOME ON THE RANGE. "Despite the
blatant hocus pocus of the manipulation, and the language which
has nothing special, the overall result was a quite moving recitation
that curiously did seem to touch the chords of racial history."

X, Marvin. "Everything's Cool--An Interview with LeRoi Jones." BLACK
THEATRE 1 (n.d.): 16-23.

Important statements made by Jones on the language of his plays,
his movement toward more pantomime and ritual in his recent drama.

X, Marvin, and Faruk. "Islam and Black Art: An Interview with Ameer Baraka."
JOURNAL OF BLACK POETRY 1 (Fall 1968): 2-14.

Reprint of interview with LeRoi Jones from BLACK THEATRE, with
a foreword and afterword by Askia Muhammad Toure.

_____. "Islam and Black Art: An Interview with LeRoi Jones." NEGRO
DIGEST 18 (January 1969): 4-10, 77-80.

LeRoi Jones discusses the influence of Islam on his art in an interview conducted by Marvin X and Faruk.

WILLIAM MELVIN KELLEY

Kelley, William Melvin. DANCERS ON THE SHORE. Garden City, N.Y.:
Doubleday, 1964. 201 p.

A collection of sixteen short stories.

_____. DEM. Garden City, N.Y.: Doubleday, 1967. 210 p.

The story of Mitchell Pierce and his wife Tam, who gives birth to
fraternal twins, one white, one black. The husband searches for
the black father in an attempt to persuade him to take the black
child.

_____. A DIFFERENT DRUMMER. Garden City, N.Y.: Doubleday, 1962. 223 p.

The story of Tucker Caliban, a black who decides to heed Thoreau's
"different drummer." He burns his house, sows his farmland with
salt, kills his animals, and moves north. His departure causes the
mass exodus of other Negroes in the state.

_____. A DROP OF PATIENCE. Garden City, N.Y.: Doubleday, 1965.
237 p.

The story of a blind Negro jazz musician, Ludlow Washington, his
rise to fame, his distrust of the white world.

_____. DUNFORDS TRAVELS EVERYWHERES. Garden City, N.Y.: Double-
day, 1970. 201 p.

Highly imaginative chronicle of an "Ivy League Negro" in the real
world "beyond the Ivory Tower."

MARTIN LUTHER KING, JR.

Baldwin, James. "The Dangerous Road before Martin Luther King." HARPER'S 222 (February 1961): 33-42.

A personal, intimate, and sometimes controversial view of Martin Luther King, Jr.

Cleaver, Eldridge. "Requiem for Nonviolence." RAMPARTS 6 (May 1968): 48-49.

Cleaver comments on the murder of Martin Luther King and gives his views on what it meant for the future of America.

"The Execution of Dr. King." RAMPARTS 6 (May 1968): 47.

An editorial on the murder of King by the editors of RAMPARTS. "King's vision of nonviolent action was profoundly radical and threatening to men of power in America."

King, Martin Luther, Jr. "Honoring Dr. DuBois." In BLACK TITAN: W.E.B. DUBOIS, edited by John Henrik Clarke et al., pp. 176-83. Boston: Beacon Press, 1970.

King's tribute to the great black leader.

_____. STRENGTH TO LOVE. New York: Harper & Row, 1963. 146 p.

The Christian ideals and philosophy that motivated King.

_____. THE TRUMPET OF CONSCIENCE. New York: Harper & Row, 1968. 78 p.

King's creed as he formulated it a few months before his assassination.

_____. WHY WE CAN'T WAIT. New York: Harper & Row, 1964. 178 p.

Contains King's "Letter from a Birmingham Jail" and his explanation of the Negro's immediate demands for his rights.

Spratlen, Thaddeus H. "Martin Luther King, Jr.--The Man and His Legacy."
NEGRO DIGEST 17 (August 1968): 36-40.

A tribute to the work of King.

Williams, John Alfred. THE KING GOD DIDN'T SAVE. Boston: Little,
Brown, 1970. 221 p.

Controversial examination of King's civil rights movement.

ETHERIDGE KNIGHT

Knight, Etheridge. POEMS FROM PRISON. Preface by Gwendolyn Brooks.
Detroit: Broadside Press, 1968. 31 p.

Poetry.

_____, ed. BLACK VOICES FROM PRISON. New York: Pathfinder Press,
1970. 189 p.

Collection of articles, poems, and statements made by prisoners
collected by Knight.

Wilcox, Preston. Review of Etheridge Knight's BLACK VOICES FROM PRISON.
BLACK SCHOLAR 2 (April-May 1971): 54-55.

Wilcox notes Knight's "ability to extract humanity from what most
readers have been conditioned to perceive as being degradation."

DON L. LEE

Giddings, Paula. "From a Black Perspective: The Poetry of Don L. Lee."
In AMISTAD 2: WRITINGS ON BLACK HISTORY AND CULTURE, edited by
John A. Williams and Charles F. Harris, pp. 297-318. New York: Random
House, 1971.
    An analysis of Lee's poetry. Giddings sees Lee as a poet of
survival.

Lee, Don L. "The Bittersweet of Sweetback, or, Shake Yo Money Maker."
BLACK WORLD 21 (November 1971): 43-48.
    A review of Melvin Van Peebles' film, SWEET SWEETBACK'S
BAADASSSS SONG. Criticizes the film for being counterrevolu-
tionary and for its commercial exploitation of sex and violence.

———. BLACK PRIDE. Introduction by Dudley Randall. Detroit: Broadside
Press, 1968. 34 p.

———. DIRECTIONSCORE: SELECTED AND NEW POEMS. Detroit: Broadside Press, 1971. 208 p.
    Poetry.

———. DON'T CRY, SCREAM. Introduction by Gwendolyn Brooks. Detroit:
Broadside Press, 1969. 64 p.
    Poetry.

———. DYNAMITE VOICES I: BLACK POETS OF THE 1960'S. Detroit:
Broadside Press, 1971. 92 p.
    Contains comments on Conrad Kent Rivers, Mari Evans, Margaret
Danner, Sonia Sanchez, Etheridge Knight, Nikki Giovanni, and
many others.

_____. FOR BLACK PEOPLE (AND NEGROES TOO): A POETIC STATEMENT ON BLACK EXISTENCE IN AMERICA WITH A VIEW OF TOMORROW. Chicago: Third World Press, 1968. 4 p.

A broadside containing three poems: "In the Beginning," "Transition and Middle Passage," and "The End Is the Real World."

_____. THINK BLACK. Chicago: NuAce, 1967. 24 p.

Poetry.

_____. "Toward a Black Aesthetic: Black Poetry--Which Direction?" NEGRO DIGEST 17 (September-October 1968): 27-32.

Lee examines the various problems that must be confronted by the new black poets.

_____. "Toward a Definition: Black Poetry of the Sixties (After LeRoi Jones)." In THE BLACK AESTHETIC, edited by Addison Gayle, Jr., pp. 235-47. Garden City, N.Y.: Doubleday, 1971.

Lee makes comparison between black music and the new black poetry of the sixties.

_____. "Voices of the Seventies: Black Critics." BLACK WORLD 19 (September 1970): 24-30.

The black critic must have both a knowledge of world literature and a specialized knowledge of black literature.

_____. WE WALK THE WAY OF THE WORLD. Detroit: Broadside Press, 1970. 71 p.

Poetry.

Miller, Eugene E. "Some Black Thoughts on Don L. Lee's THINK BLACK! Thunk by a Frustrated White Academic Thinker." COLLEGE ENGLISH 34 (May 1973): 1094-1102.

Argues that the "black aesthetic Don Lee espouses shows us a way to bridge the gap between the 'avant-garde' concern for art in its own right, and the more traditional, humanistic view of art as 'criticism of life.'"

JULIUS LESTER

Lester, Julius. Introduction to LES BLANCS: THE COLLECTED LAST PLAYS OF LORRAINE HANSBERRY, pp. 3-32. New York: Random House, 1972.

Lester's introduction contains an appreciation of Hansberry as a dramatist as well as comments on A RAISIN IN THE SUN, THE SIGN IN SIDNEY BRUSTEIN'S WINDOW, and the three plays contained in the book: LES BLANCS, THE DRINKING GOURD, and WHAT USE ARE FLOWERS?

_____. LOOK OUT WHITEY! BLACK POWER'S GON GET YOUR MAMA! New York: Dial Press, 1968. 152 p.

An angry examination of the development of the black power movement in America. Lester believes that the present system in America must be destroyed.

_____. THE MUD OF VIETNAM: PHOTOGRAPHS AND POEMS. New York: Folklore Center, 1967. 12 p.

Poetry.

_____. "Race and Revolution." BLACK REVIEW 1 (1971): 68-86.

Lester examines the significance of the white youth culture in the context of black revolutionary goals. He sees ideological connections between the white hippie and the young black militant.

_____. REVOLUTIONARY NOTES. New York: Richard W. Baron, 1968. 209 p.

The first part of the book presents essays on the peace movement, the death of Che Guevara, the International War Crimes Tribunal, and the revolutionary. The second part presents "what I consider to be the most relevant of the weekly columns I have written for the GUARDIAN since the fall of 1967."

_____. SEARCH FOR THE NEW LAND. New York: Dial Press, 1969. 196 p.

Lester calls his book a "three part fugue, with variations." The three parts are (1) a history of America from Hiroshima to the present; (2) autobiography, including excerpts from letters and a journal; (3) "found poetry" drawn from newspaper and magazine articles. Most of the material reflects Lester's experience in the 1960s.

_____. TO BE A SLAVE. New York: Dial Press, 1968. 160 p.

A children's book made up of quotations from slave narratives connected by a running commentary on the black experience in America.

_____. TWO LOVE STORIES. New York: Dial Press, 1972. 180 p.

Two novellas, "Basketball Game," and "Catskill Morning."

_____. "The Valley of the Shadow of Death." BLACK REVIEW 2 (1972): 107-35.

A short story about love and death and black revolutionaries in Mississippi.

CLARENCE MAJOR

Major, Clarence. ALL-NIGHT VISITORS. New York: Olympia Press, 1969. 203 p.

The adventures of Eli Bolton in the Vietnam war and in black ghettos in Chicago and New York.

_____. THE DARK AND FEELING: REFLECTIONS ON BLACK AMERICAN WRITING. Chicago: Third World Press, 1974. 153 p.

A collection of essays on aesthetics, literary criticism, and on contemporary black writers such as Baldwin, Ellison, Cleaver, and Reed.

_____. NO. New York: Emerson Hall, 1972. 207 p.

Experimental novel attacking all the taboos in Western culture. Utilizes magic, mysticism, witchcraft, superstition, folklore, and Afro-American slang.

_____. PRIVATE LINE. London: Paul Bremen, 1971. 24 p.

Poetry.

_____. SWALLOW THE LAKE. Middletown, Conn.: Wesleyan University Press, 1970. 64 p.

Poetry.

_____. SYMPTOMS AND MADNESS. New York: Corinth Books, 1971. 76 p.

Poetry.

MALCOLM X

Breitman, George. "Malcolm X's Murder and the New York Police"; "More
Questions on Malcolm X's Murder"; and "Why Isn't Daily Press Interested in
Who Killed Malcolm X?" MILITANT, 12 July, 9 August, and 23 August 1965.

A three-part series of articles raising questions about the circum-
stances of Malcolm's assassination.

_____. THE LAST YEAR OF MALCOLM X: THE EVOLUTION OF A REVO-
LUTIONARY. New York: Merit Publishers, 1967. 169 p.

In this second book on Malcolm X, Breitman argues that Malcolm
X did change his philosophy before his assassination, becoming a
true revolutionary and internationalist.

_____, ed. BY ANY MEANS NECESSARY: SPEECHES, INTERVIEWS AND A
LETTER BY MALCOLM X. New York: Pathfinder Press, 1970. 184 p.

A companion volume to MALCOLM X SPEAKS, Breitman presents,
with brief editorial comments, Malcolm's interest in the Third
World countries and the bond between black people in the United
States, Asia, and Africa.

_____. MALCOLM X SPEAKS: SELECTED SPEECHES AND STATEMENTS.
New York: Grove Press, 1965. viii, 226 p.

Contains the major speeches of Malcolm X.

"Brother Malcolm: His Theme Now Is Violence." U.S. NEWS AND WORLD
REPORT, 23 March 1964, p. 19.

Brief reportage after Malcolm left the Muslims to form a "black
nationalist party" and to begin urging blacks to learn the use of
firearms in order to defend themselves.

Capouya, Emile. "A Brief Return from Mecca." SATURDAY REVIEW OF
LITERATURE 48 (20 November 1965): 43-44.

Malcolm personified both the nation's desire to rise above its sordid history and its degradation.

Clarke, John Henrik. "Malcolm X: The Man and His Times." NEGRO DI-GEST 18 (May 1969): 23–27, 60–65.

An adaptation of Clarke's introductory essay to a book on Malcolm X edited by Clarke and subsequently published (see below).

_____, ed. MALCOLM X: THE MAN AND HIS TIMES. New York: Mac-millan, 1969. 384 p.

Edited with an introduction and commentary by Clarke. Contains a bibliography (pp. 352–56) compiled by Peter Bailey, and articles and personal reflections by Malcolm's contemporaries.

Crawford, Marc. "Ominous Malcolm X Exits from the Muslims." LIFE, March 1964, p. 40.

Reportage on the rift between Malcolm X and Elijah Muhammad that resulted in Malcolm's separation from the Black Muslims.

"Death and Transfiguration." TIME, 5 March 1965, pp. 23–25.

A brief review of Malcolm's life from childhood to his murder in New York at the Audubon Ballroom.

"Death of a Desperado." NEWSWEEK, 8 March 1965, pp. 24–25.

Reportage of the murder of Malcolm X.

Epps, Archie. THE SPEECHES OF MALCOLM X AT HARVARD. New York: William Morrow, 1968. 191 p.

Transcripts of Malcolm X's three speeches at Harvard, transcripts of question-and-answer sessions between students and Malcolm X, and rebuttals of last two speeches by Harvard faculty members. Long and important introductory essay by Epps.

Gardner, Jigs. "The Murder of Malcolm X." MONTHLY REVIEW 16 (April 1965): 802–5.

An anticapitalist appraisal by a Socialist magazine of the facts of Malcolm's murder.

Goldman, Peter Louis. THE DEATH AND LIFE OF MALCOLM X. New York: Harper & Row, 1973. 458 p.

Includes bibliographical references.

Goodman, Benjamin, ed. THE END OF WHITE WORLD SUPREMACY. New York: Merlin House, 1971. 148 p.

Four speeches edited and with an introduction by Benjamin Goodman.

Haley, Alex. THE AUTOBIOGRAPHY OF MALCOLM X. New York: Grove Press, 1965.

The autobiography of Malcolm Little, written largely with the assistance of Haley, with an epilogue by Haley.

Hentoff, Nat. "Elijah in the Wilderness." REPORTER, 4 August 1960, pp. 37-40; 29 September 1960, p. 10.

Contrasts Malcolm X to his former leader, Elijah Muhammad.

_____. "Odyssey of a Black Man." COMMONWEAL 83 (28 January 1966): 511-12.

A review of THE AUTOBIOGRAPHY OF MALCOLM X.

Illo, John. "The Rhetoric of Malcolm X." COLUMBIA UNIVERSITY FORUM 9 (Spring 1966): 5-12.

"Malcolm combined magnificence and ethnic familiarity to demonstrate what he asserted: the potential majesty of the black man even in America, a majesty idiosyncratic but related to all human greatness."

Jamal, Hakim A. FROM THE DEAD LEVEL: MALCOLM X AND ME. New York: Random House, 1972. 272 p.

A personal recollection by a man who was a fourteen-year-old drug addict when he met Malcolm X. Describes Malcolm's early years, his break with Elijah Muhammad, and his murder.

Kgositsile, William Keorapetse. "Brother Malcolm and the Black Revolution." NEGRO DIGEST 18 (November 1968): 4-10.

An appreciation of Malcolm X by a South African exile, poet, and essayist.

Lacy, Leslie Alexander. "African Responses to Malcolm X." In BLACK FIRE, AN ANTHOLOGY OF AFRO-AMERICAN WRITING, edited by LeRoi Jones and Larry Neal, pp. 10-38. New York: William Morrow, 1968.

Lacy traces the immediate responses to Malcolm's presence in Africa. Included are attitudes of the students, government officials, and leading newspapers.

"Lesson of Malcolm X." SATURDAY EVENING POST, 12 September 1964, pp. 30-52.

Excerpt from THE AUTOBIOGRAPHY OF MALCOLM X.

Malcolm X. MALCOLM X TALKS TO YOUNG PEOPLE. New York: Young Socialist, 1965.

Pamphlet containing Malcolm's thoughts and advice.

Massaquoi, H.J. "Mystery of Malcolm X." EBONY, September 1964, pp. 38-40.

Concerned with Malcolm's decision to defect from the Black Muslims and the formation of his own Muslim Mosque, Inc.

Mitchell, Sara. BROTHER MALCOLM. New York: Malcolm X Memorial Committee, May 1965.

A commemorative pamphlet issued by the memorial committee.

Ohmann, Carol. "The Autobiography of Malcolm X: A Revolutionary Use of the Franklin Tradition." AMERICAN QUARTERLY 22 (Summer 1970): 131-49.

Comparison and contrast of Malcolm X and Benjamin Franklin's goals and values.

Parks, Gordon. "I Was a Zombie Then--Like All Muslims I Was Hypnotized." LIFE, 5 March 1965, pp. 28-30.

A prophetic essay by Parks of the violence to follow the murder of Malcolm X.

Plimpton, G. "Miami Notebook: Cassius Clay and Malcolm X." HARPER'S, June 1964, pp. 54-61.

The influence of Malcolm on Cassius Clay is examined at the time of the Clay-Liston fight.

"Satan in the Ghetto." NEWSWEEK, 15 November 1965, pp. 130-32.

A review of THE AUTOBIOGRAPHY OF MALCOLM X.

Saxe, Janet Cheatham. "Malik El Shabazz: A Survey of His Interpreters." BLACK SCHOLAR 1 (May 1970): 51-55.

A criticism of various authors' views on Malcolm X.

Seraile, William. "David Walker and Malcolm X." BLACK WORLD 22 (October 1973): 68-73.

A comparison of the careers of David Walker and Malcolm X, both of whom believed that black liberation would never be possible if a significant number of blacks worked with the power structure to maintain the status quo.

Southwick, Albert B. "Malcolm X: Charismatic Demagogue: Interview." CHRISTIAN CENTURY 80 (5 June 1963): 740-41.

An essay and interview with Malcolm X while he was still associated with Elijah Muhammad and the Black Muslim organization.

Spellman, A.B. "Interview with Malcolm X." MONTHLY REVIEW 16 (May 1964): 14-24.

Interview conducted by Spellman, black poet and jazz critic, on 19 March 1964. Malcolm defines revolution as something that destroys the system and replaces it with something better; the Negro Revolution, he says, "condemns the system and then asks the system that it has condemned to accept them into their system." That is no real revolution.

Sudan, Nazzam Al. "Malcolm X: A Mirror of Our Soul." BLACK DIALOGUE 6 (Winter 1967-68): 7-8.

Examines the "myth" of Malcolm X as a "fulfillment of Divine Prophecy."

"The Violent End of the Man Called Malcolm." LIFE, 5 March 1965, pp. 26-27.

Brief text and photographs taken of Malcolm's body after his murder.

Warren, Robert Penn. "Malcolm X: Mission and Meaning." YALE REVIEW 56 (Winter 1967): 161-71.

Warren feels that whatever the historical importance of Malcolm Little, the AUTOBIOGRAPHY has "permanence" and "something of tragic intensity and meaning."

White, Milton. "Malcolm X in the Military." BLACK SCHOLAR 1 (May 1970): 31-35.

Efforts to establish the Malcolm X association in the military.

JULIAN MAYFIELD

Mayfield, Julian. THE GRAND PARADE. New York: Vanguard Press, 1961. 448 p.

Concerned with the tragedy of a reform mayor in a southern town.

_____. THE HIT. New York: Vanguard Press, 1957. 212 p.

A black building superintendent attempts to escape his restrictive life by betting the month's electric and gas money on the numbers.

_____. THE LONG NIGHT. New York: Vanguard Press, 1958. 156 p.

Initiation novel concerned with a boy's quest for both his real father and a spiritual father who will give him a sense of his racial identity.

JULIAN MOREAU (J. DENIS JACKSON)

Jackson, J. Denis [Julian Moreau]. THE BLACK COMMANDOS. Atlanta: Cultural Institute Press, 1967. 228 p.

Blend of science fiction and popular culture with a revolutionary treatise. Concerned with secret black army, trained by black scientists, to avenge black people whenever they are oppressed.

WILLARD MOTLEY

Giles, James R., and Klinkowitz, Jerome. "The Emergence of Willard Motley
in Black American Literature." NEGRO AMERICAN LITERATURE FORUM 6
(Summer 1972): 31-34.

> Study based on the Motley papers and correspondence housed at
> the University of Wisconsin and at Northern Illinois University.

Klinkowitz, Jerome, and Wood, Karen. "The Making and Unmaking of KNOCK
ON ANY DOOR." PROOF 3 (1973): 121-37.

> "Critical problems with Willard Motley's first novel (1947) are
> more properly attributable to the complexities of its publishing
> history."

Motley, Willard. KNOCK ON ANY DOOR. New York: Appleton-Century,
1947. 504 p.

> Nick Romano's progression from an altar boy to a life of crime
> that involves him with prostitutes, gamblers, and homosexuals.

_____. LET NO MAN WRITE MY EPITAPH. New York: Random House,
1958. 467 p.

> Plot is concerned with Nick Romano, the illegitimate son of the
> criminal who died in the electric chair in Motley's KNOCK ON
> ANY DOOR, and with various social pariahs and rejects.

_____. LET NOON BE FAIR: A NOVEL. New York: G.P. Putnam's Sons,
1966. 416 p.

> Concerned with an Edenic Mexican fishing village and its spoiling
> by rich American tourists.

_____. WE FISHED ALL NIGHT. New York: Appleton-Century-Crofts, 1951.
560 p.

Concerned with three young political figures in Chicago, class
hatred, and political machinations.

Wood, Charles. "The ADVENTURE Manuscript: New Light on Willard Motley's
Naturalism." NEGRO AMERICAN LITERATURE FORUM 6 (Summer 1972): 35-
38.

A study of an unpublished work, extant in a 474-page typescript,
entitled ADVENTURE.

GORDON PARKS

Parks, Gordon. IN LOVE. Philadelphia: J.B. Lippincott, 1971. Unpaged.
A collection of photographs and poetry.

_____. A POET AND HIS CAMERA. New York: Viking Press, 1968. 92 p.
Poetry and photographs.

_____. WHISPERS OF INTIMATE THINGS. New York: Viking Press, 1971.
96 p.
Poetry.

ANN PETRY

Petry, Ann. COUNTRY PLACE. Boston: Houghton Mifflin, 1947. 266 p.

Concerned with the traumatic effects of World War II on the society of a small New England town.

_____. MISS MURIEL AND OTHER STORIES. Boston: Houghton Mifflin, 1971. 305 p.

Short stories based on Petry's youth in a small New England town, and her experiences in Harlem.

_____. THE NARROWS. Boston: Houghton Mifflin, 1953. 428 p.

Racial theme is coupled with the influence of the past. In its treatment of time, the novel bears certain similarities to the works of Huxley and Faulkner.

_____. THE STREET. Boston: Houghton Mifflin, 1946. 435 p.

Concerned with a young black woman's desperate attempts to survive in the ghetto.

DUDLEY RANDALL

Randall, Dudley. "Black Poetry." In BLACK EXPRESSION, edited by Addison Gayle, Jr., pp. 109-14. New York: Weybright and Talley, 1969.

The new black poets differ from previous generations of black poets in their new-found black consciousness.

_____. CITIES BURNING. Detroit: Broadside Press, 1968. 16 p.

Poetry.

_____. LOVE YOU. London: Paul Bremen, 1970. 16 p.

Poetry.

_____, ed. BLACK POETRY: A SUPPLEMENT TO ANTHOLOGIES WHICH EXCLUDE BLACK POETS. Detroit: Broadside Press, 1969. 48 p.

Poetry.

Randall, Dudley, and Burroughs, Margaret G., eds. FOR MALCOLM X. Preface and Eulogy by Ossie Davis. Detroit: Broadside Press, 1967. 127 p.

Poems on the life and death of Malcolm X.

CLARENCE REED

Reed, Clarence. NOT FOREVER TEARS. Newark, N.J.: Jihad Productions, 1969.
Poetry.

ISHMAEL REED

Ambler, Madge. "Ishmael Reed: Whose Radio Broke Down?" NEGRO AMERI-
CAN LITERATURE FORUM 6 (Winter 1972): 125-31.

An examination of the theme in Reed's YELLOW BACK RADIO
BROKE DOWN.

Cade, Toni. "Review of 'The Free-Lance Pallbearers.'" LIBERATOR 9 (June
1969): 20.

Review of Ishmael Reed's surrealistic antiutopian novel.

Reed, Ishmael. CATECHISM OF A NEOAMERICAN HOODOO CHURCH.
London: Paul Bremen, 1970. 28 p.

Poetry.

_____. CONJURE: SELECTED POEMS, 1963-1970. Amherst: University of
Massachusetts Press, 1972. 95 p.

Poetry.

_____. THE FREE-LANCE PALLBEARERS. Garden City, N.Y.: Doubleday,
1967. 155 p.

Satiric novel concerned with the fantastic world of HARRY SAM
and Bukka Doopyduk and a chaos of liberals, crusaders, militants,
and "bloods."

_____. MUMBO JUMBO. New York: Doubleday, 1972. 223 p.

Concerned with Papa LaBas, astrodetective and head of the "hoodoo"
kingdom, Mumbo Jumbo Kathedral, and an expert of Jes Grew--a
kind of "life spirit." Examines the technological interpretation of
intercultural relations in the world, satirizes Freudian psychology
and white assumptions about black culture.

An anthology of "original American writing for the 1970's." Reed
believes the American experience is "rooted in slang, dialect,
vernacular, argot" as if the "common man . . . would in his
speech assert his humanity against the powers that be." Contains
pieces by David Henderson, Ronald Fair, William Melvin Kelley,
Ishmael Reed, and others.

_____. "When State Magicians Fail: An Interview with Ishmael Reed."
JOURNAL OF BLACK POETRY 1 (Summer-Fall 1969): 72-77.

An interview with Reed, with a negative "afterword" by editor
Joe Goncalves.

_____. "The Writer As Seer: Ishmael Reed on Ishmael Reed." BLACK
WORLD 23 (June 1974): 20-34.

A "self-interview" conducted by Reed concerning his "Hexorcism
of Noxon D. Awful." Also contains a long discussion on the
Afro-American male.

_____. YELLOW BACK RADIO BROKE-DOWN. Garden City, N.Y.: Double-
day, 1969. 177 p.

Satiric novel concerned with the Loop Garoo Kid and the war
between old and new ideas. Utilizes the stereotypes of the
Western movie and other elements of American pop culture.

_____, ed. 19 NECROMANCERS FROM NOW: AN ANTHOLOGY OF
ORIGINAL AMERICAN WRITING FOR THE 70'S. Garden City, N.Y.:
Doubleday, 1970. 369 p.

CONRAD RIVERS

Rivers, Conrad Kent. THE STILL VOICE OF HARLEM. London: Paul Bremen,
1968. 24 p.

   Poetry.

_____. THESE BLACK BODIES AND THIS SUNBURNT FACE. Cleveland:
Free Lance Press, 1962. 28 p.

   Poetry.

CAROLYN RODGERS

Rodgers, Carolyn M. PAPER SOUL. Introduction by Hoyt Fuller. Chicago: Third World Press, 1968. 20 p.

Poetry.

_____. SONGS OF A BLACKBIRD. Chicago: Third World Press, 1969. 34 p.

Poetry.

SONIA SANCHEZ

Brooks, A. Russell. "The Motif of Dynamic Change in Black Revolutionary Poetry." CLA JOURNAL 15 (September 1971): 25-36.

> The poetry of Sonia Sanchez contains a "note of expectancy, of hope for a better world through the coming into fruition of the black man's national aspirations."

Clarke, Sebastian. "Sonia Sanchez and Her Work." BLACK WORLD 20 (June 1971): 45-48, 96-98.

> Sanchez's poetry is a "literature of commitment"; there is the desire to live, fully coupled with the nationalist/political strain. She is also concerned with the "white woman liberation movement and its subversive relationship to Black women."

Sanchez, Sonia. HOME COMING: POEMS. Detroit: Broadside Press, 1969. 32 p.

> Poetry.

_____. LOVE POEMS. New York: Third World Press, 1973. 101 p.

> Poetry.

_____. WE A BADDDDD PEOPLE. Introduction by Dudley Randall. Detroit: Broadside Press, 1970. 72 p.

> Poetry.

MELVIN B. TOLSON

Tate, Allen. Preface to LIBRETTO FOR THE REPUBLIC OF LIBERIA by Melvin Tolson, pp. 1-3. New York: Collier Books, 1970.

> Tate feels that for the first time "a Negro poet has assimilated completely the full poetic language of his time and, by implication, the language of the Anglo-American poetic tradition."

Tolson, Melvin B. HARLEM GALLERY. New York: Twayne Publishers, 1965. Unpaged.

> Poetry.

————. LIBRETTO FOR THE REPUBLIC OF LIBERIA. New York: Twayne Publishers, 1953. Unpaged.

> Poetry.

JOHN WIDEMAN

Frazier, Kermit. "The Novels of John Wideman." BLACK WORLD 24 (June 1975): 18-38.

An analysis of Wideman's A GLANCE AWAY, HURRY HOME, and THE LYNCHERS.

Wideman, John Edgar. A GLANCE AWAY. New York: Harcourt, Brace & World, 1967. 186 p.

Exhibits strong influence of T.S. Eliot; central character is Prufrockian and the tone and style of the novel are reminiscent of Eliot.

_____. HURRY HOME. New York: Harcourt, Brace & World, 1970. 185 p.

Controlling metaphor of the novel is a painting by Hieronymous Bosch.

_____. THE LYNCHERS. New York: Harcourt Brace Jovanovich, 1973. 264 p.

Exhibits Wideman's interest in myth, ritual, and symbol. Concerned with the attempt of a group of blacks to lynch a white southern policeman.

JOHN A. WILLIAMS

Brenner, Jack. "BUTCHER'S CROSSING: The Husks and Shells of Exploitation."
WESTERN AMERICAN LITERATURE 7 (Winter 1973): 243-59.

Williams is most interested in the West; BUTCHER'S CROSSING is
not a debunking novel, but rather it "asks us to see that the con-
ceptions with which we have invested Westering have cheapened
the value that we insist it epitomizes."

Cash, Earl A. "Captain Blackman: An Interview with John A. Williams."
BLACK WORLD 22 (June 1973): 51-52, 86-89.

Interview discusses influences on CAPTAIN BLACKMAN, Williams'
narrative technique, and his intention in writing the novel.

Fleming, Robert E. "The Nightmare Level of THE MAN WHO CRIED I AM."
CONTEMPORARY LITERATURE 14 (Spring 1973): 186-96.

Fleming sees Williams' use of gothic elements ("the nightmare
vision") as freeing the novelist "from the naturalistic format which
for a time seemed the sole metier of the black novelist."

Henderson, David. "THE MAN WHO CRIED I AM: A Critique." In BLACK
EXPRESSION, edited by Addison Gayle, Jr., pp. 365-71. New York: Weybright and Talley, 1969.

Henderson points out that Williams' novel is not just an entertain-
ing and suspense-filled book and warns that "a plan for the ex-
termination of American Blacks would not be contrary to American
History."

Klotman, Phyllis R. "An Examination of the Black Confidence Man in Two
Black Novels: THE MAN WHO CRIED I AM and DEM." AMERICAN LITERA-
TURE 44 (January 1973): 596-611.

Kelly's DEM shows the influence of the character Rhinehart in
Ellison's INVISIBLE MAN, while John A. Williams' THE MAN

WHO CRIED I AM "develops that relatively new fictional character, the black espionage agent."

O'Brien, John. "Seeking a Humanist Level: Interview with John A. Williams." ARTS IN SOCIETY 10 (Spring-Summer 1973): 94-99.

Williams discusses his art and the problems confronted by black novelists.

Scott, Henry, Jr. "'King Alfred' Reconsidered." BLACK WORLD 25 (January 1976): 34-47.

A comparison between the genocidal plot in Williams' THE MAN WHO CRIED I AM and America's law enforcement agencies. Argues that the only thing lacking is "the political climate within which to launch the plan."

Skerrett, Joseph T., Jr. "Novelist in Motion." BLACK WORLD 25 (January 1976): 58-67, 93-97.

An interview with John A. Williams conducted in his Manhattan apartment, 5 March 1973.

Smith, Anneleise H. "A Pain in the Ass: Metaphor in John A. Williams' THE MAN WHO CRIED I AM." STUDIES IN BLACK LITERATURE 3 (Autumn 1972): 25-27.

A discussion of the symbolic use of the protagonist's cancer of the rectum.

Walcott, Ronald. "The Early Fiction of John A. Williams." CLA JOURNAL 16 (December 1972): 198-213.

An examination of the autobiographical roots of Williams' art and an analysis of THE ANGRY ONES (1960), NIGHT SONG (1962), and SISSIE (1963).

_____. "THE MAN WHO CRIED I AM: Crying in the Dark." STUDIES IN BLACK LITERATURE 3 (Spring 1972): 24-32.

"Williams' story, the one he tells again and again in his five novels, is the story of the sixties, the obsessively, obscenely political decade, the decade in which to be an artist and an American was to sense the ominous oppressiveness of social weight. . . ."

Williams, John A. THE ANGRY ONES. New York: Ace Books, 1960. 192 p.

Concerned with the efforts of the protagonist, Steve Hill, to gain his social and economic rights.

_____. CAPTAIN BLACKMAN. Garden City, N.Y.: Doubleday, 1972.
336 p.

Wounded black officer in Vietnam goes into a hallucinatory coma
in which he passes through the various avatars of the black soldier's
role in American history, from the American Revolution through the
Battle of New Orleans, the Civil War, the Indian wars, the Spanish-
American War, World War I, World War II, and the Korean War
to the action in Vietnam. Captain Blackman becomes a black
Everyman in his recapitulation of the black soldier's history.

_____. Introduction to WHITE MAN, LISTEN! by Richard Wright, pp. ix-xii.
Garden City, N.Y.: Doubleday, 1964. Paperback.

Williams' introduction to the reissue, in paperback, of the original
Doubleday edition of 1957. Although Williams admits that the book
echoes in places the theory of dialectical materialism, the Marxian
conflict of the classes "could certainly be converted and used to
describe the conflict of the colors."

_____. "The Literary Ghetto." SATURDAY REVIEW, 20 April 1963, pp. 21,
40.

Williams objects to the stereotyping of black authors by white
critics and the failure of white authors to create credible black
characters in their fiction.

_____. THE MAN WHO CRIED I AM. Boston: Little, Brown, 1967. 403 p.

A black writer becomes involved with a conspiracy to annihilate
the black populace.

_____. THE MOST NATIVE OF SONS: A BIOGRAPHY OF RICHARD WRIGHT.
Garden City, N.Y.: Doubleday, 1970. 141 p.

A biography written for young readers.

_____. MOTHERSILL AND THE FOXES. New York: Doubleday, 1975.
239 p.

Novel set during the turmoil in the black communities of the 1950s
and 1960s and concerned with the sexual initiation and subsequent
awareness of the book's hero, Odell Mothersill.

_____. NIGHT SONG. New York: Farrar, Straus & Cudahy, 1961. 219 p.

A novel set in the jazz world of Greenwich Village and centering
on the life of Richie Stokes, heroin addict and famous jazz saxo-
phonist.

_____. "Ralph Ellison and INVISIBLE MAN: Their Place in American Letters." BLACK WORLD 20 (December 1970): 10-11.

An appreciation of Ellison's great opus, INVISIBLE MAN.

_____. SISSIE. New York: Farrar, Straus & Cudahy, 1961. 277 p.

Concerned with the struggles of Ralph Joplin to overcome the influences of racism on his personality.

_____. SONS OF DARKNESS, SONS OF LIGHT. Boston: Little, Brown, 1969. 279 p.

Concerned with political assassination and a black revolution in New York City.

_____. "Wright, Wrong and Black Reality." NEGRO DIGEST 18 (December 1968): 25.

A eulogy of Richard Wright.

CHARLES WRIGHT

Wright, Charles. ABSOLUTELY NOTHING TO GET ALARMED ABOUT. New
York: Farrar, Straus & Giroux, 1973. 215 p.

A collection of journalistic pieces, some slightly altered, which
originally appeared in the VILLAGE VOICE.

_____. THE MESSENGER. New York: Farrar, Straus, 1963. 217 p.

Concerned with the desperate attempt of the protagonist, Charles
Stevenson, to realize the American Dream.

_____. THE WIG. New York: Farrar, Straus & Giroux, 1966. 179 p.

Protagonist Lester Jefferson seeks to immerse himself in the Great
Society and reap its benefits. He wears a wig and even submits
to castration because "having children is the greatest sin" in America.

RICHARD WRIGHT

Bakish, David. RICHARD WRIGHT. New York: Ungar, 1973. 114 p.

A biographical monograph; contains bibliography.

Baldwin, James. "Alas, Poor Richard." In his NOBODY KNOWS MY NAME, pp. 200-215. New York: Dial Press, 1961.

Wright ultimately was a victim of the war between whiteness and blackness; "he eventually found himself wandering in a no-man's land between the black world and the white."

———. "Eight Men." In his NOBODY KNOWS MY NAME, pp. 181-89. New York: Dial Press, 1961.

Baldwin's appraisal of Wright's collection of stories, EIGHT MEN.

———. "Richard Wright." ENCOUNTER 16 (April 1961): 58-60. Reprinted in his NOBODY KNOWS MY NAME, as "The Exile," pp. 190-99. New York: Dial Press, 1961.

Baldwin traces part of the difficulty between Wright and himself to the fact that he was much younger than Wright and was not a southern Negro.

Berry, Faith. "On Richard Wright in Exile: Portrait of a Man As Outsider." NEGRO DIGEST 18 (December 1968): 26-37.

Berry contends "that the content, and perhaps the volume, of the late author's work would have been different had he never left the United States."

Bone, Robert. RICHARD WRIGHT. Minneapolis: University of Minnesota, Pamphlets on American Writers, 1969. 48 p.

Brief study of Wright. Bibliography, pages 47-48.

Brignano, Russell Carl. RICHARD WRIGHT: AN INTRODUCTION TO THE MAN AND HIS WORKS. Pittsburgh: University of Pittsburgh Press, 1970. 201 p.

> A study of Wright's novels, essays, poetry, and nonfiction, especially as they depict his attitudes on race, his Marxism, and his personal philosophy.

Brown, Cecil. "Richard Wright's Complexes and Black Writing Today." NEGRO DIGEST 18 (December 1968): 45-50, 78-82.

> Brown rejects Wright's "negative protest." He also analyzes the implications in the difference between Wright's attitude toward white women in his fiction and his attitude towards them in his autobiographical works.

Caxton, Horace. "The Curtain." NEGRO DIGEST 18 (December 1968): 11-15.

> A personal memoir of a train trip through the South with Richard Wright by Caxton, an old friend of Wright.

Dickstein, Morris. "Wright, Baldwin, Cleaver." NEW LETTERS 38 (December 1971): 117-24.

> "Attacked, abandoned as a literary example by Baldwin and Ellison, whose early work he had typically encouraged, Wright has now become, after long eclipse and a decade after his death, the favored ancestor of a great many black writers, who reject his successors and feel much akin to his militant spirit."

Emanuel, James A. "Fever and Feeling: Notes on the Imagery in NATIVE SON." NEGRO DIGEST 18 (December 1969): 16-24.

> An analysis of the symbolism and imagery in NATIVE SON.

Fabre, Michel. "Impressions of Richard Wright: An Interview with Simone DeBeauvoir." STUDIES IN BLACK LITERATURE 1 (Autumn 1970): 3-5.

> An interview conducted on 24 June 1970.

_____. THE UNFINISHED QUEST OF RICHARD WRIGHT. Translated from French by Isabel Barzun. New York: William Morrow, 1973. 652 p.

> Fabre's study is based on primary materials made available to him by Wright's widow.

Fabre, Michel, and Margolies, Edward. "Richard Wright (1908-1960): A Bibliography." BULLETIN OF BIBLIOGRAPHY 24 (1965): 131-33.

> This bibliography is reprinted in Constance Webb's RICHARD WRIGHT: A BIOGRAPHY (New York, 1968) and in NEGRO

DIGEST 18 (January 1969): 86-92.

Ford, Nick A. "The Ordeal of Richard Wright." COLLEGE ENGLISH 15 (1953): 87-94.

Sees more "emotional control" in THE OUTSIDER than in NATIVE SON.

Gayle, Addison, Jr. "Richard Wright: Beyond Nihilism." NEGRO DIGEST 18 (December 1968): 4-10.

"Richard Wright believed always in the 'community of man,' and he realized that complete dedication to nihilism would make impossible the building of such a community."

Kent, George [E.]. "On the Future Study of Richard Wright." In his BLACK-NESS AND THE ADVENTURE OF WESTERN CULTURE, pp. 93-103. Chicago: Third World Press, 1972.

A review of biographies, bibliographies, monographs, and critical essays concerning Wright already published, and suggestions for needed future studies of Wright.

Kinnamon, Keneth. THE EMERGENCE OF RICHARD WRIGHT: A STUDY IN LITERATURE AND SOCIETY. Urbana: University of Illinois Press, 1972. 200 p.

Primarily, Kinnamon's text is not a biography but a critical study of Wright's early works down to the publication of NATIVE SON, although biography and intellectual history are included to elucidate the textual analysis.

Lawson, Lewis A. "Cross Damon: Kierkegaardian Man of Dread." CLA JOUR-NAL 14 (March 1971): 298-316.

"A close analysis of Wright's use of Kierkegaard's work, especially THE CONCEPT OF DREAD, is helpful in demonstrating that Wright is offering essentially Christian, rather than an atheistic existential view."

McCall, Dan. THE EXAMPLE OF RICHARD WRIGHT. New York: Harcourt, Brace & World, 1969. 202 p.

An analysis of Wright's work, his influence on later black writers, and political and moral implications of his art. Concentrates primarily on NATIVE SON and BLACK BOY.

Margolies, Edward. THE ART OF RICHARD WRIGHT. Carbondale: Southern Illinois University Press, 1969. 180 p.

Examines Wright's nonfiction as well as his short fiction and novels.

Martin, Kenneth. "Richard Wright and the Negro Revolt." NEGRO DIGEST 15 (April 1965): 39-48.

>The "voice of nationalism is a voice of desperation, a voice calling to color because the cry to countrymen has fallen on deaf ears."

Musgrave, Marion E. "Triangles in Black and White: Interracial Sex and Hostility in Black Literature." CLA JOURNAL 14 (June 1971): 444-51.

>An examination of the relationship between sex and aggression in Richard Wright's THE OUTSIDER.

Primeau, Ronald. "Imagination as Moral Bulwark and Creative Energy in Richard Wright's BLACK BOY and LeRoi Jones' HOME." STUDIES IN BLACK LITERATURE 3 (Summer 1972): 12-18.

>"The Romanticism of Richard Wright and LeRoi Jones as well as modern Romanticism on the whole invest massively in the unseen in order to transform old and create new realities."

Ray, David, and Farnsworth, Robert M., eds. RICHARD WRIGHT: IMPRESSIONS AND PERSPECTIVES. Ann Arbor: University of Michigan Press, 1973. 207 p.

>A collection of essays concerning Wright, and a bibliography of his work. The theme of the collection is that Wright "suffered from reductive literary criticism before achieving a well-deserved rediscovery by angry blacks of the late 1960's."

Reilly, John M. "LAWD TODAY: Richard Wright's Experiment in Naturalism." STUDIES IN BLACK LITERATURE 2 (Autumn 1971): 14-17.

>"Partial understanding of Wright's conscious development of his art can be gained by examining his early experiment in naturalism-- the novel LAWD TODAY." (Wright worked on LAWD TODAY between 1935 and 1937, but it was not published until 1963.)

"Richard Wright: A Bibliography." NEGRO DIGEST 18 (January 1969): 86-92.

>Supplement to the December 1968 issue of NEGRO DIGEST, which was a special issue on life and works of Richard Wright. A reprint of the bibliography which appeared in Constance Webb's biography of Richard Wright.

Scott, Nathan A., Jr. "The Dark and Haunted Tower of Richard Wright." In BLACK EXPRESSION, edited by Addison Gayle, Jr., pp. 296-311. New York: Weybright and Talley, 1969.

>Wright's "agonia" led him to attempt "to shape the story of the American Negro into something whose tragic sorrow might quicken

Richard Wright

the conscience of our time."

_____. "Search for Beliefs: Fiction of Richard Wright." UNIVERSITY OF KANSAS CITY REVIEW 23 (1956): 19-24.

Wright was destined to be a rebel because of the universe of cruelty and violence to which he was exposed.

Webb, Constance. "What Next for Richard Wright?" PHYLON 10 (1949): 161-66.

A review of the early criticism of Wright and a summary of his life up to the time of his departure for France.

Williams, John A. "Wright, Wrong and Black Reality." NEGRO DIGEST 18 (December 1968): 25.

A tribute to the late Richard Wright by a leading black novelist.

Wright, Richard. BLACK POWER: A RECORD OF REACTIONS IN A LAND OF PATHOS. New York: Harper, 1954. 358 p.

A report on the new African nationalism based on information gathered after Wright's visit to the Gold Coast of Africa.

_____. THE COLOR CURTAIN: A REPORT ON THE BANDUNG CONFER-ENCE. Cleveland: World Publishing Co., 1956. 226 p.

Based on his visit to the conference. Wright's analysis is that the two elements holding the conference together were the same things which separated the countries represented at the conference from the Western powers: race and religion.

_____. EIGHT MEN. Cleveland: World Publishing Co., 1961. 250 p.

Eight stories (some previously published) dealing with the struggles of eight black men against a deterministic universe.

_____. Foreword to BLUES FELL THIS MORNING by Paul Oliver. New York: Horizon Press, 1961. Oliver's book was republished as THE MEANING OF THE BLUES. New York: Collier Books, 1963. 283 p.

Writing in Paris in 1959, Wright says that "the American environ-ment which produced the blues is still with us, though we all labour to render it progressively smaller."

_____. THE GOD THAT FAILED. New York: Harper and Bros., 1949. 273 p.

A book of essays by writers who were at one time affiliated with the Communist party (Richard Wright, Arthur Koestler, Ignazio Silone, Andre Gide, Louis Fischer, and Stephen Spender). Wright's essay is found on pages 115-62.

_____. Introduction to IN THE CASTLE OF MY SKIN by George Lamming, pp. ix-xii. New York: McGraw-Hill, 1953.

Hails Lamming as an artist who possesses "a quiet and stubborn courage."

_____. LAWD TODAY. New York: Walker, 1963. 189 p.

Posthumously published novel was actually written before NATIVE SON. Concerned with a day in the narrowly circumscribed life of Jake Jackson, a Chicago postal clerk.

_____. THE LONG DREAM. Garden City, N.Y.: Doubleday, 1958. 384 p.

Action concerned with Fishbelly's coming of age in a Mississippi town full of racism, lynching, and violence.

_____. THE OUTSIDER. New York: Harper and Bros., 1953. 405 p.

Naturalistic novel about a Chicago postal employee who changes his identity, moves to New York, joins the Communist party, becomes a murderer, and is finally killed.

_____. PAGAN SPAIN. New York: Harper, 1957. 241 p.

Reflection on his trip to Spain in 1954; travel-journalism which reveals much about the author himself.

_____. SAVAGE HOLIDAY. New York: Award Books, 1965. 222 p.

A suspense novel concerned with sex and violence and centering on the character Erskine Fowler.

_____. WHITE MEN, LISTEN! Garden City, N.Y.: Doubleday, 1957. 190 p. Reissued in paperback. Introduction by John A. Williams. Garden City, N.Y.: Doubleday Anchor, 1964. 137 p.

Wright's book is based on a series of lectures given in Europe from 1950 to 1956 and concerned with international implications of the race question.

FRANK YERBY

Yerby, Frank. BENTON'S ROW. New York: Dial Press, 1954. 346 p.

Tom Benton rides from Texas to a sleepy Louisiana bayou town, where he takes another man's wife and alters the course of the town.

_____. BRIDE OF LIBERTY. Garden City, N.Y.: Doubleday, 1954. 219 p.

Love story set in the period of the American Revolution.

_____. CAPTAIN REBEL. New York: Dial Press, 1956. 343 p.

Historical novel about Tyler Meredith, a New Orleans captain of a fleet of blockade runners during the Civil War.

_____. THE DAHOMEAN. New York: Dial Press, 1971. 383 p.

Novel about a black prince of Dahomey who is sold into slavery.

_____. THE DEVIL'S LAUGHTER. New York: Dial Press, 1953. 376 p.

Historical romance set in eighteenth-century revolutionary France. Concerned with the adventures of Jean Paul Marin.

_____. FAIROAKS. New York: Dial Press, 1957. 405 p.

Romantic novel about southern aristocrats, plantations, and the slave trade.

_____. FLOOD TIDE. New York: Dial Press, 1950. 342 p.

The story of Ross Pary and his rise in Natchez society in the mid-nineteenth century.

_____. THE FOXES OF HARROW. New York: Dial Press, 1946. 534 p.

The rise from poverty to riches (and ultimate ruin) of Stephen Fox in the Civil War period in Louisiana.

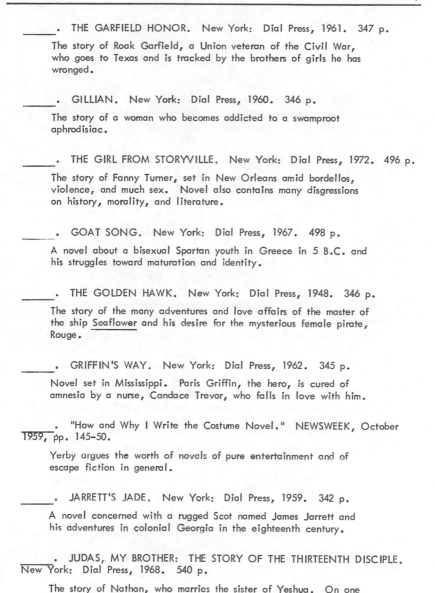

_____. THE GARFIELD HONOR. New York: Dial Press, 1961. 347 p.

The story of Roak Garfield, a Union veteran of the Civil War, who goes to Texas and is tracked by the brothers of girls he has wronged.

_____. GILLIAN. New York: Dial Press, 1960. 346 p.

The story of a woman who becomes addicted to a swamproot aphrodisiac.

_____. THE GIRL FROM STORYVILLE. New York: Dial Press, 1972. 496 p.

The story of Fanny Turner, set in New Orleans amid bordellos, violence, and much sex. Novel also contains many disgressions on history, morality, and literature.

_____. GOAT SONG. New York: Dial Press, 1967. 498 p.

A novel about a bisexual Spartan youth in Greece in 5 B.C. and his struggles toward maturation and identity.

_____. THE GOLDEN HAWK. New York: Dial Press, 1948. 346 p.

The story of the many adventures and love affairs of the master of the ship Seaflower and his desire for the mysterious female pirate, Rouge.

_____. GRIFFIN'S WAY. New York: Dial Press, 1962. 345 p.

Novel set in Mississippi. Paris Griffin, the hero, is cured of amnesia by a nurse, Candace Trevor, who falls in love with him.

_____. "How and Why I Write the Costume Novel." NEWSWEEK, October 1959, pp. 145-50.

Yerby argues the worth of novels of pure entertainment and of escape fiction in general.

_____. JARRETT'S JADE. New York: Dial Press, 1959. 342 p.

A novel concerned with a rugged Scot named James Jarrett and his adventures in colonial Georgia in the eighteenth century.

_____. JUDAS, MY BROTHER: THE STORY OF THE THIRTEENTH DISCIPLE. New York: Dial Press, 1968. 540 p.

The story of Nathan, who marries the sister of Yeshua. On one level the novel is a revisionist document against the Gospels.

_____. AN ODOR OF SANCTITY. New York: Dial Press, 1965. 563 p.

Novel concerned with Alaris, a tenth-century Gothic nobleman in Spain who ultimately ends his life as a Christian saint when he is martyred by the Moors.

_____. PRIDE'S CASTLE. New York: Dial Press, 1949. 382 p.

The rise and fall of Pride Dawson, who rose from poverty to become a robber baron before his ruin and suicide.

_____. THE SARACEN BLADE. New York: Dial Press, 1952. 406 p.

Historical novel, set in the time of Emperor Frederick II, about the picaresque adventures of Pietro di Donati in Sicily, Italy, Germany, France, and the Holy Land.

_____. THE SERPENT AND THE STAFF. New York: Dial Press, 1958. 377 p.

Novel set in turn-of-the-century American South about Duncan Childer's struggle from poverty to success as a surgeon.

_____. SPEAK NOW. New York: Dial Press, 1969. 227 p.

Novel concerned with a black jazz clarinetist in Paris who befriends a pregnant white southern heiress who has been abandoned by her lover.

_____. THE TREASURE OF PLEASANT VALLEY. New York: Dial Press, 1955. 348 p.

A combination of historical romance and mystery novel dealing with the adventures of Bruce Harkness, son of a Carolina planter, and the two women in his life, Jo Peterson and Juana Cordoba.

_____. THE VIXENS. New York: Dial Press, 1947. 347 p.

The story of Laird Fournois, a New Orleans aristocrat, his marriage to a mad woman, and his love for another woman. Set in mid-nineteenth century New Orleans.

_____. A WOMAN CALLED FANCY. New York: Dial Press, 1951. 340 p.

Nineteen-year-old Fancy leaves her Carolina hill family, goes to Georgia, and meets a series of men, one of whom makes her a carnival girl, before she marries Courtland Brantley.

AL YOUNG

Young, Al. SNAKES. New York: Holt, Rinehart and Winston, 1970. 178 p.

An initiation novel concerned with a black high-school boy who gains his identity by discovering his past.

_____. THE SONG TURNING BACK INTO ITSELF. New York: Holt, Rinehart and Winston, 1971. 87 p.

Poems expressive of Young's experiences and moods in the 1960s; draws heavily on Afro-American music of the period.

INDEXES

AUTHOR INDEX

This index includes all authors, editors, and other contributors cited in the text. This index is alphabetized letter by letter.

Author Index

Benoit, Bernard 8, 160
Benson, Steven 144
Berger, Monroe 21
Berry, Faith 252
Berson, Lenora E. 69
Berube, Maurice 69
Bigsby, C.W.E. 15, 133, 184, 200
Billingsley, Ronald G. 147, 176, 189
Blackburn, Sara 23
Blauner, Robert 108
Blaustein, Arthur I. 60
Bloch, Alice 160
Bloice, Carl 60
Bluefarb, Sam 133
Bly, Robert 205
Boggs, Grace Lee 29
Boggs, James 29, 60
Bogle, Donald 45, 74
Bond, Jean Carey 115, 120
Bond, Julian 5, 24, 29, 37, 38
Bone, Robert 15, 85, 134, 137, 160, 252
Bontemps, Arna 68, 85, 90
Booth, William H. 70
Borders, William Holmes, Sr. 106
Borenstein, Larry 82
Boskin, Joseph 108
Boulware, Marcus H. 94
Bowen, Dan R. 110
Boyle, Kay 134
Bradford, Melvin E. 134
Branch, William 4, 5
Brashler, William 21
Brecht, Stefan 200
Breitman, George 227
Brenner, Jack 247
Brignano, Russell Carl 253
Broderick, Francis L. 29, 113, 156
Brooks, Gwendolyn 85, 90, 98, 140, 142, 222
Brooks, Russell 80, 176, 244
Brown, Cecil 13, 200–201, 253
Brown, Claude 5
Brown, Clifton L. 107
Brown, Frank L. 87
Brown, Lloyd I. 106
Brown, Lloyd W. 182, 201
Brown, Roscoe C. 63

Brown, Sterling A. 68
Brown, Theodore 4
Browne, Ray B. 76
Brustein, Robert 201
Bryant, Jerry H. 176
Buckley, William F., Jr. 70, 125, 134
Bullins, Ed 3, 4, 54, 55, 59, 119, 143–45, 206
Burns, Haywood 23
Burrell, Walter 180
Burroughs, Margaret 90, 238

C

Cade, Toni 54, 120, 240
Cain, George 147
Caldwell, Ben 3, 4, 5, 59, 145, 146
Cambridge, Godfrey 41
Campbell, Dick 117
Campbell, Leslie 72
Caplan, Nathan S. 108
Capouya, Emile 130, 184, 227
Carawan, Candie 78
Carawan, John 78
Carmichael, Stokely 5, 30, 40, 95
Carson, David L. 161
Carson, Josephine 113
Carter, Steve 4
Cartey, Wilfred 134
Cash, Earl A. 161, 247
Caxton, Horace 253
Chandler, Sue 11
Chapman, Abraham 91
Chapman, Dorthy 4
Charles, Martie 5
Charney, Maurice 134
Charters, Samuel 78
Cheatwood, Kiarri 94
Chevigny, Paul 24
Childress, Alice 4
Chisholm, Shirley 94, 120
Chrisman, Robert 30
Christian, Barbara 161
Ciardi, John 135
Clarebaut, David 43
Clark, Kenneth B. 49, 100, 113
Clarke, John Henrik 13, 156, 161, 183, 219, 228

Author Index

Author Index

Author Index

Author Index

TITLE INDEX

This index includes all titles of books which are cited in the text. Titles of articles are excluded. In some cases, lengthy titles have been shortened. This index is alphabetized letter by letter.

Title Index

Title Index

Title Index

SUBJECT INDEX

This index is alphabetized letter by letter. Underlined page numbers refer to main areas within the subject.

A

Acting companies, lists of 143. See also names of acting companies (e.g. Negro Ensemble Co. [New York City])

Actors. See Entertainers and performers

Aesthetics. See Literature, aesthetics of

A.F.R.I.C.A. See African Americans for Friendship and Retainment of Our Image, Culture and Arts (A.F.R.I.C.A.)

Africa 157
    art forms of in black poetry 153
    black identity with and effect upon 40, 47, 169
    black impressions of 129
    in drama 183
    history of 193
    movements aimed at return to 28, 37
    nationalism of 256
    the origins of Afro-American music and 81, 202
    response of to Malcolm X 229
    roots of Afro-American religion and 105, 106, 107
    See also Dahomey; Liberia, Republic of; Pan-Africanism; names of African tribes (e.g. Nok; Ife)

African Americans for Friendship and Retainment of Our Image, Culture and Arts (A.F.R.I.C.A.) 73

Afro-American literature. See Literature

Aggression, as a result of social conditioning 102

Albee, Edward 131, 217

Aldridge Players/West (San Francisco) 56

Ali, Muhammad 75, 208, 230

Alienation, theme of in fiction 176

Allegory. See Fables, allegorical

Alonzo 4X 21

American Revolution in Fiction 258

Anderson, Alston 87

Anderson, Blair 24

Angelou, Maya 66

Anti-hero in fiction 170

Antisemitism among blacks 69-73, 128, 130, 212

Appollo Theater (New York City) 92

Architecture 193

Armstrong, Louis 78, 79

Art 33
    in drama 204
    of Harlem 152
    indexes to 9, 11, 12
    See also Painters and painting; Sculpture

Artaud, Antonin 216

Subject Index

Subject Index

Subject Index

Subject Index

Subject Index

Police
  Black Panthers and 25, 26
  brutality of 133
  as a cause of riots 111
  in drama 159, 211
  in fiction 190, 197, 246
  in New York City 227
Political prisoners 99, 150
Politicians
  biography of black 95
  white 148
Politics 69, 94-96, 113, 114, 127,
    207, 211, 215, 216
  bibliography 96
  black power movement and 29, 30,
    31, 32-33, 35, 37, 39, 41
  civil rights movement and 51-52
  coalitions in 94
  of Harlem 150
  indexes to black 11
  linkages to Afro-American arts 18
  of literature 254
    in fiction 169, 189, 235, 250
    in poetry 244
  responsibility of white Christians to
    black 34
  of riots 111
  in the Southern states 29, 39,
    51-52, 95
  women and 120
  See also Democratic Party. Na-
    tional Convention; National
    Black Political Convention,
    March 10-12, 1972 (Gary,
    Ind.); Government; Voter
    registration
Poussaint, Alvin F. 13
Poverty in drama 143
Powell, Adam Clayton 50, 70
Power (social science). See Black
    power movement; Politics
Preachers. See Ministers
Prejudice. See Race problems
Preservation Hall, New Orleans 82
Press, portrayal of blacks by 39
Prisons
  black interest in reform of 46
  black studies in 45
  fiction about 128, 189
  political awareness in 35
  writings from 97-99, 149, 221

Propaganda
  lack of in fiction 87
  literature as 14, 38
  drama 202
Prophet Cherry. See Cherry, Prophet
Prose poetry 215
Prostitution in fiction 234, 259
Protest and protest movements, indexes
    to the literature of 9, 11.
    See also Black power move-
    ment; Civil rights movement;
    Welfare rights movement;
    names of protest groups (e.g.
    Black Panthers)
Protestantism, responsibility of toward
    black politics 34
Psychology 100-104, 130
  of black power 38, 102
  in drama 58-59, 201, 210
  in fiction 176, 189, 240
  of rioters 110
  of sex 101, 102
  See also Educational psychology;
    Mental health; Self-image
Public welfare. See Social welfare
Publishers and publishing, Afro-
    American literature and 16
Pulitzer Prize for poetry 211
PUSH. See People United to Save
    Humanity (PUSH)

R

Ra, Sun 80, 83, 84
Raab, Earl 72
Race problems 29, 35, 70, 71, 72,
    73, 114, 207, 213, 253,
    256
  Black Muslim solutions to 22
  changes in from 1940-1964 52
  in drama 202, 206, 216
  economics of 60, 62
  in education 30-31
  in fiction 13, 190, 194, 206,
    237, 250, 257
  in poetry 142, 208
  psychology of 100, 101, 102,
    103, 114
  sexual aspects of 75
  in the Southern states 28, 164

Subject Index

Walker, Margaret 90, 91, 93
War. See American Revolution in
    fiction; Civil War in fiction;
    Vietnamese War; World War
    II in fiction
Ward, Douglas Turner 4, 5, 55
Ward, Theodore 7
Waring, James 208
Warren, Robert Penn 162
Washington, Booker T. 62
Washington, D.C., black dialect in
    44
Waters, Ethel 67
Watson, Albert E. 61
Watts
    riots in 31, 108, 109, 110-11
    writers' workshops in 6
    See also Douglas House (Watts)
Welfare rights movement 34
Wells, Warren 24
Weschsler, James 182
Wesley, Richard 3, 54, 144
West, Jerome 24
West Indies 193
Wheatley, Phillis 192
Whitman, Walt 169-70
Whittall (Gertrude Clarke) Foundation
    164
Wideman, John 246
Wilkins, Roy 156
Williams, Hosea 106
Williams, John A. 13, 88, 102,
    247-50
Williams, Robert F. 94, 148
Williams, Samuel W. 105
Winston-Salem, N.C., black politics
    in 95
Wit and humor 43
    in drama 194
    in fiction 170, 171, 191, 192,
        194-95, 196
    in poetry 91, 93
Witchcraft in fiction 226
Women 120-22, 202
    bibliography 12, 122
    black attitudes toward white 253
    black power and 34
    in drama 20
    education of 121

in fiction 6, 125, 140, 151,
    237
in films 75
indexes to 12
media images of 115, 120, 122
in poetry 121, 173, 213
in politics 120
in the Southern states 113
white liberation movement and
    black 244
as writers 12, 120
See also names of women writers
    (e.g. Nikki Giovanni)
World War II in fiction 237
Wright, Charles 76, 86, 251
Wright, Nathan, Jr. 5
Wright, Richard 6, 9, 85, 86, 87,
    88, 90, 102, 127, 132,
    134-35, 137, 138, 166,
    168, 250, 252-57
    bibliography 253-54, 255
Writers. See Authors; names of Afro-
    American authors

Y

Yerby, Frank 6, 86, 87, 90,
    258-60
Yoruba (African tribe), revival of
    religious rites of 106
Young, Al 261
Young, Whitney M., Jr. 37, 38, 94
Younge, Sammy, Jr. 32
Young Lords Party 24
Youth
    as authors 169, 184, 214
    in fiction 127, 140, 261
    influences on radical white 38,
        150
    motivation of militant 102
    poetry by 92
    poetry for 90
    See also Children

Z

Zinn, Howard 164
Zuber, Ron 5